DISABLED UPON ARRIVAL

Disabled Upon Arrival

Eugenics, Immigration, and the
Construction of Race and Disability

Jay Timothy Dolmage

THE OHIO STATE UNIVERSITY PRESS · COLUMBUS

Library of Congress Cataloging-in-Publication Data

Names: Dolmage, Jay, author.

Title: Disabled upon arrival : eugenics, immigration, and the construction of race and disability / Jay Timothy Dolmage.

Description: Columbus : The Ohio State University Press, [2018] | Includes bibliographical references and index.

Identifiers: LCCN 2017048378 | ISBN 9780814213629 (cloth : alk. paper) | ISBN 0814213626 (cloth : alk. paper) | ISBN 9780814254677 (pbk : alk. paper) | ISBN 0814254675 (pbk : alk. paper)

Subjects: LCSH: United States—Emigration and immigration—Social aspects. | Canada—Emigration and immigration—Social aspects. | Eugenics—Social aspects—United States. | Eugenics—Social aspects—Canada. | Rhetoric—Social aspects—United States. | Rhetoric—Social aspects—Canada. | People with disabilities—Social aspects.

Classification: LCC JV6475 .D65 2018 | DDC 325.7309/041—dc23

LC record available at https://lccn.loc.gov/2017048378

Cover design by Christian Fuenfhausen
Text design by Juliet Williams
Type set in Adobe Minion Pro

For the survivors of the Huronia Regional Center

CONTENTS

ACKNOWLEDGMENTS

THANKS FOR the generous support of the University of Waterloo Faculty of Arts Office of Research, the Social Sciences and Humanities Research Council of Canada, and the West Virginia University Department of English. Thanks to Jen Rinaldi for her collaboration on parts of this manuscript. Thanks to Steven Schwinghamer for his very inspiring support at Pier 21. Parts of this book previously appeared in the journals *Cultural Critique* and *Enculturation.*

Immigration has never been about immigration

IN NORTH AMERICA, immigration has never been about immigration.

That was true in the early twentieth century, when anti-immigrant rhetoric led to draconian crackdowns on the movement of bodies. That is true today as new measures seek to impede this movement and to construct migrants as dangerous and undesirable.

In this book, we will explore some of the spaces, technologies, and discourses of immigration and of immigration restriction in an effort to understand these spheres rhetorically. And what rhetorical study reveals, over and over again, is that something as seemingly concrete as a received message, or an action, is often not as important as the hidden ideas, future actions, and intentions circulating around it.

Immigration has never been about immigration.

Yes, immigration restriction has always had real, tangible effects. It reaches into and rearranges bodies, violently. And we have images, laws, manuscripts, maps, and other documents to reveal the ways that immigration restriction in North America reshaped geographies, populations, and institutions all over the world. But we can also tie immigration restriction to larger ideologies like racialization, eugenics, and xenophobia. We can recognize those who shape rhetoric around immigration working to make arguments that are in fact much larger, and that reach into all bodies. In this book, immigration rhetoric will be linked to eugenics, the flawed "science" of controlling human populations based on racist and ableist ideas about bodily values. Immigration restriction from the peak period of North American immigration in the early twentieth century right up to today will be linked to a global and ongoing series of eugenic movements. These movements will be studied through their discourses, spaces, and technologies, and eugenics will be understood as, in return, powerfully shaping technology, space, and discourse. Specifically, we will examine how disability and race were both constructed through these processes; how people became disabled and racialized upon arrival.

Rhetoricians focus on how language is used to persuade. More than this, rhetoric focuses on the ways that rhetoric shapes not just utterances or inscriptions, but also beliefs, values, and even bodies. Rhetoricians foreground the persuasive potential of all texts and artifacts, linking language to power and reminding us that sometimes, unfortunately, the ways that messages are shaped, delivered, repeated, and recirculated can be just as important as their veracity, facticity, or truthfulness. Aristotle famously suggested that rhetoric is "the faculty of discovering in any particular case all of the available means of persuasion" (1). Rhetors and teachers of rhetoric thus want and need to build flexibility and adaptability in finding the best ways to get a point across. But this has actually come to mean much more in an era of intense rhetorical spin—this has actually come to mean much more across *eras* of intense rhetorical spin. We need to question how messages can be camouflaged, how our attention might be diverted from one message by another, how a message desires a particular form of engagement to retain its power, and so on. Immigration has never been about immigration.

So I define rhetoric as the *strategic study of the circulation of power through communication.* Here, the word *strategic* is important because the study is about more than just singular uses of language or discourse: I am studying rhetoric as a social phenomenon, as something that connects to power much more broadly than just within a sentence or an utterance. And this is what *strategic* really means: the larger patterns and plans that orchestrate possibilities. So I suggest that immigration restriction, for instance, is *strategically* about much more than immigration.

I also argue for a close connection between disability studies and rhetoric. As I have written elsewhere, disability studies demands that rhetoricians pay close attention to embodied difference; in return, rhetorical approaches give disability studies practitioners means of understanding the debates that in part shape these bodies. Rhetoric needs disability studies as a reminder to pay critical and careful attention to the body. Disability studies needs rhetoric to better understand and negotiate the ways that discourse represents and impacts the experience of disability (*Disability Rhetoric*). We badly need rhetoric to make sense of a domain of meaning as powerful and impactful as immigration restriction.

But we also need a sense of rhetorical history. When Donald Trump argues that Mexican or Muslim immigrants are violent or criminal, or that countries send their "worst" people as immigrants or refugees, he's not saying anything new. For over a hundred years (and certainly much longer than this) these claims have been made, to stoke anti-immigrant sentiment. I will show how, for the last century, the claims have been both totally false and scarily effective at inciting hate.

So, as mentioned, we need to search for the meanings hiding in texts and artifacts through submersion and subterfuge—and disability studies offers an ideal set of methodological tools for wading through this rhetoric. Most notably, this book channels disability studies methodologies of "reading" sideways, of searching for "crooked" meanings, of continually asking more questions around bodily values, of valuing the meaning that comes from bodily difference even as we recognize the ways that bodily difference is used to stigmatize, remove human rights, and relocate bodies.

For instance:

In late January 2017, Donald Trump signed a series of executive orders aimed at immigration restriction: an order to build a border wall, a temporary ban on immigrants and refugees from specific Muslim nations, a focus on "saving" the religious minorities within these countries (meaning Christians). The orders were subsequently reshaped in a variety of ways following legal challenges. So, the executive orders may not have any legal enforceability. Or they may prove to be tremendously effective, legally and politically. But, unfortunately, they will certainly have very powerful rhetorical effectiveness. Why? This book will show how this has all happened before, most notably almost one hundred years ago, in the early 1920s, when eugenic rhetoric led to the shutdown of North American borders, with immigration restrictions similarly linked to specific national origins. Such bans or shutdowns mean that immigrants and refugees cannot land in North America. It means that there will be deportations and interminable detentions. But, more than this, it means that these bodies, their beliefs and behaviors, become the subject of a very public process of stigmatization.

Making America Great Again, Trump's tagline; keeping Canada a *White Man's Country*, Prime Minister William Lyon Mackenzie King's line in the 1930s; the *Return to Normalcy*, President Warren Harding's line in the early 1920s: these powerful rhetorical phrasings have all relied on scapegoating, denigrating, and making a spectacle of bodies deemed un-American or un-Canadian. Each of these slogans will be examined carefully in this book. The immigration laws and measures that these lines justify have also had a huge impact on the shape of the world, and they will be examined as well. But the eugenic, racist, xenophobic beliefs that the slogans have empowered and that their speakers have told citizens to enforce have had an even more sweeping and dangerous effect. It is this rhetorical power that this book is most interested in uncovering—because it is unpredictable yet strategic, because it is subject to multiple interpretations, because although we can find images and texts and other artifacts in an archive, we can only guess at their possible uses. The most educated guesses refuse just a single interpretation or narrative, and disability studies gives us the power of crooked reading, the ability to value difference, and this lateral and skeptical approach will be modeled on these pages.

Just days after Trump's executive order, a Canadian white nationalist terrorist killed seven Muslim citizens praying at a mosque in Quebec City, Canada. In the early part of the twentieth century, when anti-immigrant sentiment was being similarly stirred up by politicians, mobs murdered thousands of Mexicans in the United States, with 547 cases recorded but many more occurring. These lynchings occurred not only in border states but also far from the border in places like Nebraska and Wyoming. Chinese miners were frequently beaten and murdered, including an attack in Omaha, Nebraska, in 1909 in which men were killed and their houses burned. Hundreds of Italian immigrants were burned out of their homes, clubbed, and expelled from Frankfort, Illinois, in 1920 (access Jaret). Anti-immigration rhetoric and its connection to violence have been pervasive—one of the most dangerous forces in North America over the last hundred years. Reading sideways and backwards across these histories—reading rhetorically—helpfully steals away the comfort we might gain from keeping these events separate or historically distant.

This book is about the disabling and racializing force of anti-immigration rhetoric, the tools used to circulate and reproduce the rhetoric, and how we can make sense of its spread and its violent impact. Importantly, this book is not arguing that history is repeating itself, though it certainly feels that way. Instead, the book is about the fact that these eugenic ideas about the value of bodies have never gone away.

There are two specific quotes about eugenics that we will return to throughout this book. First, Angus McLaren argues that for Canadian eugenicists, their final "chief success" was not necessarily a drastic increase in restriction and deportation focused on specific groups of immigrants, though eugenic rhetoric allowed this to happen. Instead, the chief success was "in popularizing biological arguments" (McLaren 61). More simply, eugenics was successful mainly as an idea about the value of bodies. And, as Francis Galton wrote in his 1909 *Essays in Eugenics,* the first goal of eugenics is simply to get people to understand this rhetoric about the value of bodies: "Then let its principles work into the heart of the nation, who will gradually give practical effect to them in ways that we may not wholly foresee" (43). Given the idea of eugenics, the public continues to use it. These popular "biological arguments" and their unforeseen but widespread, ongoing effects are the subject of this book.[1]

Disabled Upon Arrival is divided into four sections. The sections—*island, pier, explosion,* and *archive*—describe spaces and processes, and name processual spaces (spaces that are subject to change). Within each large section, there are smaller subsections that we might call a series of snapshots, postcards, or slides, each given a header to identify it. But these individual snapshots can be read in any order, accessed in a variety of ways. In general, the reader could open this book in almost any place and be offered a version of North American immigration history, or a snapshot of North American eugenics, that dominant historical narratives have suppressed, and that conventional archives and memorializations will not make available. The postcard or snapshot approach is also intended to model a disability studies methodology, an approach to history that resists normativity. If we center the nonnormative body in research, we realize that all of the writing we do is uncertain, contingent, reliant on others, and bound to be interpreted and utilized differently by the different bodies that access it. Julie Avril Minich suggests that disability studies methodology "involves scrutinizing not bodily or mental impairments but the social norms that define particular attributes as impairments, as well as the social conditions that concentrate stigmatized attributes in particular populations" ("Enabling" n. pag.). Further, as Margaret Price argues, disability studies methodology has at its center this embodied "reshaping of relations of power" within research (160). Thus in this book, hopefully, I will model how the social conditions of immigration and immigration restriction have constructed disability and race but also how these relations can be reshaped. Once you have experienced enough of these snapshots or postcards, it should become less and less easy to impose a spatial or historical distance between yourself and the stories that are told here. The snapshots are offered in part because they are a way to resist a purely linear narrative and instead they involve you more actively in this historical process; they reshape relations of power. Hopefully, the body is implicated in this work in ways that highlight

1. A note to readers: Because immigration rhetoric is currently changing so rapidly, there will absolutely, undoubtedly be developments that this book cannot address but may be able to predict. The hope is that these developments come in the form of effective resistance to the racist, ableist, xenophobic legacy that this book traces. But this book is bound to feel incomplete.

how the "idea" of immigration has been so formative to the "idea" of disability, but also its *experience*. As the reader will come to understand, this book is about real bodies and real experiences. Also, hopefully there is space for the body of the reader to make their own choices about how to move through the text and through these histories and arguments.

Later, I will discuss how snapshot images were used in "magic lantern shows" in the early twentieth century—the images were juxtaposed with lecture materials to inform and entertain people. The shows were viewed in their time as somewhat magical, as capable of moving the viewer into a seamless, embodied, spiritualized understanding of the material. My own slides and snapshots are intended perhaps to do the opposite. to jar us out of the inclination or desire to either write or to experience a smooth history.

In keeping with this spirit of moving sideways, throughout the book, instead of including actual photographs, I have included thick visual descriptions of the photographs that I write about. This allows me to invert the usual relationship between the photograph and the means we use to make it accessible. The caption or description comes first; it's not an afterthought or a retrofit. And the images themselves are held together in a "shadow archive" on the Ohio State University Press website. This means that because experiencing these photographs may be difficult for some readers, the reader has a choice. I am not simply forcing the reader to view images that were used, originally, to mark out difference and to rhetorically construct the undesirable. Instead, you can choose how you want to interact with these images, or if you need to interact with them at all, off the page.

The method, the methodology, the key terms, and the theory underlying the book will become more apparent as we go. These engines for analysis do not exist separately from the artifacts and narratives contained in these pages, so they are best explained and developed through application.

What makes this work somewhat unique is that it brings with it an entreaty to its audience. This book asks an important favor. The responsibility of the reader is to work to recirculate these snapshots through their own research, teaching, and advocacy, and to do so in a careful, respectful, and responsible way. *Disabled Upon Arrival* was written because these artifacts and images are on the edge of our collective memory, on the precipice of forgetting. But *Disabled Upon Arrival* was also written because eugenics itself has never gone away. The book was written because, just like the historical era of its focus, we could best characterize contemporary North America as a site and an era in which immigration, and in particular in which racist and xenophobic attitudes about immigration, are at the forefront of not just discourse but of national identities. Immigration is constructed by its opponents as a pressing, dangerous threat. But instead, immigration rhetoric can itself be viewed as one of the most dangerous, threatening spheres of discourse in recent history.

In this way, this book is only about immigration to the degree that immigration itself has ever been about immigration. Simply: immigration has been about creating a dominant, normative identity; it has been about translating written and spoken and visual arguments about the value of bodies into physical action, mapping them onto other, bigger ideas like continents; it has been about land, and specifically the theft of it and its justification; it is about laughably bad science and shaky, opportunistic "facts," working together with the rhetoric that it is impossible to separate from any of these claims.

The book then asks the reader to interrogate all of these discourses and processes, and to respond to them with a counter-rhetoric that can best be shaped through an understanding of the careful, camouflaged, diverse, and powerful ways that these ideas circulate, arrive, and thrive.

Ellis Island and the inventions of race and disability

I'M GOING TO ask you to come with me on a short trip. We'll travel to New York City, approaching from the west, over the southern tip of Manhattan and out across New York Bay to Ellis Island, the waystation for millions of new Americans at the turn of the twentieth century. During our visit to Ellis Island for this section, I will examine what the Ellis Island experience entailed, paying attention specifically to the ways that Ellis Island policed and limited immigration in the early twentieth century, leading up to the highly restrictive immigration laws of the 1920s. This tour will concentrate on the ways that Ellis Island rhetorically constructed disability and race. Today, you can go on a tour of the grounds, and you can learn about the success stories of plucky migrants, on the cusp of freedom and opportunity. You can buy a mug and a T-shirt. But, in the past, if you were traveling to Ellis Island from the other direction, your experience of the island might have been quite different. It is estimated that 40 percent of the current American population can trace their ancestry through Ellis Island.[1] More than 22 million people entered the country through this immigration station. In the years of peak immigration, from the

---

1. Of course, another way to state this statistic is to say that 60 percent of Americans cannot and do not trace ancestry through the Island—which calls into question the myth of Ellis Island's originary status. Yet the island had a powerful rhetorical effect even on those who had never been there, even as there have always been many other spaces and stories and histories of origin, arrival, or lineage that have also exerted rhetorical influence over the formation of the American body.

late 1800s until the clampdown on immigration in the 1920s, you might have arrived as one of thousands of steerage passengers on an ocean liner from Europe. Were you of eastern European, southern European, African, or Jewish heritage, you would have been subject to a restrictive squeeze not unlike the cramping you felt in your boat's close quarters as you came across the Atlantic.[2] As you were processed through Ellis Island, you became part of an indelible marking, your body was interrogated, written across, and read into.

In this section I will examine Ellis Island from a rhetorical perspective—rhetoric defined here as a framework for exploring "the relationship of discourse and power, a rhetoric [. . .] being a set of rules that privilege particular power relations" (Berlin 12). I define rhetoric as the function and circulation of power in language, and I will use this definition to guide my inquiry here and throughout the book. Further, I will look at Ellis Island as what Roxanne Mountford calls a "rhetorical space." Mountford urges us to consider "the effect of physical spaces on communicative event[s]"; the ways that "rhetorical spaces carry the residue of history upon them, but also, perhaps, something else: a physical representation of relationships and ideas" (42). She argues that space "carries with it the sediment of cultural tradition, of the social imaginary" (63). Richard Marback elaborates, claiming that a given space can be viewed as a "nexus of cultural, historical, and material conditions" of oppression, and can become a "physical representation of . . . injustice" (1). Thus, in revisiting Ellis Island, rhetorical analysis will allow me to pay attention not just to how power structures and travels through proliferating discourses of ability, ethnicity, racialization, and citizenship but also to how this charging and circulation imbricates, and is proscribed by, the space of Ellis Island. That is, we will study how power travels through Ellis Island, but also how Ellis Island, as a space and as an idea, structures and shapes power.

Marback has written that any island is a "special rhetorical space" (1). Ato Quayson, in his study of Robben Island in South Africa, also argues that, in looking at this island as a space for the detention of society's unwanted, we should "take both the totality of its history and the rhetoricity of its space seriously as points for productive cross-fertilization" (175). Robben Island housed a hospital for leprosy, a hospital for the chronically sick, and a lunatic asylum, and became a sequestered colony. I will show that Ellis Island, like Robben, was a space where, in Quayson's words, "stipulations of undesirability placed in close and volatile proximity ideas of illness, deformity, insanity, and criminality, sometimes interweaving the various terms and leaving none of them stable" (176). The legacy of both of these islands echoes today as "denomina-

---

2. You wouldn't have been arriving from China, after the Chinese Exclusion Act of 1882, the legislative move that became a precedent for much of this "squeeze," and for later legislation that would close U.S. doors to immigrants.

tions of bodily difference . . . have been [repeatedly] incorporated into racial and other hierarchies" (176). Foucault has suggested that our epoch's primary spatial concern has been "knowing what relations of propinquity, what type of storage, circulation, marking and classification of human elements should be adopted" (Foucault and Miskowiec 25). This obsession with sorting has led us to create what he calls "*heterotopias of deviation*: those in which individuals whose behavior is deviant in relation to the required mean or norm are placed" (25; italics mine). These spaces are "capable of juxtaposing in a single real space several spaces, several sites that are in themselves incompatible" (25). Unlike the postmodern notion of the heterotopia as an ideal in which "nothing is left out of the grand mix," a heterotopia of deviation divides and isolates difference, suggesting that this situation (of purifying by extraction) is ideal for the "normals" in mainstream society, yet also creating a dystopian space for the minoritized (Siebers, *Heterotopia* 32; access also Vattimo; Hetherington). Ellis Island was just such a space.

Interestingly, the word *heterotopia* was first used (and is still used) in a biological and pathological sense to refer to abnormal anatomy—a displacement, a missing or extra element, a tumor that appears out of place, an alien growth (access *OED*, "heterotopy"; Hetherington 42). The social processing that Ellis Island engendered was all about identifying and sometimes manufacturing abnormal bodies: these elements are out of place; these bodies are disordered. Ellis Island created a physical space in which abnormality could be arrested or deposited. But it also created powerful social practices of stigmatization. A heterotopia of deviation was placed at the edge of North America, and alienation was placed upon racial groups and individuals. At Ellis Island, the categories of defect and disability that adhere today were strongly grounded if not created, as was the diagnostic gaze that allowed for the nebulous application of the stigma of disability as we know it today.

Sharon Snyder and David Mitchell also put forward the idea of "cultural locations of disability"—locations "in which disabled people find themselves deposited, often against their will" (3). These locations are revealed to be "sites of violence, restriction, confinement, and absence of liberty" (x). Ellis Island became a place in which disability, and people who were constructed as disabled, could be detained or deposited. Importantly, we will explore how "formulas of abnormality develop and serve to discount entire populations as biologically inferior," rooted to specific sites of enforcement like Ellis Island, become capable of great rhetorical influence (3). By understanding disability as not fixed, but rather as culturally located, we can also understand that the formulas can be rhetorically challenged and the spaces can be renovated and reimagined.

The space of Ellis Island circumscribed certain patterns of movement and practices of visualizing the body. The product was, often, the spectacle of Otherness. And all who passed through Ellis Island also became subject to—and then possessor and executor of—a certain gaze and a certain bodily attitude. Ellis Island functioned as a heterotopic space. And not simply so—always in a tangle of definitions and as a repository of bad science and overlapping oppressions.

I will examine Ellis Island in the early twentieth century as a "special rhetorical space," a heterotopia for the invention of new categories of deviation. And I will suggest that Ellis Island floats into every aspect of contemporary American society. As Robert Chang has argued, "The border is not just a peripheral phenomenon [. . .] To be an immigrant is to be marked [always] by the border." Further, "it is through its flexible operation that the border helps to construct and contain the nation and the national community" (27). Ellis Island has been rhetorically used, internalized, incorporated, embodied.

To summarize: here and in the remainder of the book, spaces, discourses, artifacts, and technologies of immigration will be examined according to a series of key methodological and theoretical tools. Those tools include the idea that spaces are rhetorical, and that some spaces are particularly imbued with meaning—as heterotopias of deviation, special rhetorical spaces, or cultural locations of disability. What happens when we examine immigration from this rhetorical perspective, with rhetoric defined as the function and circulation of power in language? We will find out.

Ellis Island was designed to process the immigrant body—through an industrialized choreography, through a regime of vision, and through layers of anti-immigration discourse. Ellis Island became the key laboratory and operating theater for American eugenics, the scientific racism that can be understood to define a unique era of Western history, the effects of which can still be felt today. I will argue that Ellis Island, as a rhetorical space, can be viewed as a nexus—and a special point of origin—for eugenics and the rhetorical construction of disability and race in the early twentieth century. Importantly, constructions of class, sex, and sexuality were also always part of this racializing and normalizing process.[3] Race and disability are always tangled and connected with gender, sex, sexuality, and class. And, as Eithne Luibheid suggests, "Immigration scholarship virtually ignores the connec-

---

3. For instance, questions about sexual preferences and histories were part of almost every medical inspection at Ellis Island. The 1917 Immigration Act listed "abnormal sex instincts" as a "constitutional psychopathic inferiority" (History Research Center 29). As Jennifer Terry has written, "Eugenic doctrine of the first half of the twentieth century placed both racial and sexual purity at the top of its agenda. . . . White phobia about miscegenation and racial passing paralleled a growing sex panic that inverts and perverts were everywhere, but difficult to detect visually hence, an apparatus for identifying and isolating them could be justified as a matter of social hygiene" (138). Ellis Island offered just such an apparatus.

tions among heteronormativity, sexuality, and immigration" ("Heteronormativity" 227). It is not my intention to further this occlusion or ignorance here. Indeed, the categories of "defect" used to sort bodies at Ellis Island always also referenced gender, sex, and sexuality norms, and were also always classed. This section lays out the foundation upon which further analysis of these constructions can develop.

As I begin, I will provide a legend for the key concepts of this exploration, not just for this section, but for the entire book—beginning with a definition of eugenics. Charles Davenport, perhaps the eugenics movement's greatest proponent, defined the movement as "the science of the improvement of the human race by better breeding" (1). Disability studies scholars Sharon Snyder and David Mitchell define eugenics as "the hegemonic formation of exclusionary practices based on scientific formulas of deviancy" (73). And Nancy Ordover notes that in the early twentieth century, "eugenics gave racism and nationalism substance by bringing to bear the rationalizing technologies of the day" (6). Looking at Ellis Island, then, allows me to recognize the development and use of these rationalizing technologies in a specific rhetorical space, as well as the discursive currents that surrounded and buttressed the island; the flow of relationships and ideas, the sediments of cultural tradition, and the social imaginary swirling around Ellis Island between 1890 and 1925. Ellis Island was a genetic experiment. This genetic experiment has, in many ways, created the frame for how we now understand both race and disability. What eugenics reveals is that race and disability are rhetorical constructions, inventions, with very real material effects. As Constance Backhouse reminds us: "Race is a mythical construct. Racism is not" (7). Much of the time, as I will show, the ways that eugenics constructs race and disability, often together, can seem ridiculous—exemplary of very bad "science." But the impacts of these constructions, which some theorists may wish to reject, are violent material effects that the historian and the rhetorician cannot ignore.

Building on my definitions of rhetoric and rhetorical space, the idea of the "rhetorical construction" of disability develops out of the social and the postmodern models of disability, both put forward in the field of disability studies—I'll define these ideas next. The social model of disability posits that disability is purely social, an oppression stacked upon people *on top of* their impairments, which are real. The view is that, as Michael Oliver writes, "Disablement is nothing to do with the body, impairment is nothing less than a description of the body" (34). Adrienne Asch qualifies that "saying that disability is socially constructed does not imply that the characteristics are not real or do not have describable effects on physiological or cognitive functions that persist in many environments" (18). Bodies and spaces are undeniably material, yet they are also undeniably rhetorical. The point is to draw attention to the fictive and oppressive cultural meanings of disability, without diminishing the lived experience of disability. Yet so-called postmodern disability studies contradicts this social model by suggesting that the strict separation of impairment and disability is an illusion or trick (access Tremain). Judith Butler's definition of a "partial" social construction of the body, from her introduction to *Bodies That Matter,* nicely distills this idea: "To claim that discourse is formative is not to claim that it originates, causes, or exhaustively composes that which it concedes; rather, it is to claim that there is no reference to a pure body which is not at the same time a further formation of that body" (5). More simply, language makes us who we are. This "making" is never complete or total—but no body is untouched and unshaped by language and by rhetoric.

Following this argument, I suggest that we can view the "formation" of disability as being both material and rhetorical—characterized in vital ways by my definition of rhetoric as the "circulation and function of power in language." To understand bodies as rhetorically constructed rather than socially constructed is to focus more closely on the power dynamics of the process of construction itself, rather than on its products, however transient. That is, if we can agree that rhetoric shapes bodies, even partially, then we should study this shaping very carefully. In the history and the geography that I chart, we will focus on how rhetorically invested the creation of disability has been— shaped by material spaces and corporeal experiences, and also by languages and grammars. This move to comprehend disability rhetorically justifies a focus on the architectures and discourses surrounding bodies. A rhetorical perspective suggests that these spaces and discourses must be understood as formed by bodies and as, in part, *forming* bodies. I refer to rhetoric here and throughout the book in a capacious or generous sense—not as the duplicitous or obscurant or dishonest art that we often view rhetoric as, but as the investigation of how meaning is made and negotiated, focusing not on reified or solid products and transcendent truths, but on the power dynamics involved in the effort to make meaning. This rhetorical perspective disallows the canonization of any one definition of disability, yet allows me to challenge the negative meanings that gather around disability as well as the social structures that have defined and policed the limited experience of disability. Finally, this rhetorical method asks each of us to examine critically the spaces and discourses that shape *any* body.

This rhetorical perspective also interacts with a critical perspective on race—allowing me to examine the ways that race is (at least partially) constructed through spaces and discourses. To say that race and disability are rhetorically constructed, importantly, is not to deny either concept materially or ontologically—but rather to bring into focus their shifting cultural meanings and their power and importance. Further, in aligning race and disability in this analysis, I am seeking to understand their rhetorical connections, not to conflate or compare, and never to deny the particularity and complexity of either race or disability. Yet these constructions of race and disability overlap, I will show, throughout the history of American eugenics. Their entwined narrative is best examined, I will also show, through the structures, practices, bodies, and discourses that make Ellis Island and other border locations such compelling rhetorical spaces.

ASSEMBLY LINES

Cursory medical inspections most strongly characterized the experience of Ellis Island for the arriving alien. In the years of peak immigration, as immigrants landed at Ellis Island they were almost immediately paraded up a set of steep stairs, some immigrants still carrying all their possessions in their arms, afraid to leave them unattended in the baggage room. Here the inspection began. Immigration agents positioned themselves so that they could view individual bodies from several angles, and so that they could pick out deficient bodies as they labored up the stairs and into the registry room. As Victor Safford, a medical doctor and officer at Ellis Island in this peak period, wrote in his memoir, "A man's posture, a movement of his head or the appearance of his ears . . . may disclose more than could be detected by puttering around a man's chest with a stethoscope for a week, [thus] an attempt was made to utilize this general scheme" at Ellis Island (247). The "scheme" allowed for views of each immigrant "systematically both in rest and in motion at a distance of about twenty or twenty-five feet"; carrying his or her bags, hopefully, because "carrying baggage makes lameness from any cause more noticeable"; and creating a situation wherein each immigrant "while under inspection [would] make two right hand turns" to help "to bring out imperfections in muscular coordination" (Safford 247–49). Officers would also stamp cards, and then hand the cards to immigrants. Because the immigrant was curious about what the stamp said, this was an opportunity for further inspection: "The way he held [the card] showed if his vision was defective" (Safford 249).

The inspection process, facilitated by the space of the Ellis Island immigration station, looked like the choreographic and architectural brainchild of Jeremy Bentham and Henry Ford—a panopticon and an assembly line. Henry Ford's Model T assembly lines began to produce cars in 1914. The appeal of mechanized industry was huge in this period, and the idea of mechanization had import even outside the automobile plant—it became a cultural logic. Christina Cogdell, in a tremendously important book on the confluence between eugenics and American modern architecture and design, goes a step further, drawing attention to "the interconnectedness of streamline design with eugenic ideology," in particular through the analogy of digestion (ix). Ellis Island works as an excellent application of this metaphorical alliance: eugenicists wanted the nation, and thus its immigration, to "run like an unobstructed colon" (Cogdell 132). Ellis Island could not be constipated, as "constipation was seen as stunting national evolutionary advancement" (133). Thus the spectacle of expulsion and a steady diet of restriction at the Island could be viewed as healthy.

Indeed, Safford used the automobile metaphor at great length in describing Ellis Island inspections, and justifying the use and the efficacy of the glancing appraisal employed by inspectors to recognize defective bodies, what Anne-Emanuelle Birn calls "snapshot diagnosis" (281). Safford wrote that "it is no more difficult a task to detect poorly built or broken down human beings than to recognize a cheap or defective automobile" (244). This metaphor equates the functioning of the body to that of the machine, as it argues for the efficiency of the assembly line: "One can see on glancing at an automobile at rest that the paint is damaged or a headlight broken . . . [likewise] defects, derangements, and symptoms of disease which would not be disclosed by a so-called 'careful physical examination' are often easily recognizable watching a person twenty-five feet away" and in action (245). Thus only cursory physical examinations—known as the six-second physical— were imposed upon newly arriving immigrants, and the agents were trained to notice, immediately, inferior stock. These practices effectively "turned entry into the U.S. into a passage partially defined by a medical vocabulary and pathology of health" (Markel and Minna Stern 1315). This medical lexicon was repeatedly imprinted upon the immigrant, and this printing was done hastily, efficiently, mechanically.

PHYSIQUES

Erica Rand has argued that there are "limited resources about sex, normative or otherwise, regarding Ellis Island" and thus "studying sex at Ellis Island requires strategies of embodiment, with attention to the particular bodies inhabited and to the complexity, messiness, and contradictions of sexed bodies in their historical specificity" (15). Yet in the line inspection process at Ellis Island, to begin with, one category of immigrant was always isolated: single women immigrants were viewed in starkly eugenic terms, "positioned as 'surplus,' 'redundant' members of society, drains on the economy, problems to be exported," as Penny Richards reminds us, citing Kranidis, Flad, and O'Connell (n. pag.). Eugenicists also believed that "the high fecundity of foreign-born women augmented the menace of" mass immigration and "since the immigrants were innately and biologically inferior," restrictive measures were necessary, and to be applied especially to women (Pickens 195). A single pregnant woman was perhaps the least desired, and they were carefully weeded out. As Alan Kraut recounts in his book *Silent Travelers,* Dr. Victor Heiser instructed inspectors that "on the left side of any immigrant woman's head was a strand of hair which under normal conditions, was more or less lustrous. If it hung dull and lifeless over her ear, it marked her at once as possibly pregnant" (63). Richards points out that these devaluations offer "analogy and resonance to studies of people with disabilities" (n. pag.). The development of specific categories for the exclusion of disabled people likewise relied on the idea that some immigrants would not be economic contributors, and thus would be undesirable, however fallacious this assumption was.

In the beginning at Ellis Island, pre-1900, there were few categories of physical (and perceived mental) defect that would warrant marking aliens out for further inspection and possible rejection. The first capacious terminology was the category "LPC," or "likely to become a public charge," introduced in 1891. Inspectors could use their judgment to determine whether an immigrant looked like he or she could work for a living. William Williams, the Ellis Island commissioner at the time, wrote in his annual report that he hoped that this category would allow inspectors to weed out the "worst" immigrants (n. pag.). Jane Perry Clark has suggested that the LPC designation was "shaken on deportation cases as though with a large pepper shaker" (309). Yet by 1904 the commissioner was suggesting that the LPC terminology be expanded, as it was difficult to prove that someone would become a public charge, particularly once individual cases made it to boards of inquiry on the island, and family members, church representatives, or others were willing to vouch for immigrants. This desire for expansion of the LPC label shows that perhaps the calculus of exclusion was never purely economic, as the LPC label might suggest—there needed to be other ways to exclude the genetically "threatening." And in this period, we begin to understand the ways that eugenic ideas of bodily "fitness" begin to structure the rhetoric of Ellis administrators. In 1904 Commissioner Williams called for the use of categories for exclusion such as "poor physique" or "low vitality," with one's appearance itself warranting rejection, without having to be mediated through an overt economic consideration. A body with a "poor physique" was defined as "ill proportioned, with defective circulatory system and poorly developed relaxed muscular system and flabby muscles . . . frail . . . a slender build, whose physical proportions with respect to chest and weight fall below the minimum requirements of the naval service, who are deficient in muscular development" ("Definitions of Various Terms"). In 1905 F. P. Sargent, commissioner general of the Bureau of Immigration, notified inspection officers and boards of special inquiry that

> "poor physique" means afflicted with a body but illy adapted not only to the work necessary to earn his bread, but is also poorly able to withstand the onslaught of disease . . . undersized, poorly developed . . . physically degenerate, and as such not likely to become a desirable citizen, but also very likely to transmit his undesirable qualities to his offspring. . . . Of all causes for rejection, outside of dangerous, loathsome, or contagious diseases, or for mental disease, that of "poor physique" should receive the most weight, for, in admitting such aliens, not only do we increase the number of public charges by their inability to gain their bread . . . but we admit likewise progenitors to this country whose offspring will reproduce, often in an exaggerated degree, the physical degeneracy of their parents. (n. pag.)

This type of starkly eugenic language came to characterize much of Ellis Island policy. And, clearly, very little about these definitions could be reliably sensed, visually. Yet this was no impediment to their implementation.

The classification of "poor physique" would expand when, in 1907, the category of "feebleminded" was also officially adopted. Howard Markel and Alexandra Minna Stern show that "poor physique" became a "favorite wastebasket" label of nativist groups and was highly diagnosed during inspections in the 1910s (1319). They also reveal "the fluid nature of exclusionary labels themselves. If one label failed to work in rejecting the most objectionable, a new one was soon created, whether of contagion, mental disorder, chronic disability, or physique" (1327). The category of the "feebleminded" soon became the new wastebasket. As Sharon Snyder and David Mitchell show, "'feebleminded-ness' became the primary category that allowed eugenics to consolidate a host of defective types under a shared heading" (79). Importantly, as Anna Stubblefield has shown, "White elites deployed the concept of feeble-mindedness to link the different versions of white impurity" (163). As well, the insinuation of *mental* disability was conflated with a semiotics of exterior markers. In the heterotopia of deviation created at Ellis Island, undesirable bodies were shaded with attributions of disability; and disabled bodies were "raced" as nonwhite, or as disqualified whites.

Further aiding in the flexible application of stigma, as Safford's description suggests, these cursory inspections were largely a matter of intuition, a kind of magical medical view—in his words, "From long experience physicians some-times acquire[d] a most remarkable intuitive power" (245). As Samuel Grubbs wrote, recalling his work as an officer, "I wanted to acquire this magical intu-ition but found there were few rules. Even the keenist [sic] of these medical detectives did not know just why they suspected at a glance a handicap which later might require a week to prove" (qtd. in Fairchild 91). Other stories from immigrants who passed through the space are equally arresting, and reveal a process that was often more arbitrary than "magical." Jean Suksennik, who arrived in 1929, wrote in a letter to the Ellis Island Oral History Project, dated May 19, 1986, that "my family got a clean bill of health but I was rejected for entrance. I had a few bald spots on my head and was to go back to Czech. Or be detained in a medical service there on the island for a cure. The fam-ily decided on treatment and I was taken away crying and screaming [but] I will forever be grateful to God, America, and my parents for their foresight of this great country. Will always love America. P.S The bald spots on my head were caused by me crawling under a wagon that was being hot tarred to retard wood rot. All farmers did that."

Regardless of the provenance of the process, suspect bodies were identified and sorted out from the stream of immigrants, these individuals were marked with chalk codes, letters written on the lapels of their jackets, inscrutable to those immigrants who had been inscribed. As Mullan describes in his men-tal inspection guide, "Should the immigrant appear stupid and inattentive to such an extent that mental defect is suspected, an X is made on his coat at the anterior aspect of his right shoulder. Should definite signs of mental disease be observed, a circle would be used. In like manner, a chalk mark is placed . . . in all cases where physical deformity or disease is suspected" (740). Some of the other code letters were "L" for lameness, "Pg" for pregnancy, and "H" for heart. Thelma Matje, an immigrant who arrived in August 1912, wrote of her experience that, "on disembarking upon our arrival at Ellis Island we were herded through the portals of this haven for the lost and destitute souls and tagged with more labels on our clothing than a pedigreed dog" (n. pag.).

SPECTACLES OF DIFFERENCE

At Ellis Island, following line inspection, the marked were removed for further mental and physical examination. I won't look in great detail at the further testing and examination that took place beyond the initial inspection here. Instead, I'll suggest that, though line officers could not deport immigrants, their inspections and markings had an indelible rhetorical effect. This effect reached three distinct audiences:

1. Those immigrants who were not marked, and yet learned something about the danger of difference, gained a self-consciousness of their own possible defects, and were empowered and encouraged to diagnose others.

2. Those who were marked and were thus in danger of rejection.

3. The medical doctors themselves, who would later inspect the immigrants in greater detail.

As Safford writes, the cursory inspection processes may actually have had greater power than the detailed inspections that followed upon detainment. For instance, he suggests that "if after taking into an examination room a person regarding whom suspicion has been aroused" due to the snapshot diagnosis "appears normal," then "the medical officer knows the passenger should not be released without looking further" (248). Without alleging that defect was manufactured by this process, clearly Safford and other officers strongly believed in the power of the medical glance. And the power of the glance was transferred to every immigrant who passed through this space.

Ellis Island, then, can be viewed as a rhetorical space in which Foucault's history of "punishment" reaches a sort of climax. Ellis Island provided a classical "spectacle"—the body was publicly inscribed and marked out for its difference when it was rejected (access *Discipline and Punish* 32–69). But Ellis Island also solidified new forms of self- and other-surveillance (access *Discipline and Punish* 32–69).[4] The alien body could be publicly stigmatized and displayed, or removed to the back rooms at Ellis Island for further medical inspection, or passed along; yet, no matter what, the immigrant was always infected with the spirit of the investigation and the power of the gaze. Each of these acts carried significant rhetorical power, structuring the "heterotopia of deviation." Foucault wrote that the classical use of the spectacle to discipline and punish was "a manifestation of the strongest power over the body" of the condemned, whose punishment "made the crime explode into its truth" (Foucault and Miskowiec 227). When you can hold a rejected body up as a spectacle, the process of inspection is given great power. Yet Foucault suggests that through modernity, "the ideal point of penality would [evolve to become] an indefinite discipline: an interrogation without end, an investigation that would be extended without limit to a meticulous and ever more analytical observation" (Foucault and Mis-

---

4. Mae Ngai also suggests that the alien has always been a "kind of specter" (*Impossible Subjects* 7). I find the metaphorical interaction between the spectacle and the specter interesting here—the spectacle being the hypervisible text, the specter being the ghostly presence. Through the spectacles of Ellis Island, it seems that specters of racialized and disabled otherness were given rhetorical power. In this way, Ellis Island continues to ghost our understandings of citizenship, the body, race, normalcy, and so on.

kowiec 227). That is, the power that was even greater than the rejection of some bodies was the power given to the immigrants to see themselves and others as potentially rejectable. While Ellis Island centered many spectacles, it also diffused innumerable investigations and unlimited surveillance into the nation.[5]

As Terry and Urla write, "The scopic regimes associated with looking for semantic markings of deviance position the expert simultaneously as objective scientist, informed interpreter, and voyeur" (11).[6] A "scopic regime," in simpler terms, is a way that an entire society looks or gazes at one another. The scopic regime at Ellis Island began with the line inspector. When other immigrants also became privy to this gaze, they were granted the same diagnostic power. This visual access to Other bodies, combined with access to these mechanisms of Othering, was a formative American experience. Through this processing and marking, and through the possibility of detainment, Ellis Island made a spectacle of inspection and exclusion, made the focus on defect *the* initiation rite for hopeful immigrants. When H. G. Wells visited Ellis Island in 1906, he commented on the "wholesale and multitudinous quality of that place and its work" (43). He left with an overwhelming impression that Ellis Island was a "dirty spectacle of hopeless failure" (44). His impressions summarize the ways that Ellis Island manufactured and focused an exclusionary gaze. And his feelings perhaps understate the general impression of the immigrant, as Wells was just a visitor, and a welcome visitor at that. Of course, the dominant cultural memory of Ellis Island celebrates the process as a rite of passage, arrival as celebratory. I am arguing against this whitewashed narrative, even as I would acknowledge that hope and triumph also always circulated in this space—as did subversion. For all of the interpellative power of this gaze, for all of the ways it trained people to look down on one another, one would expect that there was also resistance to its power.[7]

---

5. As Eithne Luibhéid asserts, the examination process at Ellis Island "individuated" each person examined, and "tied [her or him] in to [a] wider network of surveillance," placing "immigrants within lifelong networks of surveillance and disciplinary relations" (*Entry Denied* xii, xvii).

6. Often the Public Health Service stationed its newest doctors to work as inspectors at Ellis Island as an extension of their training, thus initiating these doctors through the Ellis Island diagnostic process. Many inspectors were also former immigrants themselves, who had come through Ellis Island and then returned to work there. Thus while the inspection process may have inculcated an ableist and "racist" scopic regime, many inspectors may also have seen Ellis Island more positively, as a gateway to opportunities they hoped to share with other immigrants.

7. We know, for instance, that immigrants often stole the same blue chalk that was used to mark the lapels of the potentially rejected, and used the chalk to write graffiti (Trausch).

SPECTACULAR LABORATORIES

Alexandra Minna Stern has also shown that similar "spectacular" techniques were also expanded for use at the border of Texas and Mexico in the first decade of the century (at El Paso, Naco, Nogales, Douglas, Tucson, Laredo, Eagle Pass, Rio Grande, Brownsville, and Hidalgo). At stations on this border, every immigrant was stripped, their clothing "chemically scoured," their hair clipped and burned; they were showered with kerosene and water, and then subjected to a medical exam and psychological profile (Minna Stern, 63). Ostensibly this process was used because of the threat of typhus. But these processing stations, called "sanitation plants," were later "enlarged and further equipped [. . .] despite the disappearance of any typhus threat" (65). This spectacular rendering allowed for the "pathologization of Mexicans" and the "association of immigrants with disease" to expand "into new racial and metaphorical terrain" (67). The embodied rhetorical effects of these plants and their processing then "contributed to the culture of segregation, suspicion, and violence that took shape in the Southwest and California in the first half of the twentieth century" (70). In other sections to follow, we will look more closely at this border and its rhetorics. There is some evidence that similar showers were used on ships traveling to Ellis Island. Emmie Kremer, an immigrant reflecting on her Ellis Island experience in 1986, wrote that "third class passengers had to go through a disinfecting shower" on a boat coming from Germany in 1926. "I believe about two years later or so, they did away with that process," he wrote (Kremer n. pag.). In the space of Ellis Island, the space of the ship, and the space of the U.S.–Mexico border, initiation through inspection and inoculation served key rhetorical purposes.

DISABLED BEFORE ARRIVAL

Mary Grace Quackenbos was the first female United States Attorney, known as "Mrs. Sherlock Holmes" for cracking cold cases, and founder of the People's Law Firm, dedicated to the cases of the working poor and immigrants. In an article in *Pearson's Magazine* in 1910, Quackenbos suggested that the steamship lines were involved in a planned, mechanical process of alienation. She writes that the majority of undesirable immigrants were transported to the United States via the "superior power of a vast and intricate 'machine.' In its main outlines this 'machine' may be likened to an enormous dredging apparatus stretching forth gigantic cranes to every port of Europe, catching up

and heaving back loads of emigrants collected from every corner of the Eastern Hemisphere by the tireless efforts of no less than fifty steamship agents
and their canvassers. The fuel which energizes this colossal structure is an
equally colossal greed for yearly dividends, and the combined intellects controlling [these companies] . . . may be said to represent the engineer. The pivot
upon which the entire mechanism turns is fraud and evasion of the United
States' Immigration Law" (737). She concludes that, finally, all immigrants are
"tarnished by the corroding influence of the 'machine'" and suggests that this
influence will always affect their ability to become good citizens (737).

In her analysis of the work of Hortense Spillers on the disabling impact
of slave ships, Nirmala Erevelles shows that this impact was about physical
and rhetorical disablement: "it is precisely at the historical moment when one
class of human beings was transformed into cargo to be transported to the
new world that black bodies became disabled and disabled bodies became
black" (40). Similarly, the very act of traveling across the Atlantic was often
a violent, traumatic experience for immigrants to North America. The process of immigration itself created disabling conditions, tracing these intentions upon certain bodies. The environmental conditions of the regions of the
world from which immigrants came were mapped as zones of environmental and embodied undesirability, but these seeming misfortunes of birth also
subjected immigrants to conditions on the ships that exacerbated or in fact
created the signs of poor health that inspectors and the general public were
already expecting to find upon their bodies. To paraphrase Erevelles, immigrant subjectivity became disabled subjectivity on these ships (40).

As Doris Weatherford points out, "Not only sailors but also many male
passengers considered women traveling alone to be fair game" and "even if a
man did not succeed in forcing his affections, he could cause serious trouble
by lying about her rejection of him" (284). Or, as Mae Ngai points out, "the
Immigration service considered lapses of misfortune subsequent to entry to
be the teleological outcome of a prior condition, which it adduced by way of
retroactive judgment" ("Strange" 32). More simply, if one was injured, became
sick, or became pregnant on the trip overseas, this was immediately attributed
to individual behavior before boarding and never blamed on the conditions
of the journey. While minor crimes or "sexual immorality" on the ship on the
way over were not deportable offenses, they could lead to immigrants being
marked as "LPC before entry" (Ngai, "Strange" 32). The trauma of the trip
was understood as a natural consequence of inhabiting the social station of
the immigrant.

Immigrants wrote of specific spectacles, seemingly designed to highlight
their status as potentially contagious, as well (access Kremer). Mexican and
Chinese laborers were specifically targeted, and "more frequently poked for

blood and urine samples, and disinfected with chemical agents" once they arrived at Ellis Island (Markel and Stern 1320). But before ships were able to land, sometimes entire ocean liners were disinfected with chemical agents, or entire ships were held in quarantine, if disease was suspected. This quarantine and inoculation served as a form of marking-out, just as it served medical purposes. In oral histories, immigrants told stories of these processes, and also repeatedly mention the rumors circulating about the many immigrants who had been rejected committing suicide on their return trip ("Suicide").

Immigrants were not just rhetorically disabled upon arrival. The entire process was disabling.

DISABILITY AND "NEW" RACISM

While, on ships and at borders, bodies were physically disabled by immigration, rhetorical forces were also at work in concert with physical ones. Throughout history, as Aristide Zolberg shows, American immigration policy has always had a double logic: "boldly inclusive" *and* "brutally exclusive" (432). He argues that the United States has never been laissez-faire about immigration (2). That is, immigration has always been a matter of keen public and political concern—as the public has shaped immigration, so has it shaped the public. Yet, starting in the late 1800s, the stakes were raised. Immigration debates became a rhetorical arena through which one of the most powerful and dangerous ideas of our civilization took form: eugenics. The Immigration Restriction League (IRL) began in 1894 and was to have a remarkable influence on the political, intellectual, and business leadership of the country, and on the U.S. public. The immigrant was reframed as a menace, as a possible strain on resources, and as an undesirable undercurrent in the national gene pool. Eugenics, the "science" of positively advocating for particular forms of human regeneration, coupled with the negative restriction of the propagation of certain classes and ethnicities, beginning at the turn of the twentieth century, was the modus operandi of North American national health and immigration policy. Eugenics was "anointed guardian of national health and character," as Nancy Ordover has shown, "constructing immigrants as both contaminated and contaminators" (xiv). IRL co-founder Prescott F. Hall, in his article "Immigration Restriction and World Eugenics," wrote at the time that "immigration restriction is a species of segregation on a large scale, by which inferior stocks can be prevented from both diluting and supplanting good stocks. . . . The superior races, more self-limiting than the others, with the benefits of more space and nourishment will tend to still higher levels" (126). Robert DeCourcy Ward, another co-founder (with Hall) of the IRL, wrote at the time of the ways that America would map out its eugenic future: "A policy of national eugenics, for the United States as for every other nation, means the prevention of the breeding of the unfit native. For us it means, in addition, the prevention of the immigration of the unfit alien" (38). Ellis Island was a key reference point for this new mapping of America.

The rhetoric employed by the IRL and other proponents of eugenics held that certain races and ethnicities were characterized by embodied deviance. Such uses of disability as a mode of derogation grafted onto Other bodies might be understood as one of the primary corporeal grammars available to us. Douglas Baynton has shown that "the *concept* of disability has been used to justify discrimination against other groups by attributing disability to them" ("Justification" 33).[8] The disabled body becomes a loose, flexible, and magnetic symbol easily layered over insinuations of deficiency of all colors, shapes, and locations. In this negative sense, disability functions rhetorically. Eugenic rhetoric, seeking to identify inferior genes, necessarily constructed deviant phenotypes, creating investigatory techniques, a visual shorthand for identifying and marking out undesirable elements. Baynton has since gone on to suggest that immigration restriction wasn't primarily about race, at least never without reference to ability: "the menacing image of the defective was the principal catalyst for the rapid expansion of immigration law and the machinery of its enforcement" (*Defectives* 1). But there is real danger inherent in these forms of comparative writing and argument. How is it possible to disentangle race and defect as rhetorical forces? The histories I am recounting here insist that such disentanglement, or clear prioritization ("principal") is impossible and fruitless. As Natalia Molina has shown, it is "not only that race, immigration, and disability studies are intimately connected but also that often it is difficult to discern where one ends and the other begins" (33). In her words, and through her historical work on Mexican immigration: "inquiry in these fields is relational" (33).

As Nancy Stepan has shown, "as a science of 'race improvement,' some concept of race was of course built into eugenics from the start. At times, 'race

---

8. It is worthwhile to quote Baynton at greater length here to clarify this point. He suggests that "disability has functioned historically to justify inequality for disabled people themselves, but it has also done so for women and minority groups." For instance, "opponents of political and social equality for women cited their supposed physical, intellectual, and psychological flaws, deficits, and deviations from the male norm" (Baynton, "Justification" 33). In similar ways, "disability was a significant factor in the three great citizenship debates of the nineteenth and early twentieth centuries: women's suffrage, African American freedom and civil rights, and the restriction of immigration. When categories of citizenship were questioned, challenged, and disrupted, disability was called on to clarify and define who deserved, and who was deservedly excluded from, citizenship" (33).

improvement' meant merely the genetic improvement of the 'human race' or 'our people'; more often, however, eugenicists were concerned with particular portions of the human population, which they saw as being divided into distinct and unequal 'races'" (11). This division is clear in the histories recounted here, and shows that race—or more accurately racism—can never be separated from discussions of eugenics, and there is absolutely nothing rhetorically useful that can come from prioritizing other concerns ahead of race.

DICTIONARIES OF RACE

At Ellis Island, through the inspection process, a medical and a penological (criminalized) gaze were incorporated, in the service of both identifying some bodies for detention and rejection, and in the process, through a logic of negation, constructing the U.S. citizen. As Matthew Frye Jacobson shows, for anyone who arrived at Ellis Island before 1924, "Race was the prevailing idiom for discussing citizenship and the relative merits of a given people" (9). Within this racial idiom, disability was the accent applied to differentiate and hierarchize. Race and disability rhetorically reinforced each other and worked together to stigmatize. Markel and Minna Stern summarize this propensity: "In an era in which differences of skin color and physical characteristics were becoming increasingly medicalized, it is not surprising that exclusionary labels of disease and disability became an essential aspect" of immigration restriction (1328). Jacobson adds that the categories of the physically and mentally defective were created and used in service of racism, as a means of darkening a group of ethnic others with the stigma of disability. Jacobson writes that the "scientific probabilities for such conditions [of mental and physical defect] were themselves determined by a calculus of race" (69). The use of disability as a darkening mark applied to the singular body of an arriving immigrant later allowed for the accent of disability to be applied to entire (designated) racial groups. The probability of exclusion was determined by an exponential interaction of race and disability. As Anna Stubblefield has shown, "[disability and] ability [were] constructed as the touchstone in a way that linked race to class and gender and created the tangled mess that we are still untangling today" (179).

Racialized immigration restriction officially began with the Page Law of 1875 and the Chinese Exclusion Act of 1882, through which the nation effectively halted Chinese immigration. From this point on, restriction tightened as quickly as the immigration machine itself expanded. Roger Daniels argues that, although Chinese exclusion is often viewed as a small or minor matter, affecting only Chinese Americans, it is "now apparent that [this exclusion] became the pivot upon which all American immigration policy turned, the hinge upon which the 'golden door' of immigration began its swing towards a nearly closed position" (Daniels and Graham 8). This exclusion also characterizes the enduring fusion of racism and attributions of disability. The February 28, 1877, "Report of the Joint Special Committee to Investigate Chinese Immigration" to the U.S. Congress found that "there is not sufficient brain capacity in the Chinese to furnish motive power for self-government [. . .] Upon the point of morals, there is no Aryan or European who is not far superior" (159). This synthesis of race classification and attributions of inferiority would set a powerful precedent for future prejudice, prejudice that would become medicalized, industrialized, and bureaucratized through Ellis Island.[9] Between 1891 and 1906, the immigration bureaucracy in the United States grew by 4,200 percent (Daniels and Graham 15).[10] This explosion would be matched by an unprecedented "production of racial knowledge" (Ngai, *Impossible* 7). As this knowledge grew, its flaws would also multiply, as racial knowledge tangled with emerging eugenic ideas about bodily fitness; confusion between race, ethnicity, and nationality; and the bad science that Ellis Island allowed.

A major aspect of this proliferation of flawed racial knowledge was the Dillingham Immigration Commission's "Dictionary of Races or Peoples." The atmosphere of eugenic panic in the United States in this period led to the creation of this special commission, made up of eugenics proponents such as Henry Cabot Lodge, to investigate immigration. The commission presented this famous (and huge) document as part of an even larger report to Congress in 1911. The goal of the "Dictionary" was to classify races, and it did so according to physical and linguistic difference from the Caucasian norm. The "Dictionary" presented as part of the 1911 Dillingham Report relied on "ethnical factors" and "racial classification" to identify immigrant groups, signaling a shift from the old system of classification based on country of birth or nativity. The commission focused on color (white, black, yellow, red, and brown); on head measurements; and on not just language but also perceptions of literacy. This "Dictionary" both borrowed from and slightly evolved

---

9. Of course the American Naturalization Act of 1870 was a precedent for, yet also consonant and contemporaneous with, the sentiment of this document—limiting American citizenship to "white persons and persons of African descent" and thus excluding the Chinese specifically, even as it extended citizenship rights to African Americans, overwriting the 1790 act, which limited citizenship to "any alien, being a free white person" (House of Representatives, 41st Congress, 2nd Session).

10. Unlike any other federal bureaucracy before it, these officials were tasked not with serving as advocates or service providers, but with *protecting* America *from* certain constituents (Daniels and Graham 15).

from the key preceding ethnological text, William Z. Ripley's 1899 *The Races of Europe,* which divided Europe into Alpines, Nordics, and Mediterraneans, basing these divisions on physiognomy, somatotype, and skin color, as well as social and cultural distinctions, and rooting all divergence in heredity. The key innovation of the "Dictionary" was its subcategorization: moving beyond the five primary colors of ethnology to create hierarchies within ethnic groups.

The "Dictionary" was built out of an informal "list of races or peoples" that Ellis Island officials had been keeping for years, and using to compile a crude count of immigrants for statistical purposes (Weil 370). But the "Dictionary" signals a shift in that it makes a concerted effort to create divisions that might be useful beyond counting and broadly classifying newcomers—the text repeatedly strives for further divisions and discriminations. For instance, under the entry for "Negro, Negroid, African, Black, Ethiopian or Austafrican," the "Dictionary" begins by describing "that grand division of mankind distinguished by its black color" (100). The document's authors concede that "in a simple classification for immigration purposes it is preferable to include all of the above under the term 'Negroes.' They are alike in inhabiting hot countries and in belonging to the lowest division of mankind from an evolutionary standpoint" (100). Yet the "Dictionary" offers ever more qualified and subtle categorizations when considering the "bewildering confusion in terms used to indicate the different mixture of white and dark races" (101). As a huge group of Others, "Negroes" seemingly required minimal taxonomy. Yet when the challenge was to differentiate within many shades of black and white, the project of generating "racial knowledge" gained momentum—at stake was exposure to the "lowest division of mankind," from a eugenic perspective. As Thomas Guglielmo, David Theo Goldberg, Anna Stubblefield, Matthew Frye Jacobson, Jennifer Guglielmo, and others have shown, this "new" racial "knowledge" manufactured shades of non-whiteness, using darkness to symbolize genetic inferiority and using the implication of genetic inferiority to rescind whiteness. A result was that "black color" and "dark races" came to be loaded rhetorical terms and tools, facilitated in their usage by eugenic constructions of disability.

As Patrick Weil has argued, the "Dictionary" was used primarily "for the purpose of demonstrating the inferior capacity of certain races and peoples, primarily from Eastern and Southern Europe" and Africa. Notably, the influence of the document "on the future course of immigration policy was enormous" (Weil 373). Just as the bureaucracy of immigration was multiplying, so too were the powers given to immigration officials to differentiate between individuals. There were now many more ways to be racially abnormal.

Roger Daniels shows that the Dillingham report "popularized, if it did not invent, the category of 'old' and 'new' immigrants" with new immigrants being "both different from and inferior to" old (pre-1880) immigrants (62). And Foucault suggested that the proliferation of categorization that the "Dictionary" engendered also typifies a "new racism": "a racism against the abnormal, against individuals who, as carriers of stigmata, or any defect whatsoever" allows them to be detected and constructed as a danger. This, in his words, "is an internal racism that permits the screening of every individual within a given society" (*Abnormal* 317). This "new" racism always interacts with the "old" racism of identifying differences *between* larger ethnic groups. As Martin Pernick points out, there are historical bases for this shift—movements more gradual and diffuse than Foucault suggests, yet still recognizable. Pernick writes that early twentieth-century eugenic rhetoric helped to convert ethnicity into race—linking race to the idea of "heredity as immutable" (56). For instance, people of the Jewish religion from varying backgrounds and geographies became Jews; then they also became, as Ellis Island doctor J. G. Wilson wrote in 1911, "a highly inbred and psychopathically inclined race," whose defects are "almost entirely due to heredity" (493). Jewish ethnicity may have been characterized by the religious and cultural habits that made a "people" unique. The Jewish "race" would be classified by genetic characteristics that mark a group as defective. Race became a "*project* in which human bodies and social structures [were] represented and organized" (Chang 29). Racialization was both a project (noun) in that it was the result of concerted and organized rhetorical action on the part of groups like the IRL and a *projection* of the nation's fear of difference onto the bodies of immigrants.[11] As Catherine Kudlick has written, every Ellis Island rejection "reinforced the ideal of a healthy nation" (61).

Robert Chang suggests that immigrants *became racialized* as they entered Ellis Island. Chang calls this new racism "nativistic racism" because racism and nativism became "mutually constitutive" (30).[12] Ellis Island was a key part of this process, conveniently extracting (or manufacturing) from the stream of newcomers a range of dark, disabled, sexually ambiguous others who, when

---

11. This reinforcement of course was repeatedly unsuccessful, as any desire for normalcy goes unrequited. As David Gerber adds, "When we see normality asserted in regards to the body and the mind, we are usually seeing anxious and aggressive projections of boundary-drawing that are meaningful in understanding a society's felt need and points of stress" (50).

12. Chang's definition of "nativistic racism" emerges from the work of Étienne Balibar and of Omi and Winant, the latter developing the idea of "racial formation," the former the concept of this new "differentialist racism" (qtd. in Chang 30). Lisa Lowe also cites Omi and Winant in her book *Immigrant Acts,* and she similarly suggests that racialization happens "along the legal access of definitions of citizenship" (11).

marked out, allowed a white, Western European, heteronormative, and normal, able (and wholly fictional) American body to rise out of the negative space. The "new racism" at Ellis Island gave this process prominent grammars of race and ethnicity, with the accent of defect and disability. Foucault argued that these two types of racism—old and new—were most fully "grafted" by Nazism. Yet Ellis Island was perhaps the place where these forces were first successfully grafted, and *used*. Of course, immigrants carried ideas about race and racisms across the Atlantic with them, and disability was not created immediately or solely upon their arrival; but the Ellis Island rhetorical space was constitutive of both race and disability in important (though never monolithic) ways.

As Foucault has noted, medicine constructs bodies by "limiting and filtering" what we can sense and what we pay attention to, through classification systems, and then transcribing difference into language (*Birth* 135). This limiting and filtering might proceed according to what Foucault called "the nomination of the visible," wherein the definition and coherence of difference is located in the skin and skull (132). Recall the inspection process itself. But also recall that the language used to attribute defectiveness to Chinese immigrants referred to brain capacity, based on skull measurements.[13] The situated practices of Ellis Island were enabled by texts like the "Dictionary," just as the situated practices of Ellis Island provided the pseudoscientific basis for such texts to be created—rhetorical discourse and rhetorical space were mutually constitutive. Ellis Island manufactured both newly nominal and newly visible difference. The island, as a "heterotopia of deviation" and as a "special rhetorical space," processed the aforementioned "new racism." In this new cartography, Ellis Island functioned to filter and remap the bodies of immigrants.[14] To figure out who was American, one had to scientifically create, locate, mark, and showcase the expulsion of he and she who were not.[15] Thus Ellis Island,

---

13. Martha Gardner also suggests that the "Dictionary" "argued for a link between sexual deviance and visible racial-ethnic otherness" (66). Through this "Dictionary," "immigration officials . . . defined moral deviance as a *visible procedure long* before federal courts would confirm the visual common sense of racialized and sexualized identities" (51; italics mine).

14. James Tyner argues that "the idea that bodies belong to specific places is a peculiar construct of . . . the last few decades of the nineteenth century" (23). This was "a period of knowledge production that centered on embodied spaces" and "the disciplining of bodies through space" (24). Indeed, the connection of a given body with a "naturalized" ethnicized space was a relatively new concept. This was one of the main functions of the "Dictionary," linking bodies to geographic regions—spaces were given bodies, but bodies were given spaces, too.

15. Snyder and Mitchell suggest that the "commonality" of the majority "was marked not in the likeness of their valued citizens, but rather in the existence of a common social dis-ease with the biologically stigmatized. In this way racialized and disabled others were catapulted to the status of transatlantic pariahs" (129). To be American was to be *not* the racialized, disabled

as a rhetorical space, was a conduit or centrifuge through which race and defect could be redefined. Ellis Island offered a page—not a blank page, but an available surface—upon which racial Others could be newly mapped, always located offshore from an American ideal.[16]

Kevin Hetherington writes of heterotopias that "they exist only in relation" (43). A heterotopia is established based on its opposition to other sites, not based on an Otherness derived solely from itself. Ellis Island perfectly exemplifies this relation—its rhetorical purpose was always to establish the normalcy of the American mainland, the white mainstream. Looked at in and of itself, Ellis was just an island. But viewed from within North America—then, and now—it is something much different, something capable of setting terms through which difference is established and mandated.

THE TERMS OF RHETORICAL DISABILITY

When, in 1907, the term "feebleminded" was adopted as a class for exclusion at Ellis Island, eugenicists and immigration restrictionists found a broad brush for the application of derogation and the attribution of deviance. Feeblemindedness was classified as "an awkward mentality which is beyond much hope of improvement [. . .] Appearance, stigmata, and physical signs may confirm such diagnosis" (Mullan 101). This term had been used in America since the 1850s, when state asylums emerged. Anyone deemed unproductive or otherwise "backward" could be excluded from society and housed in these asylums, or "idiot schools" (Kline 15). Then, as at Ellis Island, the term "feebleminded" was useful for its flexibility. The term took on greater meaning in the early twentieth century, when it was charged with eugenic rhetoric. Undesirable people were now not just to be kept out of sight—they needed to be kept out of the genetic pool as well. "Feeblemindedness" was often interpreted as a purely statistical—and usefully tautological—category. The *Eugenical News,* in 1916, stated that the lowest 3 percent of the community at large "determined by definitely standardized mental tests, are to be called feeble-minded" ("Definition"). The authors admitted that "objections may be urged against such a standard

---

alien. As Étienne Balibar writes, "The racial-cultural identity of 'true nationals' remains invisible, but it can be inferred (and is ensured) a contrario by the alleged, quasi-hallucinatory visibility of the 'false nationals.' . . . In other words, it remains constantly in doubt and in danger; the fact that the 'false' is too visible will never guarantee that the 'true' is visible enough" (60).

16. The heterotopia of deviation and the special rhetorical space come together at Ellis Island as what Gareth Hoskins calls a "racialized landscape," "where racial categories frame a discourse of national identity" and where race was a "geographical project," "a social category constructed to consolidate claims to space by alienating others from it" (96; 109, paraphrasing Mitchell 230).

based on the 'community at large,' which would differ from area to area and time to time." But "incidentally, the new method solves the problem of estimating the proportion of feeble-minded in the population. It is three per cent by definition." Of course, this is perhaps the strongest evidence of the bad science of eugenics, as it is also clear evidence of the subjective nature of this eugenic project: the goal was not to diagnose clearly and scientifically or to understand feeblemindedness, it was to exclude a certain quotient of the population.[17]

Howard Knox, arguably the most powerful man at Ellis Island and the number-one surgeon at Ellis Island from 1912 to 1916, in the textbook he created for his officers on the mental testing of aliens, wrote that "fortunately the term 'feeble-mindedness' is regarded by most alienists as a sort of waste basket for many forms and degrees of weak-mindedness, and since it is incorporated in the law as a mandatorially [*sic*] excludable defect, it is especially suited to the needs of the examiners who for the sake of conservatism and certain fairness include many imbeciles under the term" ("Tests" 125). Knox's motivations of course were always eugenic: "Fortunately," he wrote, "the laws are such that feebleminded aliens may be certified and deported before they have had an opportunity to contaminate the blood of the nation or to commit any crime" (122).

Ellis Island, and eugenics writ large, projected suggestions of interior (mental, moral, biological) inferiority onto the surface of the body and into gesture and bearing.[18] Officers (and then every immigrant) became well versed in this symbology—this rhetoric. Howard Knox wrote that "in the higher and more refined grades of deficiency, the most important element in the diagnosis is the 'human test' or the ability of one human being to take the mental measurement of another by conversing and associating with him. This intuitive ability can be very highly developed in persons of a strong and pleasing personality and good physique" ("Tests" 127).[19] The better looking you are, the better you'll be able to pick out inferiors. The conflation of perceived mental or physical disability with differences of ethnicity, class, gender, and sexuality

17. As I will explore further, this quotient approach to exclusion would soon carry over to the enterprise of immigration legislation—when the doors to Ellis Island closed in 1921, the "quota" for immigration by nation would also be capped at 3 percent. This would later be lowered to 2 percent in 1924.

18. This became what Snyder and Mitchell call a "corporeal regime," in which "the body must be made to bear witness to an otherwise internal deviance" (141). Such a regime is, in their words, "essentially a discursive order grafted onto the body to visually articulate morals and laws," calling for an "over-reliance on readings of the symbology of the body" (142).

19. Knox continues, further explaining the construction of the norm only ever in reference to "positive cases": "It must be based on the experience of having seen and examined many positive and also normal cases and the examiner must be a broad-minded, big-souled man keenly alive to the frailties and shortcomings of the human race in general, including himself" ("Tests" 127).

gels in the development of each of these snapshot glances and frames how we look at ourselves and one another. Whether or not this outcome was desired, Ellis Island helped to strengthen or validate this propensity for body-reading in everyone.[20] This "human test" became a form of interpellation at Ellis Island—the idea that one can size up a "defective" is one of the most pervasive social attitudes about disability. In the archive of images that accompanies the book, further discussed in the third major section of the book, I offer examples from the manual that Knox developed for Ellis Island inspectors, showing the supposed facial characteristics of different forms of feeblemindedness.

When Ellis Island surgeon E. H. Mullan later wrote about the mental inspection process for *Public Health Reports,* he emphasized the ways that the mental and the physical overlapped, and the ways that "feeble-mindedness" might be a way to enforce racial typing and exclusion as well.[21] Mullan wrote that "the physical details in the medical inspection of immigrants have been dwelt on at some length, and necessarily so, because a sizing up of the mentality is not complete without considering them. Speech, pupil symptoms, goiters, palsies, atrophies, scars, skin lesions, gaits, and other physical signs, all have their meaning in mental medicine. . . . Knowledge of racial characteristics in physique, costume and behavior are important in this primary sifting process" (733). Mullan went on to echo Knox and to reinforce the idea that any good American should be able to co-identify racial, mental, and physical deficiency, suggesting that "experience enables the inspecting officer to tell at a glance the race of an alien. . . . Those who have inspected immigrants know that almost every race has its own type of reaction during the line inspection. On the line if an Englishman reacts to questions in the manner of an Irishman, his lack of mental balance would be suspected. The converse is also true. If the Italian responded to questions as the Russian Finn responds, the former would in all probability be suffering with a depressive psychosis" (733). Clearly, those who trespassed racial categories and stereotypes could be quickly and easily disciplined. The ability to view racial trespass as deficiency was meant to be made innate within the American citizen. This mandate interacted with a very active rhetorical push to identify and stigmatize racial trespass within the country, closely policing the color line through antimiscegenation laws, for instance, and attributing a perceived wayward genetic stream within the country to mixed blood.

20. The inculcation of an investigatory gaze worked its way across the Atlantic as well: by 1907 "about ten times as many people were refused transportation for medical reasons as were barred upon arrival at United States ports" ("Annual Reports of the Commissioner General" 62, 83). This movement toward "remote control," however, was just beginning.

21. You would note that the faces in Goddard's *Manual* are seemingly "white." But the vision that this text trained for would allow these "feebleminded" faces and bodies to be effectively "colored" as exceptions to the genetic superiority of Western European "white" stock.

The invention of the term "moron" then became another important move for immigration restriction. This term was invented by Henry Goddard in 1910, and the classification was key to research he performed on immigrants at Ellis Island beginning in 1913—the term should be understood as, in part, a product of this rhetorical space.[22] As Anna Stubblefield has argued, Goddard's invention of this term as a "signifier of tainted whiteness" was the "most important contribution to the concept of feeble-mindedness as a signifier of a racial taint," through the diagnosis of the menace of alien races, but also as a way to divide out the impure elements of the white race (173; 162). The moron was viewed as, in the words of Goddard's contemporary, Margaret Sanger, "the mental defective who is glib and plausible, bright looking and attractive" (210). This person "may not merely lower the whole level of intelligence in a school or in a society, but may . . . increase and multiply until he dominates and gives the prevailing 'color'—culturally speaking—to an entire community" (210). The "moron," designated as a high-functioning feebleminded individual, yet capable of "passing" as normal, being attractive to normals, highly sexualized, and thus an even greater menace to the gene pool, was a threat that created the need for greater diligence and surveillance, and inspection and worry, in the whole population and on the borders. This desire to detect, detain, and deport the confusing border creatures, and thus somehow protect the supposedly clear delineation of an untainted norm, was achieved through linguistic and symbolic finesse. "Feeblemindedness" became a useful categorical wastebasket. The "moron" upped the stakes. The "moron" was also a particularly gendered construct. As Stepan argues, people tend to act as though eugenics impacted all genders equally, when it did not—it was focused primarily on women, because their reproduction was thought of as controllable, because

---

22. Steven Gelb argues that it is important also to recognize the discourses that preceded Goddard's invention of this term. As Gelb writes:

> Henry H. Goddard first coined the term moron and applied it to mature persons who scored between eight and twelve years of mental age on the 1908 Binet Simon test. His contemporaries argued that Goddard had actually discovered a milder type of deficiency than had been identified before, and this claim is still widely accepted. However, that belief is erroneous because it ignores the development of ideas about mild states of mental deficiency in the late eighteenth and nineteenth centuries which defined and shaped Goddard's work in 1910. This mythology sanitizes the modern construct by distancing it from earlier, scientifically discredited paradigms—including faculty and religious psychologies, phrenology, degeneracy theory, and criminal anthropology—in which its roots are planted. (360)

Gelb's argument is that many have seen Goddard's coining of the term "moron" as the beginning of a modern and more valid paradigm of mental testing and classification, and he suggests we recognize the full pseudoscientific history as a way to challenge the validity of all later testing and classification.

their bodies were constructed as both particularly menacing and as possible of being contained and constrained (12). So the potential promiscuity of the "moron" drastically reshaped attitudes toward the bodies of young women.

Feeblemindedness and the classification "moron," as wastebasket terms, incorporated many biases into bodily signs. As June Dwyer has written of immigration law in this period, despite the specificity of the catalog of restrictions that each new law introduced, "generalizing phrases" such as feeblemindedness, "moral turpitude," and "psychopathic inferiority" "were easily read as catch-all terms and invited blanket condemnation" (108). "It was quite easy, for those who were so inclined, to elide . . . specific restrictions into manifestations of a root condition: the mental and physical inferiority of the immigrant body" (108). That is, the flexibility of terms allowed *any* noticeably foreign body to be made inferior.

Importantly, while the location of defect in the face of the immigrant was still the dominant visual trope of immigration restriction, the moron needed to be less detectable to be more menacing. As Goddard wrote, what "we are struggling very hard to overcome in the popular mind [. . .] is the idea that these defective children ['morons'] show their defect in their faces. The real fact [. . .] is that the most dangerous children in a community are those that look entirely normal" (*Feeblemindedness* 2). By creating a category of "defective" that eludes visual investigation, the inspection process could reach further into the bodies of immigrants, and the sweep of exclusion could be even further extended. This move also allowed for a further *combination* of the disciplining power of the spectacle, and the disciplining power of diffuse surveillance. The invention of the "moron," while originating in the special rhetorical space of Ellis Island, had the power to float into the consciousness of the nation. Thus this microhistory shows clearly how the disciplinary shift from spectacle to surveillance also results in a proliferation of discourses, architectures, and choreographies, the tangle of which is best investigated rhetorically. The discourses of power and surveillance engendered by the invention of terms like "moron" allowed the nation eventually to dispatch with Ellis Island inspectors altogether, and enlist us all in enforcing exclusions.

TRASH

In 1911 Charles Davenport wrote the extremely influential *Heredity in Relation to Eugenics,* a book that "was assigned reading in many of the eugenics courses that were springing up at colleges and universities across the country, and was cited in more than one-third of the high school biology textbooks of the era" (Cohen, *Imbeciles* 112). In the book he suggested that, "summarizing the review of recent conditions of immigration," after he has looked in depth at each group, "it appears certain that, unless conditions change of themselves or are radically changed, the population of the United States will, on account of the great influx of blood from South-Eastern Europe, rapidly become darker in pigmentation, smaller in stature, more mercurial, more attached to music and art, more given to crimes of larceny, kidnapping, assault, murder, rape, and sex-immorality" (219). This was the lesson being taught in American classrooms.

As Francis Galton wrote in his 1909 *Essays in Eugenics,* "The first and main point is to secure the general intellectual acceptance of Eugenics as a hopeful and most important study. Then let its principles work into the heart of the nation, who will gradually give practical effect to them in ways that we may not wholly foresee" (43). The spectacle of the denial or detainment of aliens at Ellis Island, and the inculcated, incorporated practices of Other-assessment, of marking the alien as defective and the assumedly defective as alien, allowed eugenics to march from Ellis Island into the heart of the nation, and indeed to lead to unprecedented practical applications. Interestingly, as eugenic sentiment flowered, as the national immigration bureaucracy grew by 4,200 percent, as the classifications within and between races multiplied, Ellis Island itself was also growing physically. Originally it had an area of 3.3 acres. In 1892 it was expanded to 11.07 acres; in 1896, 14.2; in 1898, 15.52; in 1906, 20.27; in 1924, 24.37; it now has an area of 27.5 acres (Moreno 127). Ellis Island expanded geographically as it expanded ideologically and, conversely, constricted access to the American frontier just a few miles away. Garbage and landfill from New York was added to the island to increase its size, as was soil from the construction of the new New York subway system. The garbage metaphor seems almost too apt: not just because many saw immigrants as the waste of other countries, but because the rhetorical growth of pseudosciences and racisms were matched by a physical growth that was equally odorous.[23] Another irony: this island, the end of the line for the immigrant, a cul-de-sac for many, was also built out of the dirt that was cleared away to make mass subway transit possible in New York City.

In 1921 President Warren G. Harding passed the first immigration quota law, the Emergency Quota Act, intended to be temporary. This law limited immigration numerically by nation. When such quotas were first proposed in 1919, 1910 census data were used to set thresholds—immigration was then capped at 3 percent of the total of any nation's residents in the United States,

---

23. Vice President Calvin Coolidge wrote in 1921 that America had become a "dumping ground," explaining his eugenic view that "the Nordics propagate themselves successfully. With other races, the outcome shows deterioration on both sides" (14). Coolidge wrote this in an article entitled "Whose Country Is This?" for *Good Housekeeping* magazine in 1921.

according to this census. In effect, the immigration service was able to turn back the clock, to arrest the growth of the country, and to call time-out, harking back to the years before the waves of southern and eastern Europeans and Jews began to arrive in large numbers. The quota law adopted in 1921 went back even further, using the 1890 census numbers (with the cap again at 3 percent), essentially rewinding thirty years of American immigration, in an attempt to reverse the melting of certain races into the American pot.[24] The 1921 quota law was so restrictive that Italians reached their monthly quota the second day after it passed, and thousands more Italians were stranded at Ellis Island or in ships in New York harbor waiting for the next month's allotment.[25] One immigrant from Austria wrote that "I arrived at Ellis Island in 1921 and spent some time there while waiting for a new quota. During that time I was employed in the dining hall" (Karzel n. pag.).

THE FINAL quota law, the Immigration Act of 1924, was passed in 1924. The "per centum" number was lowered to 2 percent, and again based on the 1890 census. As eugenics proponent Charles Davenport stated in a lecture on American immigration policy, the 1924 act "now added the eugenic principle in selection and new legislation was enacted which was directed toward retaining in our population a prevalence of that high quality which it had from the beginning" (2). Essentially, any group tainted by the possibility of genetic inferiority was to be excluded.[26]

With President Coolidge's passage of this National Origins Act in 1924, the door essentially shut. As Roger Daniels wrote, with this act Congress "wrote the assumptions of the Immigration Restriction League and other nativist

---

24. The final quota law of 1924 also took the added step of barring all Japanese immigrants, even though the quota would have limited their immigration to just two hundred persons a year. This move was intended as a slap in the face and was rightly interpreted as an insult by the Japanese government (access Daniels, *Not Like Us* 2002).

25. The Johnson-Reed Act, which included the National Origins and Asian Exclusion Acts, and which built on the aforementioned Emergency Exclusion Act of 1921, eventually let them in—basically allowing entry for those who were on the seas when the law passed. Still, ships would wait in the harbor and race to Ellis Island at midnight of each new month. Access "Six Big Liners in Thrilling Race to Land Aliens."

26. Restrictionist Robert DeCourcy Ward, writing in *Scientific Monthly*, celebrated the idea that although this act "contains no specific provisions looking towards a more rigid exclusion of eugenically undesirable aliens, it will accomplish a better selection than has hitherto been possible" through the "distinct improvement in the mental and physical conditions of our immigrants" (438). Eugenic principles had been largely camouflaged. The quota law also acted against the socially constructed category of "new immigrants," genetically distinct from "old immigrants" pre-1880 (access Daniels, *Not Like Us* 61).

[and eugenicist] groups into the statute book of the United States" (*Guarding* 55). The eugenic message was clear. Prescott Hall, writing on behalf of the IRL in 1920, simply stated that America must "exclude the black, the brown, and the yellow altogether. As to the white, favor the immigration of Nordic and nordicized stock." "We need to become and to remain a strong, self-reliant, united country, with the only unity that counts, viz, that of race" ("Immigration" 193). And this is essentially what the Emergency Quota Act of 1921 and the Immigration Act of 1924 did. These developments were celebrated by eugenicists on both sides of the ocean—from Henry Laughlin to Adolf Hitler.

Further, the 1924 act did not distinguish between refugees and aliens, and this really hurt postwar refugees and contradicted the legacy of sheltering those international citizens who were in danger—for instance Russian Jews fleeing pogroms, or the Irish fleeing the "black and tans," and soon Jews fleeing Hitler.

When Donald Trump signed an executive order "temporarily" banning refugees and immigrants from seven predominantly Muslim countries in 2017, once again "national origin" became the basis for discrimination. Rather, "national origin" became a cover for discrimination that is religious and ethnic. But the "temporary" nature of this order also had precedent. The 1924 act was preceded by a 1921 immigration act in the United States, which was framed as an "emergency quota act" and was temporary. Yet, as John Higham has shown, this became "the most important turning-point in American immigration policy," in part because it habituated immigration agents and institutions to a new, restrictive reality that they were more than ready for (311). Even though Trump's executive order was partially overturned by legal action from the American Civil Liberties Union, on the ground many immigration agents were seemingly all too willing to enforce it to its maximum. As this chapter has evidenced, the North American immigration processing machine has shown, over time, an incredible efficiency and willingness to enforce restriction. An incredible efficiency and willingness to advance eugenics.

NATIONAL ORIGINS AND A "MUSLIM BAN"

Eventually, the 1924 act, linking immigration to national origins, became an embarrassment to the United States. It was deemed a violation of global human rights, was under tremendous pressure from other countries, and Americans worked to ensure it couldn't happen again. The Hart-Celler Immigration and Nationality Act of 1965, setting its sights back to the 1924 law in an attempt to atone for it, banned discrimination against immigrants on the basis of national origin, evening out the quotas across countries. As David Bier points out, "in signing the new law, President Lyndon B. Johnson said that 'the harsh injustice' of the national-origins quota system had been 'abolished'" (n. pag.; access also Fitzgerald and Cook-Martin).

But then, as mentioned at the beginning of the book, and at front-of-mind at the time of this book's writing, Donald Trump signed executive orders in late January 2017 to instate a ban on immigrants and refugees from seven Muslim-majority countries. Trump has said repeatedly that the bans are not about religion or race, despite copious evidence to the contrary. We know, of course, from historians like Candace Epps-Robertson, that arguments about citizenship and immigration only ever really "masquerade" as being about something other than race (119). Further, the ban would seem to fly in the face of the 1965 Act, which was meant to protect the United States from the racism and religious persecution that Trump's order empowers. Trump's order is based entirely on national origins and, even more plainly, is aimed at one particular religious group which also, by force of rhetoric, is viewed as an ethnic group (access Modood). And it is yet to be seen what impact Trump's temporary ban will have. The legal justification for the provisions of the law will surely be tested (access Hudak). But given what we know from the early 1920s, the rhetorical power of the executive orders will be vast. This ban works in rhetorical concert with Trump's *first week* machine-gun-fire sequence of executive orders to build a border wall with Mexico and to keep a public record of crimes committed by immigrants, and with sweeping increases in the power of immigration agents and agencies to detain and deport, and it is even connected to Trump's public and personal endorsement of the idea of torture. The executive orders may be tested in Congress and the courts, but the empowerment the orders give to xenophobia and racism are effective immediately.

NORMALCY

President Warren Harding's own rise to power in America was fueled by the immigration restriction rooted at Ellis Island, and he relied on some of the same rhetorical tools that eugenicists and restrictionists had made useful and popular. In his famous 1920 speech on "Readjustment," Harding used (or perhaps even invented) the term *normalcy* to describe an idealized state, attainable once America was again at peace and had closed its doors to foreigners (access Murray). This "Return to Normalcy" was his campaign slogan, not dissimilar to Donald Trump's "Make America Great Again" or Trump's inauguration speech's repetitively shouted "America First." In these cases, the emphasis is on reclaiming a past version of the country and reorganizing around the priorities and privileges—to prioritize and protect the privileges—of a past era of immigrants. Both campaigns made it clear that a huge part of this return would be to turn back the tide of immigration. Trump's "America First," like Warren Harding's "Return to Normalcy" speech, sent a clear eugenic message. The difference is that Harding created a new word ("normalcy") to code his sentiments. Trump used an old slogan ("America First"), calling up the name of the anti-Semitic national organization that urged the United States to appease Adolf Hitler.

While many believed Harding was making a lexical mistake, the word perhaps nicely summed up a new system of making-normal. Of particular note was Harding's strong push for "not submergence in internationality but sustainment [*sic*] in triumphant nationality" (n. pag.). He was referring here both to the end of war overseas and to the end of the stream of immigration. Harding was promising to return the United States to its status before World War I. This meant winding the clock back, most notably, on immigration and racial "change"—sentiments that we know Trump was intentionally tapping into as well. Harding promised to close the gates, and he did just that. As Roger Daniels points out, his speech "served as a stimulus for congressional action on immigration restriction" (Daniels and Graham 18).[27] The rhetoric of an idealized American "normalcy" is what allowed Harding and others to paint the international world as irrational, crooked, impaired, while the new America would be straight and sure on its feet. The traditional concept of the norm, defined by Canguilhem as "a polemical concept which negatively qualifies," also applies to Harding's "normalcy"—he does not have to say what America will be, only to qualify what it will not be. In such cases, "the abnormal, while logically second, is existentially first" (243).[28]

In Canada, a decade earlier, Robert Borden won election as Prime Minister behind the slogan "A White Canada," a phrasing he had first trotted out when he was immigration minister in 1908, and which he used in his campaign in British Columbia to play to anti-Asian sentiment in that province (access Boyko). Indeed, the xenophobia was that plain, that straightforward.

---

27. It helped that the House was "dominated by radical anti-immigration forces" (Daniels and Graham 18). For instance, Albert Johnson, chair of the House Committee on Immigration in 1924, made specific reference to the danger of incoming "abnormally twisted" and "unassimilable" Jews: "filthy, un American and often dangerous in their habits" (qtd. in Daniels and Graham 20).

28. For more from the field of disability studies on the concept of normalcy, access Lennard Davis, *Constructing Normalcy.*

Of course, Harding's reference to "normalcy" pertains to a subject position around which this rhetoric of difference swivels, just as clearly as Borden's "whiteness." Disability studies scholars use the term *normate* to designate the unexamined and privileged subject position of the supposedly (or temporarily) able-bodied individual and the ways in which our culture valorizes that position. As with the concepts of whiteness or of heteronormativity, the normate occupies a supposedly preordained, unproblematic, and unexamined central position. In disability studies, this concept has come to symbolize how norms are used to control bodies—normalcy, as a social construct, *acts* upon people with disabilities. Rosemarie Garland-Thomson defines the normate as "the constructed identity of those who, by way of the bodily configurations and cultural capital they assume, can step into a position of authority and wield the power it grants them" (*Extraordinary* 8). A normate culture, then, continuously reinscribes the centrality, naturality, neutrality, and unquestionability of this normate position. Such cultures demand normalcy and enforce norms, marking out and marginalizing those bodies and minds that do not conform. Norms circulate, have cultural ubiquity, and ensure their own systemic enforcement.

The Jew, the Asian with "insufficient brain capacity," the black, the brown, and the yellow, the "tainted" white, and all other conveniently unfit or enfeebled aliens, are the ground against which some fiction of the "normal" American comes into relief. For Trump, the ground was shockingly similar— Muslims, even if they were military heroes; Mexicans, successfully criminalized through his rhetoric; disabled media members; women in positions of power; these groups and individuals all became spectacles of scorn, all that was not "great." His rhetoric was nothing new, but it was built upon attitudes that we can trace back to Ellis Island. In doing this tracing, we also need to move forward, to understand how Ellis Island was picked up and applied across other geographies.

EXPANSIVE REJECTION

What is remarkable about the "normalcy" that Ellis Island spawned in the United States was not that racist and eugenic sentiments and policies were new, but that now the mechanisms for marking out difference, and thus fortifying the "normal" position only ever in contrast, were multiplied. While the National Origins Act was blunt and finite, the bodily attitudes interpellated or passed along, contagiously, to all who passed through Ellis Island were nuanced and profligate, they were plenty and they were powerful. Post-1924, eugenics became a widespread projection of Ellis Island across the entire country. The rhetoric surrounding the Ellis Island process and spectacle helped to inculcate "normalcy" into the American everyday, to bury systems of downward comparison and stigmatization into the citizen's psyche. When Harding used the term *normalcy* in his presidential campaign of 1920, he solidified an ongoing rhetorical reality: America had defined and would continue most successfully to define itself by what it rejected, not by what it was.

Within a year of the 1924 act, the Commissioner of Immigration at Ellis Island, Henry Curran, reported proudly, though ridiculously, that "all immigrants now look exactly like Americans" (n. pag.). The dangerous hope and the seeming lack of logic in a statement such as this nicely sums up the frantic play for "normalcy" and the tragic comedy of this drama. To say that "all immigrants now look like Americans" simply reveals that, all along, the idea of Americanness has been an opportunistic projection. Restrictionists shifted more emphasis to the deportation of new Americans within the country, communists, and other threats, and the eugenic focus shifted to the lower classes within America, maintaining racial and ethnic prejudice that had been defined and applied at Ellis Island.[29]

One specific relocation for Ellis Island as a rhetorical space has been the U.S.–Mexico border. The U.S.–Mexico border patrol was founded on May 28, 1924—*just three days* after the passage of the National Origins Act. As Kelly Lytle Hernandez has shown, the patrol, to this day, allows for "perseverance of racially differentiated systems of coercive force . . . racial profiling [by the border patrol is] a wormhole of racial domination; a practice in which past articulations of white supremacy live in the present" (13). This wormhole, in part, allows Ellis Island to travel into the present. Mexican immigration reached a high point of 89,000 in 1924, and then, "*immediately* upon the passage of the law of 1924, restrictionists began a campaign to extend the quota system to the Western hemisphere" (Higham 57; italics mine). In this way, Ellis Island lives on in current American anti-immigration rhetoric.

In 1915 the Ku Klux Klan was inaugurated. By 1923, KKK membership reached 2.3 million. As Gary Gerstle has shown, it was no coincidence that "the kind of eugenics-inflected revulsion against 'mongrelization' that informed Congressional immigration debates" leading up to the 1921 and 1924 crackdowns "also triggered an expansion of and hardening of state anti-miscegenation laws," including the 1924 Virginia law, which "powerfully strengthened the nation's substantial body of racially and eugenically-based marriage laws" (114). On March 20, 1924, the Virginia legislature passed two

---

29. The rhetoric of "normalcy" and the impetus for immigration restriction also gained important momentum from the Red Scare between 1917 and 1920.

closely related eugenics laws: SB 219, entitled "The Racial Integrity Act [1]," and SB 281, "An act to provide for the sexual sterilization of inmates of State institutions in certain cases," referred to as "The Sterilization Act." The alien "feebleminded" became larger targets within the country as eugenic sterilization became widespread. By 1932 thirty states had sterilization statutes on the books, thanks in large part to the rhetoric of immigration restriction. In the United States, there were seventy thousand total known sterilizations between 1907 and the end of World War II.[30] Eugenic anti-immigrant rhetoric reached into the bodies of those racialized others made alien within the country. The "integrity" of racial groups could be qualified and policed in multiple, overlapping ways. For instance, sterilization was always explicitly linked to class, and black Americans were specifically targeted for sterilization when they could also be labeled as mentally defective, because they were then seen as more likely to be sexually promiscuous and to thus breed interracially (Holloway 56). As Holloway writes, the "class bias in sterilization" was always "openly articulated" (55). She also explains that many whites believed that "mentally unfit African Americans were especially likely to be sexually promiscuous and engage in inter-racial sex . . . [thus] this population was more likely to pollute the white races and should be sterilized" (56).

Ellis Island's rhetorical "success" allowed Americans to pick up the border, so to speak, and lay it down across the bodies of thousands of Others within the country. As Allison Carey has shown, despite the fact that most people, historians included, believe there was a long-standing, historical exclusion of people with intellectual disabilities from society, there is plenty of evidence that the eugenics era recalibrated these exclusions in profound ways: minority groups could now be "portrayed as incompetent and dependent," and yet

because the category of "feeblemindedness" provided a secure and flexible basis for exclusion, it may well be that the exclusion of people with intellectual disabilities from citizenship was central to the inclusion of other marginalised populations. As women and African-Americans fought for the rights of citizenship, in general they did not fight to overturn the dual-track system or the liberal narrative. Rather, they argued that definitions of incompetence had been misapplied to their population [. . .] and the liberal narrative could remain dominant as long some populations, including those with

---

30. At this time, Margaret Sanger wrote that "every feeble-minded girl or woman of the hereditary type, especially of the moron class, should be segregated during the reproductive period. . . . Moreover, when we realize that each feeble-minded person is a potential source of an endless progeny of defect, we prefer the policy of immediate sterilization, of making sure that parenthood is absolutely prohibited to the feeble-minded" (n. pag.).

> intellectual disabilities, remained defined as "incompetent" and outside the
> realm of practicing citizenship. (425)

Étienne Balibar has written about the ways that physical borders have become "inner borders" (78). That is, to establish "national normality," the mode of discrimination between the national and the alien "is *internalized* by individuals" (78). These inner borders allow for "some borders [to be] no longer situated at the borders at all" and to reside instead "wherever selective controls are to be found" (89). Another way of stating this, in the wake of eugenic anti-immigration programs and rhetorics, would be to say that border spaces like Ellis Island constructed disability in a particular way: as a tool to differentiate the citizen from the noncitizen. Disability has always—of course—been constructed and experienced in many other ways. That said, we should pay attention to how disability continues to be used a tool to differentiate citizens from noncitizens, those with rights from those without.

REMOTE CONTROL

Following the closing of the doors on immigration in 1924, U.S. immigration restriction efforts shifted from "filtering" arriving bodies to detecting and deporting within the country. The raids on Mexican workers in the Southwest in the 1950s (and that continue today) are one notable example of this new emphasis. But these raids were preceded (and in some ways, anticipated and allowed) by the "Palmer Raids" between 1918 and 1921, exemplified by the "Red Raids" of 1920, during which three thousand suspected communists were detained and deported, many of these bodies held at Ellis Island (access "500 Reds"). Ellis Island continued to be the space that many East Coast political dissidents (such as C. L. R. James) were "removed to" before deportation, from the 1920s through the 1960s. It is also interesting that the overwhelming emphasis of much anticommunist rhetoric was put upon the foreignness of possible dissidents, seen as what Woodrow Wilson called "hyphenated Americans."

During the "Tong Wars" of the later 1920s, many more Chinese immigrants were removed from New York to Ellis Island for eventual deportation (access "More Tong Wars"). Ellis Island became a space, like Guantánamo Bay Prison today, where suspect bodies could be held indefinitely, all rights and protections countermanded in this "special rhetorical space." The aggressiveness of current Immigration and Customs Enforcement efforts clearly relies on similar suspensions of legal protections and rights, and no longer relies on the fixity of the physical border to apply these powers. In fact, ICE detention centers can be seen as contemporary Ellis Islands, towed onto the mainland. I will explore these centers in greater detail in the final section of the book.

Daniel J. Tichenor has argued that, following the 1924 clampdown, immigration restriction also gained more "remote control" (117). Aristide Zolberg suggests that "remote control amounted to a projection of the country of destination's borders into the world at large" (224). Matthew Coleman has written about this phenomenon more abstractly, by suggesting that there has been a historical shift from the "geopolitics of containment," characterized by hard borders, to a "geopolitics of engagement," which "reaches inward to 'local' spaces and at once outward to 'regional' spaces beyond the state" (610). This selective containment and engagement was allowed not just because American restrictionists began to have more control over the ways that immigration was restricted in other countries, before an immigrant even made it to Ellis Island, but also because of the rhetorical power of the "new racial and ethnic map" drawn at Ellis Island (Ngai, *Impossible* 3).

One example of this "remote control" was that American restrictionists began to experiment with the use of field workers at American consuls overseas. These workers examined would-be immigrants in their own countries. As Henry Laughlin wrote, in a personal letter in 1921:

> We have demonstrated that in friendly countries the American Consul can, without giving international offence, make first-hand studies in the field, of the would-be immigrants. The minute of any objection to the field-studies appears, the Consul and his workers simply withdraw to the American consulate, and announce that if the would-be immigrant desires to have his passport vised [*sic*], he must provide the information concerning his own "case history" and "family pedigree." Because of the immigrants desire to come to the United States, they smooth the way for perfecting these field studies, and give their consent to medical examinations. In the future, doubtless the cost of these examinations would be placed upon the immigrant, so that ready and prompt cooperation means less expense than hesitancy or non-cooperation. (3)

He continues: "I do not expect the field studies to be as perfect as they could be made if the Law were established, [but the Consul can get information] which under no circumstances could be secured at Ellis Island" (4). Laughlin's trip abroad had been made possible by an honorary appointment by the secretary of labor, designating Laughlin as "United States Immigration Agent to Europe."

As Mae Ngai has argued, post-1924, there was a new "global racial and national hierarchy," as this new map articulated an unprecedented "production of racial knowledge" and a "new sense of territoriality, which was marked by unprecedented awareness and state surveillance" of borders (*Impossible* 7; 3). Snyder and Mitchell reveal the ways that the eugenics movement created new connections across the Atlantic. In the evolving relationship between the United States and Europe, commonality across the Atlantic "was marked not in the likeness of their valued citizens, but rather in the existence of a common social dis-ease with the biologically stigmatized. . . . Racialized and disabled others were catapulted to the status of transatlantic pariahs" (*Impossible* 129). Clearly, we can see similar influences in current transnational "exports" of American norms, and in the ways that race and ability continue to strongly inflect immigration control internationally. In the next section of the book, I will show how such exports worked just North of Ellis Island, at Canada's key immigration station, Pier 21. Further, a clear line can be drawn from Ellis Island and the rhetoric of immigration restrictionists and North American eugenicists in this period, across the Atlantic, to Germany and the Nazi T4 program. "Aktion T4" was a Nazi eugenic program that systematically killed between 200,000 and 250,000 people with intellectual or physical disabilities between 1939 and 1941 in Germany.

Nazi doctors named American eugenicists as their ideological mentors at Nuremberg. The chalk marks at Ellis Island might be understood as a precursor to the armbands and the tattooing of the Nazi regime.[31] In 1936, Nazis gave a medal to Harry Laughlin, IRL founder. He was recognized by Hitler for his "model eugenic law" (Carlson 12). Hitler also praised the eugenic provenance of the 1924 American Immigration Restriction Act in *Mein Kampf*.[32]

---

31. In 1927 Charles Davenport of the American Eugenics Society was in contact with Professor Eugen Fischer of the newly formed Kaiser Wilhelm Institute in Berlin. He made a note to send to Fischer "all publications of the Eugenics Record Office so far as they are available. The Institut was opened two weeks ago and is almost without a library. We want to work in close cooperation with them" (Davenport, "Memorandum" n. pag.). The Kaiser Wilhelm Institute, it has now been recognized, was the key location for German eugenic science and racial hygiene—undertaking mass sterilizations and performing experiments on skulls and body parts received from Auschwitz to "establish" the genetic inferiority of those killed.

32. From a 1921 letter between Laughlin and Davenport: "I have not yet received [German] Dr. Edwin Bauer's letter asking for information about sterilization. I shall attend to it promptly upon receipt. The paper on 'National Eugenics in Germany' . . . will appear in the February number of *Eugenics Review*. I shall be especially interested in the success that Dr. Bauer's committee has in developing eugenical interest in Germany. So far as legislation or constitutional provision is concerned, judging from what they have already written into their fundamental law, the time seems ripe for the further development of a national eugenic policy" (n. pag.).

While in the early 1900s immigration restrictionists felt the need to make actual policies more biological in nature, moving from relatively vague economic designations like LPC (likely to become a public charge) to more explicit terminology like "feeble-minded," current immigration reform camouflages biological arguments under economic ones. As Christina Gerken shows, both contemporary immigration opponents and immigration advocates tend to make the same neoliberal arguments about contributions to the economy, disguising "the racist effects of immigration laws and the discourse that surrounds them" through a "focus on economic objectives" (250). Regardless, the engine of immigration discourse continues to be fueled by "race and race anxieties" that we can trace back to Ellis Island (250).

The attitudes incubated or accelerated at Ellis Island led to the eugenic "racial knowledge" that can be comprehended clearly in a text such as the "Dictionary of Races or Peoples." There was a new catalog of races, ordered by deviancy.[33] The use of terms such as "moron" and "feeble-minded," applied nimbly for eugenic purposes, created the rhetorical potential for opportunistic disablement and incorporated a look and a lexicon of eugenics into the American psyche. As mentioned, the island was gradually expanded with landfill, subterranean mazes connecting every building. Ellis Island was also constantly regenerating and redoubling its rhetorical powers, connecting forms of discrimination and derogation. Its ideological spread was vast.

As a "heterotopia of deviation" and a "special rhetorical space," Ellis Island helped to invent—and rhetorically construct—disability as we know it today. This construction continues to inflect our understandings of race, "normalcy," and difference, continues to electrify and transport our borders, continues to exist as a bodily attitude, continues to shade and shadow how we look at others and ourselves. The stories of Ellis Island write and map for us much broader narratives and cultural geographies. We recognize not just the ways that spaces and discourses work together to impose social order, creating spaces in which deviation is sequestered; we also recognize how spaces and discourses in part *create* deviation and difference. Recall the original use of the word *heterotopia* to refer to abnormal anatomy—a displacement, a missing or extra element, a tumor that appears out of place, an alien growth. Ellis Island was a eugenically "hopeful" experiment wherein threats to American purity could be isolated

---

33. This racial knowledge was highly flawed of course, and in this way it was *defective knowledge*—yet it is defective also because the terms by which each race was differentiated from Caucasian or white normalcy was always through perceived defect. Only through defect did difference come into view. The alien, always somewhat spectral, always convenient for the projection of the nation's own insecurities, was also useful for his or her key role in the spectacle of inspection and exclusion—warning every citizen that they too were being watched, that their humanity might also be qualified.

and arrested, and it also inculcated an act of diagnosis, the discursive and rhetorical and spatial terms through which any "abnormal" anatomy might be marked. Recall also that the heterotopia only ever exists "in relation." Hopefully, retelling these stories and remapping this space also demands that we develop a new relation to the history of Ellis Island and to immigration that reevaluates the rhetorical uses of difference. I suggested that we all take a trip to Ellis Island. But Ellis Island visits us, too. We might recognize the ways that the chalk marks can be read on all of our bodies, the ways that Ellis Island travels with each of us wherever we go. As we recognize the ghosts and ruins of this space elsewhere, as we view its regeneration and persistence, we can make an effort to challenge its spectacles and interpellations, and to imagine the resistance and subversion it might have engendered and might still. Finally, in viewing this island as a rhetorically constructed space in which the key grammars were derogation and exclusion, we might also recognize the possible power of any rhetorical or cartographic construction for reimagining the individual, social, and political body more carefully and critically.

The shift to "remote control" over immigration was about empowering and encouraging other countries, other entities within the United States, and individual citizens to begin to enforce immigration restriction and, by extension, to become eugenic agents. But it wasn't new in 1924. It simply became more sanctioned and systematic. Moreover, even after the National Origins Act was later condemned by historians and then politicians, remote control didn't go away.

As Egbert Klautke has shown, "eugenics in the USA was not immediately abandoned after the war, but transformed and 'repackaged': to mainline eugenicists in Germany and the USA, the substance of eugenics was not discredited because of the experience of German racial and genocidal policies" (36). Eugenicists simply used new terms like *family planning* and *genetic counseling*; journals and classes and professorships of eugenics shifted their name to *genetics*.

In a sense, the latent but ongoing work of eugenic policing in North America has been waiting for the state sanctioning that it received from Donald Trump in 2017. But eugenics, and especially eugenic attitudes about immigration, has never ceased. So the historical and rhetorical awareness required to trace and combat this "remote control" must be ongoing as well.

ARCHIVAL EXCESS

The final section of the book, titled ARCHIVE, explores the affective and physical work of archival research in greater detail. But before we leave this ISLAND, it is worth reflecting on where this research comes from.

Much of the material you are reading in the surrounding pages was gathered from the archives at the American Philosophical Association (APA), in Philadelphia. The APA archives are located in a historic building just a few yards from the Liberty Bell and Independence Hall. Leaving the archives on a summer evening, after a long day reading about the scientific racism of the American Eugenics Association, its journals, and the letters between its leaders and Nazi doctors, you will pass hundreds of tourists being taken through re-enactments of scenes from American history, learning about the significance of these memorials and buildings as symbols of the "freedom of humanity." Similarly, when you access the archives at Ellis Island, you can ask ahead for a special pass to take an employee ferry to the island. Or, you can travel on the tourist ferry that leaves Manhattan regularly. On the employee ferry, you will recognize that the labor that currently keeps the monument working is predominantly provided by "new" immigrants, people who do not fit into the historical picture of American immigration that Ellis Island paints. On the tourist ferry, you approach the island from the opposite direction that immigrants would have and, when you look around you, you will invariably see a much more diverse mixture of people than would have been accepted into the country in the early part of the twentieth century.

I note these as felt disjunctions. I note these as uncomfortable ironies. I note these because, clearly, the stories we are telling ourselves about our recent history are selective and narrow.

Of course, Ellis Island is lucky to have survived at all, let alone to have an extensive archive. In 1982, after the Island had fallen into extreme disrepair, then president Ronald Reagan asked Lee Iacocca, the chairman of Chrysler, to collect private funds for restoration. It worked: over $700 million was raised, and this became the largest historical restoration in American history. The National Parks Service continues exemplary stewardship over the Island and its archive. These spaces and archives, of course, are imperiled under Donald Trump, who signed an executive order for the review of protections for these parks, and a proposed $2 billion cut to the Parks budget. Which history will be made available as we move forward?

Another archival space for this work was the Houghton Library at Harvard, where you can read letters between eugenics champion Henry Laughlin and David Starr Jordan, president of Stanford University, about how to find funding for eugenics initiatives, or discover Laughlin workshopping manuscripts with Madison Grant on why only Nordic races were truly suited for democracy. When you go to access these materials, you might proceed past the "gallows lot" in North Cambridge where, when slaves were burned at the stake in the late eighteenth century, the smoke from the fire drifted over Harvard Yard (Walters). This history of slavery at Harvard has largely been forgotten, as has the legacy of eugenics. To get to Houghton, or to leave the archive, you might also move past residence buildings named after A. Lawrence Lowell and Charles William Eliot. In this way, to go and study the racist history of American eugenics, you will also be among lasting monuments to its success.

A. Lawrence Lowell, who served as Harvard president from 1909 to 1933, was an active supporter of eugenics. If you were to examine his legacy, eugenics promotion would be his main intellectual "success." Lowell, who also worked to impose a quota on Jewish students and to keep black students from living in the Yard at Harvard, was particularly concerned about immigration. He joined other eugenicists in calling for sharp racial limits: "The need for homogeneity in a democracy," he insisted, justified laws "resisting the influx of great numbers of a greatly different race" (qtd. in Tichenor 38). Later, he was vice president of the eugenicist Immigration Restriction League, which was founded in 1894 by three young Harvard College graduates, Charles Warren, Robert DeCourcy Ward, and Prescott Farnsworth Hall.

Lowell, Warren, Ward, and Hall had an ally in Charles William Eliot, a Harvard president emeritus in the early 1910s. He also saw the mixture of racial groups through immigration as dangerous, and did all in his power to halt it: "Each nation should keep its stock pure," Eliot famously said: "There should be no blending of races" (175). As Adam Cohen has pointed out, the former Harvard president "was an outspoken supporter of another major eugenic cause of his time: forced sterilization of people declared to be 'feebleminded,' physically disabled, 'criminalistic,' or otherwise flawed" ("Harvard" n. pag.). In 1907 Indiana had enacted the nation's first eugenic sterilization law. In 1913, in the paper "Suppressing Moral Defectives," Eliot declared that Indiana's law "blazed the trail which all free states must follow, if they would protect themselves from moral degeneracy" (176). Eliot became vice president of the First International Eugenics Congress, which met in London in 1912. Two years later, Eliot helped organize the First National Conference on Race Betterment in Battle Creek, Michigan. As Cohen points out, "none of these actions created problems for Eliot [or Lowell] at Harvard, for a simple reason: they were well within the intellectual mainstream at the University" ("Harvard" n. pag.). If you are in the archives at Houghton Library, as I was when researching the role of eugenics proponent Henry Laughlin for this book, you could exit, go straight down Plimpton Street about a block, and you'd find the Eliot and Lowell houses, where students continue to live. These houses are some of the most exclusive on campus, known as the most "Brahmin," the most elite. The houses were created as part of the Harkness family Common-wealth Fund, established in 1918 and also known to support mental hygiene initiatives (Richardson 41).

Though the Eliot and Lowell houses are incredibly well-appointed and turned out, the Henry Laughlin papers that I accessed at the Houghton Library were, for years, housed in an attic at the library in a "state of consider-able decay and disorganization" (Bird and Allen 341). In a way, it is miraculous that they were saved, and thus that the history of Laughlin's coordination and orchestration of American eugenics can be told at all.

In Canada, key archival evidence of the eugenic, racist past is also cur-rently under threat. For more than a century, the Canadian government and Christian churches forced over 150,000 indigenous children into residential schools. Recently, following more than 12,000 lawsuits for compensation for the abuses that happened in these schools, which were designed to eradicate indigenous culture, Canada and the churches reached a settlement. Part of this settlement was that for the thousands of claimants, there was to be a choice about what would happen with their claim documents, but they were never given that choice. The records and the recordings of the voices of sur-vivors stand to be destroyed without the consent of the claimants. As Thomas McMahon suggests, "after they have died, it will be the last and final abuse that Canada, the churches and the courts will inflict on the residential school children" (88).

In each of these archival maps or stories, clear trends can be seen: archives of eugenics and racism are surrounded and supported by ongoing celebra-tions, memorializations, or overt manifestations of eugenics and racism; or they are juxtaposed with celebrations of inclusiveness and exceptionalism that the archives belie or negate. So, as scholars like Adria Imada suggest, we must study these archives as in-process, subject to a variety of reuses and recircu-lations, and we must make the effort to recognize when there might be what Imada calls "affective excess" in and outside of the archival space (28).

When we look for this excess, I would suggest, it is relatively easy to find in Philadelphia, Manhattan, Boston, Halifax, Ottawa, and other places, and it can be described with terms like irony, hypocrisy, and ignorance.

Canada's Pier 21 and the memorialization of immigration

PREVIOUSLY, I asked you to travel with me on a short trip to Ellis Island. We will continue this geographical journey north to Halifax, Nova Scotia, at the far eastern edge of Canada, on the coast of the Atlantic Ocean. We will carry with us our concern with rhetorical spaces, with rhetorical bodies, and with the construction of race and disability through immigration restriction. Halifax is home to Pier 21, an ocean liner terminal and home to immigration sheds that saw over a million immigrants pass through between 1928 and 1971. Pier 21 was designated a Canadian National Historic Site in 1997, became an immigration museum in 1999, and officially became a National Museum of Canada in 2011. Now, Pier 21 is *the* Canadian National Museum of Immigration.[1]

I will offer an overview of the physical history of the grounds of Pier 21, beginning with a genealogy of Canadian policies and practices of immigration restriction based on evolving eugenic ideas of race and disability in the early part of the twentieth century. As was the case in the last section, my method

---

1. The term *Shed 21*, the original name for the site, could be used throughout the book to underscore the site's origins as a cargo shed. But the now-common name Pier 21 is used instead. I footnote this mainly to call attention to the fact that even the current name of the site performs historical erasures. Further, for long periods of time, inspection and immigration processing actually happened at Pier 2, not Pier 21. Again, however, for the sake of simplicity, and to call attention to the ways that this history has always been a sort of rhetorical invention, I stick with labeling the site Pier 21.

here will be to examine Pier 21 as a rhetorical space, a cultural location of disability, a heterotopia of deviation.

I will continue to fold together legislative histories, archival documents, and popular texts to investigate the ways that new categories of race and disability were constructed and reinforced as immigration into Canada accelerated between 1900 and 1930. These policies and practices, it will be shown, were powerfully influenced by ideas about the Canadian environment and the forms of labor needed to reshape and subsist in this environment, but also profoundly influenced by at times shocking ideas about race and genetics. This history is tangled up with Canadian trade interests, colonialism, and settler colonialism, as well as eugenic philosophies influenced by industrialism and agriculture. I will offer an important backdrop not just to help understand other histories but also to put current Canadian immigration laws and policies into historical context. My focus will be on rhetorical space (Mountford; Marback; Quayson) and in particular on how bodies are rhetorically constructed (Snyder and Mitchell; Butler).

This exploration will serve to augment the traditional focus on the United States as the place where eugenics and immigration restriction were most tightly fused, allowing readers to recognize a continental "movement." Importantly, this eugenic movement does not end with the clampdowns on immigration at either Ellis Island or Pier 21. The movement is also part of how these sites are remembered and memorialized to this day. I urge readers to understand that while there are key historical, factual differences between Pier 21 and Ellis Island, it is much more useful to view them as part of the same story of eugenics than it is to separate them. And it is essential that we understand that the particular story of North American and transatlantic eugenics that I am telling in this book is one that has been obscured from the public and continues to be overwritten. We might look back on the early twentieth century and argue that this was an era *characterized* by eugenics, by anti-immigration sentiment. In Harding's case, promising to halt immigration was a way to win a presidential election. Yet we could just as aptly describe our current era as one in which eugenic, anti-immigrant sentiment is central. Harnessing this rhetorical force is still a way to get elected. Importantly, much less has changed about the discourses and rhetorical spaces of immigration than we might expect.

I mentioned in the beginning of the book that immigration has never really been about immigration. Instead, immigration has been about creating a dominant, normative identity; it has been about translating written and spoken and visual arguments about the value of bodies into physical action, mapping them onto other, bigger ideas like continents; it has been about land,

and specifically the theft of land and its justification. One of the shakiest ideas, associated with some of the largest thefts of this history, is the idea of the border. Thus my separation of Canadian and American immigration histories is in almost every way lazy. The Canada–U.S. border, laughably called the "longest unprotected border in the world," is of course very actively and diligently protected, albeit usually not by the military. But it is also protected as an idea, and as an idea that powerfully disenfranchises—for example—First Nations people who choose not to recognize this border and to refuse American or Canadian citizenship or governance. For example, Audra Simpson shows how the Mohawks of Kahnawà:ke, living across this colonial border, refuse and resist the border. This refusal reveals how easily—perhaps even urgently—others, in both countries, have been willing to accept the colonial project as complete, as finished, and thus its borders as sovereign. In what follows, in discussing Canadian immigration history, I hope to be able to *connect* the fiction of Canadian coastal borders (characterized by Pier 21) with the fiction of American coastal borders (characterized by Ellis Island). I hope to show also how the border between the two countries, as well as the border between the United States and Mexico, has been historically invented and maintained as a lie of colonialism, and how the separation between these three countries continues to be rhetorical and unsteady rather than geographical and fixed. This does not diminish but rather increases the impact of these borders, as they are picked up and applied violently across bodies, or as they are used to broker the theft of sovereignty and the theft of land, or as they carefully select the bodies that cannot move across them against the flows of capital that can. Specifically, in creating Canada as a "white man's country," the border has been used both to decide who can come into the country after colonization and to invalidate the geography that existed before colonization.

A WHITE MAN'S COUNTRY

As mentioned previously, Charles Davenport, an American cited by many as the eugenics movement's greatest proponent, defined the movement as "the science of the improvement of the human race by better breeding." Yet, alongside these genetic goals, immigration restriction gave eugenicists an opportunity to construct an improved national body by excluding undesirable races. To do so, eugenicists suggested that certain racial and ethnic groups were disabled, biologically inferior (access Ordover; Hasian, *Rhetoric*). For instance, in Canada, eugenicists such as C. K. Clarke suggested that "feeble-minded" immigrants from certain parts of Europe, "invariably mated with the mental weaklings in their own class as partners, thus perpetuating a race of defectives" (Dowbiggin 619). This threat fueled Clarke's increasingly vehement calls for immigration inspection and restriction at the Canadian borders between 1909 and his death in 1924.

Popular history tends to tie eugenics to Nazi Germany, yet I have shown that the U.S. Immigration Restriction League and the American Eugenics Society were hugely influential organizations that established rhetorics of eugenics in the United States long before the Nazi program, and in fact served as exemplars. Canadian historians tend to isolate Canadian eugenics mainly to forced sterilization programs, beginning in the late 1920s, and most popular in the West. Yet Canada had its own extremely influential but often-overlooked eugenics movement beginning at the turn of the twentieth century, one with clear connections across the country and across the Atlantic. Beginning in the early 1900s, and rooted in the geographies of immigration, Canada developed its own public figures, texts, discourses, spaces, and visual rhetorics of eugenics.

As Constance Backhouse writes, "Canadian history is rooted in racial distinctions, assumptions, laws, and activities, however fictional the concept of 'race' may be" (7). If we ignore this fact, we would "acquiesce to the popular misapprehension that depicts our country as largely innocent of systemic racial exploitation" (7). Or, worse, we would view racism in its historical context in an effort to normalize it—suggesting that we cannot judge the past based on current ideas about racism. Backhouse tells the story of Canadian census takers who, in 1901, were told to classify all Canadians with *w* for white, *r* for red, *b* for black, and *y* for yellow—with the enjoinder that no one could be white who wasn't "pure" white (3). Notice, of course, that the sanctity or purity of the other colors was not a concern. Clearly, these racial classifications are constructed—"human beings simply do not come in any of these colors" (4). So, sure, race is a construct, a fiction. But as Backhouse warns, *racism* is very real, and it is the harm of racism that I will focus on in this book. Racism is very real in Canadian history—a racism that had serious material consequences that cannot be rationalized away.

Evgeny Efremkin has written that bureaucrats like immigration agents, "informed by social Darwinist views on race and ethnicity, coupled with the Anglophone bourgeois concern over modernization brought on by the forces of industrialization and urbanization, both consciously and subconsciously developed an elaborate system of categorization of Canada's population according to prescribed criteria of ethnicity, nationality, and race" (300). In his words, Canadian cultural identity was subject to an "invisible" process in the early twentieth century, one obsessed with categorizing immigrants so as to keep them in categories separate from citizens for as long as possible.

As Janice Cavell and others have shown, Canada always had the eugenic aim of preserving "Canada's predominantly British character" (345). Read: white. Yet this aim developed into more negative eugenic goals and restrictions. One effect was the rhetorical darkening and disabling of the non-British immigrant in the public mind. William Lyon Mackenzie King wrote in 1908: "that Canada should remain a white man's country is believed to be not only desirable for economic and social reasons but highly necessary on political and national grounds" ("Report" 7). Thirty years later, now as prime minister, his opinion unchanged, he wrote: "We must seek to keep this part of the Continent free from unrest and from too much intermixture of foreign strains of blood" ("Diaries").

Overlaying this history is a negative and eugenic framing of the immigrant body as a site and source of contamination—of evil, deficiency, or disease (access Paupst; Schweik, *Ugly Laws*). That was certainly how the Asian body so feared in the early 1900s was framed (access Rinaldi and Dolmage), and this fear only expanded as new and different groups of immigrants began to seek a new home in Canada. Such a framing is haunted by and entangled with disability. For instance, in a historical analysis of early twentieth-century U.S. "ugly laws"—antivagrancy ordinances that themselves emerged from eugenic projects and sought to protect public spaces from unsightly disease and deformity—Susan M. Schweik demonstrates that legal constructions of othered embodiments at the time lumped together the immigrant with the mendicant, the criminal, and the sick. Citing Diana Courvant, she characterizes the intersection of race, poverty, and disability as a confluence of rivers: "different currents but not entirely different matter of substance" (*Ugly Laws* 61). Therefore, sociolegal histories of race and disability can be read together, through one another, to articulate the varied and complex contours to eugenics. These waves encircled both Ellis Island and Pier 21.

A dissatisfaction with Canada's immigration process has been noted from the beginning. Importantly—the practice, seemingly, has never been restrictive *enough*. Notably, what made these processes "defective" was always a lack of focus on weeding out supposed *defectives*. When Lord Durham returned to England to report on the Canadian colony to British Parliament, he made it clear that "the measures which government have adopted are deplorably defective. They have left untouched some of the chief evils of emigration" (Buller 121). Specifically, "the provision for the reception [and inspection] of emigrants are of the most inefficient and unsatisfactory character" (121). Later, restrictions pertaining to the physically and mentally infirm were built into Canada's original immigration legislation of 1869;[2] and the 1886 Immigration Act established screening and quarantine processes, where failure to report the medical conditions of inspected steamship passengers resulted in financial penalties.[3] In 1902 the statute was amended to prohibit the entry of immigrants "suffering from any loathsome, dangerous or infectious disease or malady."[4] When debating the amendment in the House of Commons, Mr. Frank Oliver held that "the first consideration [in immigration standards] should be the intellectual as well as the physical quality of those immigrants."[5] As Valentina Capurri has further explored, with the passage of this statute, persons with mental deficiencies and loathsome or infectious diseases were automatically and absolutely barred from entering the country (91).

As Alan Sears writes, "ultimately the polarization between members of the [Canadian] nation and 'outsiders' as defined by race, culture, and nationality"—divisions that were solidified in the creation of a division between, for instance "old" and "new" immigrants—"provided the state with a powerful weapon in the reproduction of a divided working class" (106). This division has been racial; has been a division between those from capitalist countries and those who are not; has been a division inflected and powered by eugenic ideas about the suitability of certain bodies for certain types of work, and the construction of unsuitable bodies for a wide range of harmful purposes. There are clear rhetorical residues.

As was the case at Ellis Island, in Canada medical inspections were spectacles that strongly influenced the first experience of Canada for most arriving aliens. In the years of peak immigration, between 1900 and 1930, the inspection process at Canadian immigration stations empowered inspectors to recognize defective bodies through just a glancing appraisal, what Anne-Emanuelle Birn calls "snapshot diagnosis" (281). These snapshot inspections were utilized at Pier 21 as well, and such inspections were also undertaken very explicitly at the Grosse Île quarantine station on the St. Lawrence River, to ensure that no "defective" or contagious immigrants made their way to Quebec City (access O'Gallagher). Similar processes were in place at the Partridge Island and Middle Island quarantines in New Brunswick, and the

---

2. Note that, when I am citing laws, I will do so in the footnotes, to avoid cluttering the text. As I do here: An Act respecting Immigration and Immigrants, SC 1869, c 10; access also Mosoff.

3. The Immigration Act 1886, RSC 1886, c 65.

4. An Act to Amend the Immigration Act, RSC 65, c 14, s 24.

5. House of Commons Debates, 9th Parl, 2nd Sess (29 April 1902) at 3740; also access Chadha.

William Head quarantine on Vancouver Island, though these have not been studied in depth.

At Pier 21, as at Ellis Island, though line officers could not deport immigrants, their inspections and markings had an indelible rhetorical effect. This effect reached three distinct audiences: Those immigrants who were not marked, and yet learned something about the danger of difference, gained a self-consciousness of their own possible defects, and were empowered and encouraged to diagnose others; Those who were marked and were thus in danger of rejection; The medical doctors themselves, who would later inspect the immigrants in greater detail, and many of whom would go on to practice medicine across the country.

At these inspection stations, a key criterion for rejection or deportation was the (perhaps intentionally) vague clause: "All immigrants who are unable to satisfy the agent or Inspector-in-charge either that they have independent means of support or that they are suited to farm work and intend to engage in such work, are liable to be excluded" (Robertson to Cory). Circulars among immigration agents beginning in 1909 detail how this clause was to be implemented. Yet nearly a decade later, in 1918, agents admitted this clause was an ongoing "source of considerable confusion" (ibid.). Their solution was to make an ad-hoc amendment to the clause in pen and ink, and then communicate this nonbinding amendment via circular among immigration agents. The correction suggested that agents "may relax" this liability for exclusion "if satisfied that the immigrant is in all other respects an acquisition to Canada" (ibid.). Then, "this amendment shall be exercised in the cases of immigrants of only the following races: English, Scotch, Irish, Welsh, French, Belgian, Scandinavian, Dutch and Swiss." "Finnish" was later added by hand (ibid.). E. Blake Robertson, the Assistant Immigration Inspector at the time, suggested that "the countries in which immigration effort is carried on, or is to be carried on, should be enumerated; otherwise the inspectors will not understand clearly what is meant" (ibid.). What this meant was that, in fact, the clause had always been intended to be applied only to immigrants from nondesired countries, and would be interpreted as such. We know that a similarly informal, but no less effectively exclusive process was being followed for refugee claims at the time, as well. As Gerard E. Dirks has shown, "immigration officials in Canadian offices on the European continent fulfilled their processing tasks in a most rigid manner" demonstrating an "enthusiastic" bias against any people who weren't Anglo-Saxon or from Northern Europe (256).

Roger Daniels shows that the protocols for racial differentiation at Ellis Island "popularized, if [they] did not invent, the category of 'old' and 'new' immigrants" with new immigrants being "both different from and inferior to" old immigrants (*Not Like Us* 62). We can comprehend this same process happening when a Canadian official appends a list of traditional immigrant groups that are sanctioned, exposing all others to extended scrutiny. Daniels is specifically referring to the difference between pre-1880 American immigrants and those who arrived afterwards. At Pier 21, this same division may have happened later, but it is clear that officials were working to turn back the clock.

The agents—in essence—decided that only immigrants from certain countries could engage in the work needed to stay in Canada. Thus immigrants from all other countries were disabled, rhetorically. If an immigrant was from one of the countries in Robertson's informal list, and thus desirably "raced," according to their calculus, inspectors could use their discretion to allow landing in Canada; if not, then there could be no discretion used at all. This listing was never legally added to the clause—yet before 1918 the list certainly existed as part of the implicit nature of the code, and after 1918 Robertson made it an explicit aspect of the code's application, albeit scribbled in by hand. These circulars can of course still be found in the Immigration Fonds (or collection of archival documents) at Library and Archives Canada (LAC).

EXTENDING THE BORDER

As was the case in the United States in the 1920s, what most Canadians really seemed to want to do was turn back the clock on immigration. There were forms of immigration that were acceptable, namely the arrival of white Western Europeans in the late nineteenth century and early twentieth century. Interestingly, this division was central to the 2015 Canadian federal election. When then Prime Minister Stephen Harper mentioned "old stock" Canadians during a nationally televised debate, many commentators linked this to the history of eugenics: stock is an implicitly (or perhaps explicitly) eugenic term, with allusions to genetics, and "old stock" most often means white, Western European immigrants (Edwards n. pag.). Stephen Harper—perhaps unwittingly or perhaps intentionally—was appealing to anti-immigrant sentiment. In particular, old stock creates a discursive division: conveying the idea that there are good and bad immigrants, and that good immigrants come from particular parts of the world and immigrated at a particular time, a belief that has deep roots in Canadian immigration (and eugenics) history. This temporal stretching back toward an "ideal" era of immigration is characteristic of the rhetorical movement of the Canadian border.

But as mentioned, as Robert Chang has argued, "It is through its flexible operation that the border helps to construct and contain the nation and the national community" (27). Borders are picked up, laid down, moved around, extended in order to discipline bodies. This shifting was temporal but also geographical. Importantly, by the late 1920s in Canada, the responsibility for medical examination was almost entirely shifted to the countries from which emigrants might come. In Britain, for example, a set of *Instructions to Medical Officers* was created in 1928. The *British Medical Journal* summarized some of these key points in 1931, suggesting that "it is of particular importance" to detect "the obvious physical or mental defective, but also those cases on the borderline between sanity and insanity—individuals who possess defective judgment, instability of the nervous system, or who are emotionally hypersensitive" though these things "may produce very few signs or symptoms" ("Medical" 1040). Much like in the American context, it was suggested that a careful observation, as well as a "pen picture" of the immigrant's medical past, could allow an inspector even to identify "borderline" cases (1041).

Further to this spirit of the temporal and spatial extension of the border, Canadian restrictionists also effectively utilized law that made possible the deportation of immigrants for up to two years after their arrival, stretching the inspection process out and redistributing responsibility across a range of social institutions. Under s. 33 of the 1906 iteration of the Immigration Act,[6] immigrants who had committed a crime "involving moral turpitude" or had been committed to a hospital or charitable institution within two years of arriving in Canadian were targeted. Municipal officials were responsible for reporting these cases to the minister of the interior, who would order deportations, whenever possible at the expense of the immigrant in question—and the Immigration Fonds at LAC are full of negotiations between agents, agencies, steamship lines, and individuals about who was to be held to account for the cost of these deportations. In fact, these particular archival records are dominated by correspondence between CN (the major Canadian steamship line at the time) and immigration officials about who is to blame for an "undesirable" immigrant landing in Canada. This coordination of industry and government led to much more stringent inspection at foreign ports before potential immigrants could even board a ship. As Angus McLaren has shown, this attention led to over ten thousand persons forbidden entry to Canada in the 1920s—a number that was "still not enough" to quell the concerns of eugenicists (64).

---

6. Immigration Act, RSC 1906, c 19, s 33.

In this way, eugenics proponents effectively utilized and sanctioned specialized public spaces and institutions to enforce immigration restriction. There were dozens of cases of public officials across the country writing to immigration agents, complaining of having to deport individuals just weeks after they had arrived because inspection itself had been "deficient." In one publicized instance, the Toronto School Board wrote to immigration officials complaining that nearly one thousand students "recommended for classes for the mentally subnormal" were either born outside of Canada, or to parents born outside of Canada, and many were "so sub-normal that they should have been noticed readily at the ports of entry" (Pearse to Egan). These complaints were repeated in a *Toronto Globe* article from November 12, 1925, with the title "Immigration Barrier Is Not Tight Enough." Importantly, as Geoffrey Reaume has shown, "people labeled 'mentally defective' covered a wide variation in human expressions and appearances that were deemed unacceptable"—including mad people, "racialized and ethnic minorities, females, and working class" (35). The public effectively believed that a tightening border could be used to reject and remove a wide variety of "undesirable" bodies, so long as some nebulous connection could be made to their country of origin.

These complaints from newspapers and public officials like those from the Toronto School Board led to a tightening at the border, and this is evident throughout the archival record of immigration agent correspondence. For instance, when there was concern that officials might be allowing in the wrong sort of biological stock, an official reminded his inspectors that "we would rather discourage five good members of a family than take in one who was subnormal" (Unattributed correspondence). In another example, immigration official Peter Bryce justified the deportation of a young girl named Daisy Fetch by writing that though her deportation would cause "a great deal of inconvenience for her relatives [. . .] you will understand that our action is taken solely in the interest of this country and for the protection of future generations" (Bryce to unnamed official). When a woman deemed insane ended up at a mental hospital in Saskatchewan as a "public charge," a letter was circulated to immigration officials chastising them, and reminding them that it was not the cost of caring for the woman that was the foremost concern. Instead, the emphasis was placed on the "menace in the future to this country from the progeny of such persons" (Jolliffe to Clark). Again, this eugenic rhetoric invoked the idea that certain bodies were in effect a contagion, and did so to relocate the selective power of the border from the immigration stations on each coast, across the social institutions in between, while expanding the power of deportation temporally. In such archival stories, we also perceive the extralegal networks in place to enforce eugenic sentiments that may not have been policy but certainly became practice.

THE NEGRO AND THE INDIAN

In North America and other parts of the world facing an influx of immigrants in the early twentieth century, religion was understood as the one key way to convert immigrants into more desirable forms, to extend the interpellating, acculturating work of the border. Importantly, the syntax of this conversion was uniform. More simply, immigrants were almost invariably described with an inventory of biological defects and deficiencies in comparison to original white, Western European settlers, and then religion was posed as the only way to balance out these deficiencies. Methodist minister J. S. Woodsworth's 1908 *Strangers within Our Gates; or, Coming Canadians* takes this tack. In the book, similar to Grose's *Aliens or Americans?*, Woodsworth offers definitions for a series of different immigrant groups, offering statistics about their numbers and distribution throughout the country and then suggesting, for instance, that when picturing an Italian, the idea "that first flashes before the mind's eye is probably that of the organ-grinder with his monkey" before this image "fades away, and we see dark, uncertain figures" (160). The Southern Italian, for example, is described as "short of stature, very dark in complexion [often] diseased and criminal" (162). All immigrants are then defined, as in the title of the book's final section, as a "Challenge to the Church." It should be noted that W. R. McIntosh's *Canadian Problems,* written in 1910, is an almost identical book, albeit from a Presbyterian perspective. This literary technique—an eugenic taxonomy of immigrant groups, combined with alarming statistics about their influx, allied to some form of religious or legal "solution"—is a genre in and of itself, echoed as well in W. G. Smith's 1920 *Study in Canadian Immigration.*

The idea that one group of immigrants could make claim to North America, and then convert those who had been there before to *their* way of life, or exterminate them, as well as judge and filter those who might come after them, creates a very specific settler-colonial backdrop. The extension of the power of deportation for those who could not be successfully converted played out in Canada in just such a manner. Woodsworth therefore devotes a chapter to "The Negro and the Indian," neither of whom are immigrants "and yet they are so entirely different from the ordinary white population that some mention of them is necessary if we would understand the complexity of our problems" (190).

This differentiation, which feels biological and eugenic, echoes the sentiment of the eventual prime minister, William Lyon Mackenzie King, and his desire for a "White Man's Country." In the words of William Duncan Scott, minister of immigration in the early 1910s, "at no time has the immigration [of Negroes] been encouraged by the Canadian government" despite the fact that immigration from the United States was strongly incentivized and targeted through propaganda and marketing campaigns (531). As with other Canadian immigration enforcement, the origin of even far-reaching restrictions was often ad hoc. R. Bruce Shepard shows how Canadians employed a "diplomatic racism"—laws that were never formally enforced nonetheless shaped practice. For instance, there was an "an order-in-council barring Blacks from entering the country" because the black race was "deemed unsuitable to the climate and requirements of Canada" (100). Even though this law was repealed, "the fact that it was approved at all indicates how serious Canada was about keeping the northern plains white," and we know that the law influenced actual practice at the border (100). The law was proposed to address and repudiate the efforts of black Oklahoman farmers to move to Canada. It wasn't just a broad, ideological statement, it was a direct attack.

As Harold Troper has shown, extremely exclusive border inspections and rejections, the collusion of railway lines, and the cooperation between American and Canadian lines all served to create a reputation for the discriminatory nature of the country's approach to black people—the border became a "prevention and a cure" (145). He suggests that "if a negro did not fit into a small box" for the purpose of rejection "it was not too difficult to find a big box into which he would fit," such as "catch-all categories like lack of funds, bad character, or physical disabilities" (145).

In his book, Woodsworth describe the "negro" as impulsive, violent, and full of sexual passion, their qualities of "intelligence and manliness" destroyed by slavery (191). "We may be thankful," he suggests, that there aren't too many "negroes" in Canada—not enough to create a "negro problem" (191). The tone seems to warn, very clearly, that if the population were larger, there would be a problem. Meanwhile, Woodsworth also argued that there were "still [and this word is *very* revealing] 10,202 Indians in our Dominion, as grossly pagan as were their ancestors, or still more wretched, half civilized, only to be debauched" (194). Clearly, in Canada, the work of careful immigration restriction, fueled by eugenic attributions of biological value, always worked in concert with settler logics of extermination and segregation. The selectivity of overseas immigration was also buttressed by very specific forms of rejection and selectivity along the land border between the United States and Canada.

THE EUGENIC CONSTRUCTION OF INTELLECT

While time and space were being marshaled and manipulated to limit immigration in North America, eugenic *language* also shaped borders and shaped immigration policy. One important facet of this eugenic language was the use of the category of the "feeble-minded," utilized as a catch-all or "wastebasket term" in Canada as well as the United States. To borrow Troper's phrase from above, restrictionists needed "big boxes" into which to "drop" undesired races and individual bodies. As modern historian Robert Menzies shows, between the 1920s and the outbreak of World War II, more than five thousand people were deported from Canada based on the "feeble-minded" diagnosis which was "bolstered by theories of eugenics and race betterment, and drawing on public fears about the unregulated influx of immigrants . . . nourished by the flood of nativist, rac(ial)ist, exclusionist, eugenicist, and mental hygenist [*sic*] thinking in Canada during this period" (135–36). Eugenics proponents effectively utilized a specific discourse and language to enforce immigration restriction.

As mentioned, the invention of the term "moron" then became another important move for immigration restriction. This term was invented by American Henry Goddard in 1910, and the classification was key to research he performed on immigrants at Ellis Island beginning in 1913. As Anna Stubblefield has argued, Goddard's invention of this term as a "signifier of tainted whiteness" was the "most important contribution to the concept of feeble-mindedness as a signifier of a racial taint," through the diagnosis of the menace of alien races, but also as a way to divide out the impure elements of the white race (162). The moron was constructed as, in the words of Goddard's contemporary and sometimes colleague, Margaret Sanger, "the mental defective who is glib and plausible, bright looking and attractive" (210). This person "may not merely lower the whole level of intelligence in a school or in a society, but may . . . increase and multiply until he dominates and gives the prevailing 'color'—culturally speaking—to an entire community" (210). The "moron" was viewed as a high-functioning feebleminded individual, yet capable of "passing" as normal, being attractive to normal individuals. The moron was often constructed as highly sexualized and thus could be held up as an even greater menace to the gene pool.

In Canada, eugenicist C. K. Clarke wrote the unpublished novel *The Amiable Morons* to drum up Canadian worry about this newly designated danger. The novel warned of "the evil consequences of importing insane and defective immigrants [and] was circulated to members of the federal cabinet in Ottawa" (Greenland 21). According to his biography, "this led to the amended Immigration Act of 1919 which extended the list of prohibited persons" (21). Clarke later spent a month in St. John's, Newfoundland, on Canada's East Coast "personally supervising the landing of some four thousand immigrants and instructing the inspectors on how to inspect them" (21). All of this is recounted in a celebratory tone in Cyril Greenland's 1966 memorial profile of Clarke.

In this way, in Canada, eugenics had its own public champions, and eugenic ideas became popular ideas. Terms like *moron,* though still very young, filled public discourse and fomented public fear of immigration. McLaren argues that for Canadian eugenicists, their final "chief success" was not necessarily even the drastic increase in restriction and deportation focused on specific groups of immigrants after 1919. Instead, the chief success was "in popularizing biological arguments" (McLaren 61). That is, not only did eugenic immigration restriction actually reshape the Canadian body, but it reshaped how Canadians thought about bodies and minds.

CLIMATIC SUITABILITY

The 1910 Canadian Immigration Act allowed the government to prohibit the landing of immigrants "belonging to any race deemed unsuited to the climate or requirements of Canada."[7] This section of the legislation was expanded in 1919 to prohibit the following immigrants:

[Those] deemed unsuitable having regard to the climatic, industrial, social, educational, labour or other conditions or requirements of Canada or because such immigrants are deemed undesirable owing to their peculiar customs, habits, modes of life and methods of holding property, and because of their probable inability to become readily assimilated.[8]

Decades later, the Immigration Act of 1952 still similarly allowed agents to exclude immigrants on the basis of "climatic suitability." In short, this solidified the sense that only certain, sanctioned races were biologically matched to the Canadian environment, even as settlers were drastically altering that very same environment in ways that were making it toxic to the peoples who had actually been living on the land for generations. For instance, James Daschuk's recent *Clearing the Plains: Disease, Politics of Starvation, and the Loss of Aboriginal Life* looks at how the arrival of disease interacted with the ecological change and harm brought first by the fur trade and later by large-scale agriculture to sow the seeds of the historical and contempo-

7. Immigration Act, RS 1910, c 27, s 38(a)(c).
8. Ibid. at s 38(c).

rary health disparities between aboriginal peoples and settlers in "Canada." Regardless, the notion that some bodies were suited to immigrate to, live in, and work in Canada has always shaped immigration law. As Frank Oliver, the one individual most responsible for the creation of Canada's first race-based immigration laws in the early 1900s, said at the time, "We did not go out to that country [western Canada] simply to produce wheat. We went to build up a nation, a civilization, a social system that we could enjoy, be proud of and transmit to our children; and we resent the idea of having the millstone of the [undesirable] population [of both natives and of non-British immigrants] hung round our necks in our efforts to build up, beautify and improve that country, and so improve the whole of Canada" (2939). Oliver, and much of the Canadian public, simply believed that non-British immigrants were racially inferior and thus incapable of doing anything but hindering the colonial project. And the solution was to halt their immigration.

After laws had been passed to clamp down on American immigration, the Commissioner of Immigration at Ellis Island, Henry Curran, reported proudly, though ridiculously, that "all immigrants now look exactly like Americans" (n. pag.). As discussed previously, the dangerous hope and the seeming lack of logic in a statement such as this nicely sums up the frantic play for "normalcy" and the tragic comedy of this drama. Very similarly, the idea that Canada would "*remain* a white man's country" was also a dangerous hope. Those Western European "immigrants" who had only a few generations before come to the country and begun violently colonizing it were now suggesting that this country was built for only their type, genetically.

Moreover, as Paulette Regan and others have pointed out, despite this history, public sentiment in Canada is that "Indigenous peoples have been the fortunate beneficiaries of altruism" (84). The truth is much more unsavory, and much more messy. Canadians first self-described the country as a "white settler colony," and this later became a useful way to understand its political and economic character (access Abele and Stasiulis). But this self-reference has now come to describe a process in which *making* Canada white, and *keeping* Canada white, worked in very much connected ways. The elimination or assimilation of Indigenous peoples happened at the same time as, and was justified with the same types of eugenic arguments as, the restriction or deportation of particular groups of immigrants. Thus, though I have shown that books about different "types" of immigrants and the problems they pose were ubiquitous, the distinctive chapter in Woodsworth's *Strangers within Our Gates* is "The Negro and the Indian," whom he feels he must point out "are so entirely different from the ordinary white population" that they "both stand out entirely by themselves" (190). This eugenic rhetoric provides clear evidence of the rhetorical co-construction of Indigenous peoples and "new" immigrants in Canada. The proud self-definition of Canada as a "white settler colony" and the later understanding of white settler colonialism as a violent and eugenic process both require that we place artifacts like Woodsworth's chapter at the center of our analysis.

MAGIC PROJECTIONS

In *The Inconvenient Indian,* Thomas King suggests that he is often asked, as an Indigenous person, what do Indians want? He suggests a better question: what do whites want? And the answer, he suggests, has always been the same: whites want land (216). As Robbie Shilliam has shown in *The Black Pacific,* this colonial obsession was a global trend: "Colonization has depended upon an interlocking super-exploitation of labour and super-dispossession of land organized along lines of race" (185). This is the answer that fuels both the violent efforts to make native people assimilate or disappear, and the effort to people the country with "the right stock" in the early part of the twentieth century; in turn, this was also an effort to drastically alter the land that whites wanted and took.

Aside from the efforts to carefully limit immigration on the borders, in the early part of the twentieth century, the Canadian government, with the help of the major rail and steamship line, CN, was also promoting immigration *into* the country. That is, Canada was promoting the immigration of desired people from desired countries, and constructing a tailored identity for Canada in the process. A big part of this push was the desire to turn the Canadian prairies into an orderly, prosperous farming area—a radical environmental shift—a shift that required taking Indigenous land and destroying Indigenous ways of living on the land, as well as recruiting thousands of immigrants to do the labor.

Canada did so by going overseas to recruit. As one agent wrote in the 1922 Canadian Department of Immigration Annual Report, "our agents would be equipped as missionaries of Canada, carrying propaganda to the smallest town and remotest Hamlet."[9] Canada's two most highly regarded photographers, William Topley and John Woodruff, were paid to take photographs of Canada that could then be used in "magic lantern slide shows" and lectures

---

9. Canada, Canadian Department of Immigration and Colonization, Annual Report, 1922 at 25.

that would promote the country to potential immigrants from the United States and Western Europe.[10] Many of the photos were of summer landscapes, crops, gigantic apples and huge tomatoes, men at work in farm fields, choice livestock. The images made clear arguments about the Canadian environment, and about the labor desired and needed in Canada. In the 2007 Cannes Lions–winning film *The Golden Door,* about an Italian family's emigration to the United States, the characters are shown to have "no frame of reference for the place save for the handful of fanciful novelty postcards that have made their way back to [their] tiny, remote village—amazing pictures of miraculous produce the size of farm animals" so that when they imagine this future, they imagine themselves "wading into a river of milk, then climbing aboard a passing carrot the size of a canoe" (Chocano n. pag.). Well, we do know that such images were part of the Canadian effort to promote immigration and likely part of U.S. efforts as well, in lantern slides as well as postcards; we also know that the very *first* Canadian ambassadors, diplomats, or representatives abroad were sent abroad to spread such images (Skilling 2). This focus on the fecundity of the land turned these slide shows and promotional materials into spectacles of settler colonialism, promising this land and these natural riches to preferred immigrant groups, if we take there to be a key distinction between settler colonialism and other forms of colonialism: that the land is the key resource at stake.

Lecturers, when they delivered the magic lantern shows, also addressed negative myths about Canada. For instance, the cold winter was reframed as having "done an enormous good in keeping out the Negro races and those less athletic races of southern Europe" (Cook). The myth of threatening "natives" was addressed by showing pictures of aboriginal youth "under control" at residential schools. Allied photographic collections also included photos, slides, or postcards of almost every "asylum" or "school for the feeble-minded" in Canada, suggesting that the segregation and institutionalization of people with disabilities would also be showcased as the hallmark of a "civilized" country to which one would want to emigrate. We now know that, as was the case at native residential schools, these institutions were machines for sexual and other forms of abuse (access Rossiter and Clarkson; Seth et al.). Preferred ethnic groups were showcased in photos taken in the moments after they had passed successfully through Pier 2, Pier 21, or another immigration station. An image of a "deformed idiot" has also been found among photos used in these slide shows, suggesting that agents also wanted to show prospective immi-

---

10. These images are credited to the "Topley Studio" or to Woodruff, but we know that at times Woodruff worked in Topley's studio, so the credit is difficult to truly discern.

grants the types of bodies and minds that were not welcome. I will offer much more consideration of this image in the final section of the book.

In *The Golden Door,* this contradiction between promise and warning is also tackled head-on: the son in the family is deaf and mute, and when they arrive at Ellis Island, "moving from room to room like a stealth tiger, the camera observes the way the health and intelligence of the immigrant is intently and disturbingly scrutinized by the cavernous gateway's workers" (Gonzalez n. pag.). The son passes an absurdist literacy test only by tricking the inspectors. But the message is clear: unlike so many other films that depict Ellis Island as a welcoming space, *The Golden Door* captures the reality of immigrants who have been promised a paradise and arrive in what feels and looks like a hospital and a prison, from which only a select few will be set free. As Skilling shows, for emigration agents, there was always a balance between promotion and "control[ling] the movement by seeking to eliminate what were considered undesirable types" (2).

The magic lantern shows, and their valorization of the Canadian landscape as a place of excessive production, as well as their placement of potential immigrant bodies on farms, tied into settler colonialism and evolving immigration law. Recall, for instance, this vague clause: "All immigrants who are unable to satisfy the agent or Inspector-in-charge either that they have independent means of support or that they are suited to farm work and intend to engage in such work, are liable to be excluded" (Robertson to Cory). Circulars among immigration agents beginning in 1909 detail how this clause was to be implemented and, as mentioned above, developed their own clear categories of desirable ethnic and racial groups.

Of course, the clear delineation between "racial" groups was stark, but so was the circularity and informality of the process itself—the fate of entire groups was determined in letters between a few men, hastily typed up and revised in pen and ink. Repeatedly, these important decisions were made, excluding entire racial and ethnic groups, in ways that were justified by extremely flawed eugenic ideas about what type of body could or should be allowed into Canada.

"SLIGHT DEGREE DARK"

As an example of the disorder of the immigration process in Canada, and its eugenic intent, in the spring of 1927 a group of seven Macedonian immigrants was issued certificates in Zagreb by the Canadian officer there, F. W. Baumgartner. When they arrived in Canada on the 24th of March, they were rejected for being "of dark type and poor physique." This description alone speaks to the idea that the category of "poor physique" was most often hinged to other ethnic or racial factors. No one could formally be rejected for being of "dark type," and yet yoking this characteristic to "poor physique" created grounds for exclusion. This shows just one way in which Canadian immigration linked racial types with insinuations of biological deficiency.

Here, the idea also was that only those with a satisfactory physique were suited to the labor, climatic, and environmental demands of Canada.

In this case, Baumgartner was essentially blamed for having issued certificates to this group of men. He responded by offering the CN continental superintendent, as well as Canada's deputy minister of immigration, a lesson on political history, geography, and race. He promised that no passenger with skin of even a "slight degree dark shade" would be given a certificate. He then went on, in great detail, to discuss the regions from which each of these men came, defending the stock from these regions as "good woodmen" or as having a "deep seated democratic spirit." Baumgartner did admit that "ethnographic conditions" in many of these regions were "extremely complicated," and he even made an effort to parse these complications. He concluded that "the selection is not easy and [neither is] the rejection of the apparently for Canada undesirable [sic] types [. . .] but a severer selection is possible." In these definitions and clarifications, we can understand the ways that certain regions of the world were being mapped as zones of environmental and embodied undesirability.

The CN responded by issuing instructions to its overseas agents that no certificates were to be given to any passengers from Southern Serbia or Dalmatia, "or to any immigrant slightly dark in colour." Baumgartner's lesson on race also resulted in the CN suggesting in 1927 to F. C. Blair, the acting deputy minister of immigration, that "it will always be difficult to define precisely the degree of colour which should bar an applicant" (Black to Blair). Dr. Black, the CN representative, then also, perhaps defensively, suggested that "in the examination of these immigrants, it is sometimes necessary to inspect the skin underneath the clothing as in many cases the arms, neck, and face are somewhat dark owing to exposure."

In these ways, agents manufactured shades of non-whiteness, using darkness to symbolize genetic inferiority and using the implied inferiority to rescind whiteness. A result was that "black colour" and "dark races" became powerful tools for eugenic immigration restriction. Many further examples of this can be found in the Canadian archival record, though these stories have been long neglected. For instance, when a young woman named Louise Abbott was rejected and deported from Canada for being "feebleminded," the nationality on her medical certificate was simply marked down as "negro." Current Pier 21 historian Jan Raska recounts the similar case of Rebecca Barnett, who faced deportation in 1907 and was labeled "Undesirable (insane) (black)."[11] In short, while other medical cards listed nationality by country, if one was "black" or a "negro," this superseded country of origin or made nationality immaterial at the same time that it was linked to mental and physical inferiority.

Opportunistic eugenic uses of the concept or label of disability have always operated as a key or central theme within Canada's colonial history. Undesirable bodies were held up at the border in service of the desire for a particular type of colonial Canadian, the valorization of certain forms of Canadian labor, and even to preserve a sense of the Canadian environment, itself rapidly changing in the period, due to settler colonialism. This history, of course, has largely gone untold. If you were to visit the Pier 21 museum, you'd find almost no sign of this eugenic past.

In this particular era, as happened at Ellis Island, Pier 21's doors effectively shut. The number of immigrants accepted into Canada dropped from 169,000 in 1929 to fewer than 12,000 in 1935 and never rose above 17,000 for the remainder of the decade. During that time European Jews fleeing Nazi Germany were denied sanctuary in Canada. The number of deportations from within the country rose from fewer than 2,000 in 1929 to more than 7,600 just three years later. Almost 30,000 immigrants were forcibly returned to their countries of origin over the course of the 1930s. Kelley and Trebilcock show that by the 1930s Canadian immigration policy "was reduced to an essentially explicit concept of *exclusion*" (249). Barbara Roberts has shown that, for instance, between the "beginning of November 1931 and the end of January 1935, the Department deported 10,805 immigrants [from within the country] as public charges," and this doesn't even include accompanying family who would have been deported as well (192). These public charge cases were most often fortified with some form of evidence of physical defect, but, in her words, "the vast majority of these people were simply unemployed" (192).

As Chadha shows, this exclusion and deportation was empowered by the rhetorical (and concurrently visualized) expansion of eugenic conceptions of disability: "By the time of Canada's 50th birthday, a litany of labels, descriptors and conditions, such as idiocy, insanity, imbecility, feeblemindedness, epilepsy, loathsome or dangerous diseases, constitutional psychopathic inferiority, chronic alcoholism, mental defects and illiteracy, were being employed in immigration legislation to justify the discriminatory ban of persons with

---

11. Raska and other Pier 21 historians have worked to recognize and represent the eugenic roots of Canadian immigration history (see ARCHIVE for more on this).

mental disabilities. We see that both psychiatric and eugenics science were relied on by legislators to justify this wholesale exclusion" (n. pag.).

Right around 1930, Canadian immigration restriction moved into high gear, and Pier 21 and other immigration stations began rejecting and deporting thousands more immigrants than they had in the previous thirty years. This clampdown can and should be connected to a range of cultural coincidences and historical developments, but it also coincided with a distinct change in the complexion of Canadian immigration—increasingly from countries other than those of Western Europe. As Aristide Zolberg shows, American immigration policy always had a double logic: "boldly inclusive" *and* "brutally exclusive" (432). Canadian history is similarly bifurcated, and immigration has always been a matter of keen public and political concern—as the public has shaped immigration, so has immigration shaped the public. As mentioned, eugenics, the "science" of positively advocating for particular forms of human regeneration, coupled with the negative restriction of the propagation of certain classes and ethnicities, beginning at the turn of the twentieth century, was the modus operandi of North American national health and immigration policy. Eugenics was "anointed guardian of national health and character," as Nancy Ordover has shown, "constructing immigrants as both contaminated and contaminators" (xiv). Importantly, "old" Western European immigrants, even though they literally brought with them to Canada diseases and agricultural practices that systematically contaminated the country, eradicating First Nations, were constructed as the bodies natural to this world, while "new" immigrants could be constructed as climatically unsuitable.

Katherine McKittrick argues that "black Canadian geographies are permanently linked to the Canadian landscape, both historically and presently. This connection between 'black' in/and 'Canada' advances two recognizable geographic processes: the domination of Canadian lands and peoples through white and European geo-political meanings, and the rupture of these geo-political meanings by the longstanding and recent places occupied by black communities in Canada" ("Their Blood" 28). So, for example, there can be no "climatic unsuitability" if there weren't the presence of black Oklahomans in Alberta. In the final section of the book, I will explore in more detail how the memorialization of Canadian immigration fails to take these dual realities into account. In the "official" historical record, we have been encouraged to forget just how restrictive Canadian immigration was, as well as to forget that there have been ongoing and important eras and flows of immigration outside of the idealized view of "old" white, Western European immigrants.

Like Ellis Island, power traveled through Pier 21, but Pier 21, as a rhetorical space and as an idea, continues to structure and shape power.

EXPLOSION

Technologies of immigration restriction

> Whatever a picture is . . . we ourselves are in it.
> —W. J. T. Mitchell

IN WHAT FOLLOWS, I look back at photographs taken at Ellis Island very early in the twentieth century. Cultural theorist Roland Barthes suggests that this was an "age of explosions"—specifically explosions of population and immigration, explosions of the personal into the public, and an explosion of technophilia, best metaphorized by the explosion of the flashbulb of the camera to illuminate a new world (98). So, looking at photography as it was utilized at Ellis Island and other immigration stations seems particularly apt when writing about this era.

Here, I develop a "rhetorical history of the visual," in the way that Cara Finnegan suggests such a project "relies upon critiques of vision and visuality to illuminate the complex dynamics of power and knowledge at play in and around images" (198). I suggest that we recognize a particular group or album of photographs as emblematic of an important rhetorical moment—the emergence of the American eugenics movement. I suggest that we comprehend these photos as charts of an important rhetorical space—Ellis Island. And I argue that we should view these photographs as the products of a technology—photography—that was creating a new archive and index for the sorting and classification of human bodies in this era. In these ways, I finally argue that Ellis Island, and the photographs taken there, helped to actually *frame and develop* both race and disability, contingently.

In early twentieth-century America, photography became a rhetorical tool of eugenicists and immigration restrictionists, and ideas about bodily fitness and defect drove the development of the technology. The photos I will examine here both capture and illuminate rhetorical trends already at work at Ellis Island, as they also facilitate, reproduce, and expand these rhetorical processes.

In keeping with the idea that this will be a "rhetorical history of the visual," I will anchor this section in examination of the "surfaces of emergence" of these images, to borrow a term from David Bate. That is, I will focus on not just the photos but also the connected practices, institutions, and relationships that must be considered when undertaking an archaeology of photography (4). Who circulated the photos, to whom, and through what venues, for instance, helped the images facilitate the rhetorical growth of eugenics as a powerful idea and practice.

I gesture to "archaeology" here (and elsewhere in the book) as a way to suggest that this work is not just historical. That is, as Jussi Parikka writes of media archaeology more broadly, the goal is to understand technological and media cultures as "sedimented and layered" but also to question the "regimes of memory and creative practices" that allow us to interpret and use media and technologies, currently (3; 2). I will attempt to analyze photographs in terms of their possible reproduction and emergence, and I will attempt to formulate a working thesis about what these images tell us about photography as a eugenic technology, in the past and in the present.

These considerations overlap with a desire to understand fully the production, reproduction, and circulation of these images, as Walter Benjamin suggests we must do in an age of mechanical reproduction ("Work of Art" 1). Finally, I will form arguments about the operant rhetorics of the photographs in question, as I link these images to the rhetoric of eugenics and to the social and cultural construction of categories of race and disability in this era—categories that still adhere today.

VISUAL DESCRIPTION

Throughout this section (and the entire book) I will be arguing that the overemphasis on the visibility or visuality of disability—how it is created and cemented through regimes of vision—is a problem, a historical problem. Therefore, I will also continue to try to avoid the uncritical use of terms like "see" and will instead substitute words like "view" or "understand" or "recognize" or "comprehend" that I hope offer less "ocularist" ways of making my point, except for when I call attention to the term through italics or scare quotes.

The historical overemphasis on the visuality of disability and race was also discriminatory in a very straightforward sense: if you couldn't "see," you were excluded at the border, deported. The evidence I present here captures this clearly, while refusing to reinforce this exclusion. So I will provide thick visual description for all the images I include in this section and the rest of the book. In the text itself, all that I provide will be these descriptions. Part of the effort here is to call attention to the fact that, perhaps especially in academic and historical work that is making an argument for the importance of images and photographs, these images and photographs are not presented in an accessible manner. The argument about the importance of the visual is thus undermined by the exclusionary practice of failing to caption and describe.

All images are available in an archive accompanying this book, housed on the Ohio State University Press website. There, the images can be presented in an accessible form. And readers will have the option of *not* viewing these images as well. In this way, I hope to honor the fact that all the images I am discussing were, originally, taken without the consent of those pictured. And the images have been used and circulated in ways that "freakify" the subjects, hold them up as abject and Other; these have been spectacles of rejection. So, simply including the images in this book, without acknowledging this history, would undermine the arguments I am making here. Making them available on the site allows the reader to retain some agency and choice in structuring their own encounter with the images. The creation of this small archive also means that these images, these people, cannot be easily forgotten.

The fact that the need to memorialize these images clashes so powerfully with the ethics of exhibiting them, this conveys the rhetorical complexity of this project. As Teju Cole writes, "What honors those we look at, those whose stories we try to tell, is work that acknowledges their complex sense of their own reality. Good photography, regardless of its style, is always emotionally generous in this way [but] weaker photography delivers a quick message [. . .] but fails to do more. But more is what we are" (n. pag.). Unfortunately, these are not, generally, photographs that acknowledge a complex sense of the subjects' reality. So the least I can do is make space to imagine, in a much more generous sense, what this reality might be. The archive opens up the opportunity to create the space to honor these realities in ways that the simple reproduction of these images in a book does not. Other researchers can and should use these images as they see fit—but for the purpose of my inquiry, I place the description first and allow the reader to choose how they want to access the images after that.

Here, then, is a description of the first image in this archive:

Image One: "Figures 2–5"

"Examples of Faces of Feeble-Minded Immigrants," *Manual of the Mental Examination of Aliens,* Treasury Department of the United States Public Health Service, Miscellaneous Publication 18, 1918. Owned by: Department of Health and Human Services (Public Domain).

There are four black-and-white images of faces tiled and spaced evenly on a page. Gender has not been assigned to any of these images. In the top left image, there is an eleven-year-old with close-cropped hair, wearing a striped shirt, labeled a "low-grade imbecile," a hand reaching from out of the frame to hold up the chin, with eyes directed to our right; in the top right image, there is a twenty-year-old with a dark mustache, wearing a suit jacket, labeled "low moron"; in the bottom right image, a teenager wearing a heavy coat is pictured, labeled "a constitutional inferior"; in the bottom left image there is a seventeen-year-old with blond hair, labeled a "high-grade imbecile."

PICTURING DEVIANCE

At Ellis Island, a key triumph of eugenics was the creation of new categories of disability, and photography readily facilitated these inventions. The terms "moron" and "feeble-minded" were both created at Ellis Island to classify immigrants. A regime of literacy and IQ testing, but also a regime of vision, was responsible for the solidification of these terms, terms that are still used to this day, despite their racist and pseudo-scientific roots. Perhaps the most overt example of this fusion can be found in the 1918 *Manual of the Mental Examination of Aliens,* published by the U.S. Public Health Service for the use of medical officers performing medical examinations at Ellis Island. The image described above comes from the pages of this *Manual.*

Most people will grant that disability has always been a highly visible or visual phenomenon, thinking mainly of the sorts of physical disabilities (and people with those disabilities) that are, in the words of Lennard Davis, "a disruption in the visual field" of the so-called normal viewer (128). But it is less widely understood how even supposedly "invisible" or less-visible mental or cognitive disabilities have historically been defined through visual regimes and technologies. Walter Benjamin argued that one of the earliest functions of photography was as a physiognomic tool, to catalog the human body in a way that translated embodied signs into insinuations of a mental hierarchy: "up to the highest representation of civilization, and . . . down to the idiot" ("Small

History" 252). This "physiognomic photography" was then linked to "comparative photography," which made all photography a "training manual": "just as there is comparative anatomy [there is] comparative photography, adopting a scientific standpoint" (253). The *Manual* is an example par excellence of this physiognomic, comparative photography. The document clearly outlines a visual grammar for discerning "feeble-mindedness." This grammar, providentially, could lead inspectors to any number of possible rhetorical usages. The *Manual* warns that

> a great many feeble-minded persons on ordinary inspection present no physical signs whatever which would indicate real lack of intelligence. Nevertheless, the examiner should have made close examination of facial expressions, both in normal and abnormal persons, especially as to whether they might be gloomy, sad, anxious, apprehensive, elated, hostile, confused, sleepy, cyanotic, exalted, arrogant, conceited, restless, impatient, etc. An examination of the photographs which appear herewith may prove interesting and instructive in this connection. (13)

The photographs then show several men (and, on other pages not shown, women) labeled as varying grades of "imbecile" or "moron." The images make direct connections between facial characteristics and defect. As Elspeth Brown suggests, eugenicists at this time assumed that "photography could map intelligence," and the *Manual* reflected this belief (118).[1] As Martin Elks has shown, there was a clear visual protocol used to classify the "feeble-minded" through photography in this era (381). Such protocols were clearly produced and reproduced at Ellis Island. These techniques then rhetorically influenced the ways that everyone, from eugenics proponents to Ellis Island inspectors to common citizens, looked at one another.

Choreographed by the *Manual,* the physical inspection process through which newly arrived immigrants were paraded at Ellis Island was also markedly visual. As Victor Safford, a medical doctor and officer at Ellis Island, wrote in his memoir about his experience as an inspector, "a man's posture, a movement of his head or the appearance of his ears . . . may disclose more than could be detected by puttering around a man's chest with a stethoscope for a week, [thus] an attempt was made to utilize this general scheme" at Ellis Island (247). I wrote at length in the first section of the book about the visual-

---

1. Brown links this belief to the era's "promise of standardization through photography" (i). She traces industrial uses of photography in the progressive era of the 1910s and 1920s and suggests that photographs were viewed as "unmediated scientific tools" because of their supposed "indexical relationship to the real" (20).

ity of this inspection process, how inspectors utilized what Anne-Emanuelle Birn calls "snapshot diagnosis" to evaluate the mental and physical state of the incoming immigrant. This "snapshot diagnosis" was indexed directly to the actual snapshots of immigrants in the *Manual*.

While this section is primarily concerned with photographic "surfaces," as Ellis Island expanded it also developed a huge contagious disease hospital, centered around "an autopsy amphitheater that enabled visiting physicians and medical students to study the pathology of exotic diseases" (Conway 9). This calls to mind Foucault's chapter in *Birth of the Clinic*: "Open Up a Few Corpses." In this chapter, Foucault shows how enlightenment science moved the gaze from the level of the skin to the deeper, previously hidden level of the tissue (135). Immigrants who had died on the trip overseas or while at Ellis Island could be exhibited, their "exotic" bodies used to develop new medical knowledge. This amphitheater is itself an analogue to the architecture of the entire island—a means of dispassionately focusing on bodies in order to alienate, Other, and exoticize difference. The hospital functioned not just as a place to heal and inoculate but also as a space for framing defect, and for deepening the medical gaze.

This said, the way to better understand this "snapshot diagnosis" is to look at consonant developments in the field of medicine. For instance, Foucault distinguishes between the medical gaze and the development, in this era, of the medical *glance*. In his words, "The gaze implies an open field, and its essential activity is of the successive order of reading; it records and totalizes . . . the glance, on the other hand, does not scan a field: it strikes at one point, which is central or decisive; the gaze is endlessly modulated, the glance goes straight to its object" (*Birth* 149). At Ellis Island, the six-second physical transformed the gaze into the glance. Inspectors needed to, very quickly, sort desirable from "defective" immigrant bodies. They also needed the glance to transform outward bodily signs into harbingers of mental inferiority. Thus these cursory inspections were largely a matter of intuition, a kind of magical medical view. In the words of Victor Safford, "from long experience physicians sometimes acquire[d] a most remarkable intuitive power" (245). As Samuel Grubbs wrote, recalling his work as an immigration officer, "I wanted to acquire this magical intuition but found there were few rules. Even the keenist [*sic*] of these medical detectives did not know just why they suspected at a glance a handicap which later might require a week to prove" (qtd. in Fairchild 91). Regardless of the provenance of the process, suspect bodies and minds were identified and sorted out from the stream of immigrants. The marked were removed for further mental and physical examination. Line officers could not deport immigrants, but their inspections and markings had an important rhetorical effect. It may have even been the case that examination on line and in intensive exam was, in the words of Amy Fairchild, "chiefly a spectacle" used to send a message to all immigrants, not necessarily to reliably discern "defect" (99). As in the automobile assembly plants being built across the country at this time, or as in a photomat, "defect" was visually developed and manufactured at Ellis Island.

As Safford writes, the cursory inspection processes may actually have had greater power than the detailed inspections that followed upon detainment—for instance, he suggests that "if after taking into an examination room a person regarding whom suspicion has been aroused" due to the snapshot diagnosis "appears normal," then "the medical officer knows the passenger should not be released without looking further" (248). In this way, the snapshot glance takes actual "scientific" or "medical" precedence over other diagnostic techniques. Foucault wrote that the classical use of the spectacle to discipline and punish was "a manifestation of the strongest power over the body" of the condemned, whose punishment "made the crime explode into its truth" (*Discipline* 227). Once the body was made a spectacle, it was totally incriminated, regardless of the individual's actual guilt or innocence. In a similar way, the Ellis Island process didn't really need or use diagnostic techniques to discover *actual* "defect." Instead, the spectacle of rejection was needed to send a message to all other immigrants. The flashbulb of the camera and the magic of the glance were used to create this "explosion into truth."

The photographs from the *Manual* can be considered a key part of the manufacture of this spectacle of rejection. The small eugenic idea that a person's intelligence (and even their human worth) can be seen quickly in their face, can be captured in a "snapshot," exploded into a much larger, pseudo-scientific, enforceable truth, a North American social value.

Susan Sontag suggests that "the industrialization of photography permitted its rapid absorption into rational—that is, bureaucratic—ways of running society" (21). This tendency can obviously be recognized in the use of photographs of mentally "inferior" types to guide line inspection at Ellis Island. Sontag elaborates: "Photographs were enrolled in the service of important institutions of control . . . as symbolic objects and as pieces of information" (21). The photographs of the "feeble-minded" functioned bureaucratically as means of control. And their "subjects" became spectacles of rejection.

Next, I explore how another series of photographs extended this work across American culture, making every non-white alien a possible eugenic menace, a body and mind to be framed according to criminological, pathological, and even freak-show referents. As Nancy Ordover explains, "American eugenicists, armed with charts, photographs, and even human skulls, were there to provide the visual and mathematical support that rendered racism scientifically valid and politically viable" (9). I show some of the key ways that photography provided this grounding and developed eugenic rhetorics that linger to this day.

IMMIGRANT TYPE PHOTOGRAPHS

What follows are visual descriptions of a series of Augustus Sherman's "immigrant type" photographs, captured at Ellis Island. The images themselves can be accessed in the archive that accompanies this book, housed on the Ohio State University Press website.

Image Two: "North African Immigrant"
National Park Service, Statue of Liberty National Monument, Pub Dom, Sher 24.4A-6

This image is labeled "North African Immigrant," and the picture shows a seemingly middle-aged, dark-skinned person with a beard, a knit or woven hat, and a large hooded jacket, frayed at the bottom and closed with buttons at the front. The subject's legs are bare. The subject also has a tag affixed to their jacket with the number 2 printed on it.

Image Three: "Eastern European Immigrant"
National Park Service, Statue of Liberty National Monument, Pub Dom, Sher 23.1A-8

This image is labeled "Eastern European Immigrant," and the picture shows a young person with a beard, wearing a woven hat with a wide brim angled to the side of the head. The subject wears a sort of cape, a vest, and a white shirt tied at the neck. The subject plays a flute that is held out in front of the subject. The subject seems quite tanned but not particularly dark-skinned.

Image Four: "Subramaino Pillay (Right) and Two Microcephalics"
(Mesenhöller and Sherman 96)

This image pictures three people, on the roof of a building (a common backdrop for Sherman's photos). At the left, seated on a bench, there is a dark-skinned person with head turned to our right, wearing a knee-length jacket; beside him another dark-skinned person stands on the bench, so as to draw attention to the subject's comparatively smaller stature—the subject stands at about the same head-level as the seated person. This middle subject is wearing an ankle-length jacket with fur trim, and their chin is raised in the air. On the far right, there is a third subject, also dark-skinned and also standing on the bench and just slightly taller than the person in the middle of the picture. This final subject wears a turban, and their head is larger than those of the other two subjects. This final subject also wears an ankle-length coat and holds their hands on their waist. The image is labeled "Subramaino Pillay (Right) and Two Microcephalics."

Image Five: "Perumall Sammy, Hindoo, ex SS Adriatica April 14, 1911, certified for congenital deformity of the abdomen, two arms and legs being joined at the abdomen . . ."

(Mesenhöller and Sherman 97)

This image shows a side angle of "Perumall Sammy," and the handwritten notation at the top of the photo suggests that Sammy was "certified for congenital deformity of the abdomen, two arms and legs being joined at the abdomen . . ." Sammy wears a long jacket, opened at the front, where a pair of legs and arms, bound and partially covered with silk, are shown to be attached to Sammy's stomach. Sammy has dark skin, a mustache, long hair, and a hat perched at the very top of their head.

Image Six: "Ruthenian Girl"

National Geographic 1907, 324

This image shows a young person (the title genders the subject as female) wearing a white headscarf, a vest, a blouse with floral stitching down the sleeves and front, and many beaded necklaces. The subject gazes directly at the camera. Though the photo is black-and-white, the eyes have an unusual, light color that has a striking effect. The subject's skin is tanned.

Image Seven: "Russian Giant"

(Mesenhöller and Sherman 99)

The "Russian Giant" stands with hands on the shoulders of two white people in suits, whose heads reach only to the Russian immigrant's waist. The subjects in suits each have mustaches. The Russian wears a top hat and tuxedo with tails. The chain of a pocket watch is visible where the suit jacket is open. There is a set of double doors behind the subject, and the Russian is clearly taller than this doorway.

Image Eight: "Burmese"
(Mesenhöller and Sherman 98)

The "Burmese" stands between two white subjects in suits, the same two subjects from the "Russian Giant" picture. The Burmese subject has dark skin and stands at waist-height of the subjects on either side, and holds a top hat. The Burmese subject wears a double-breasted suit.

SURFACES OF EMERGENCE

Beginning in 1905, Augustus Sherman, an Ellis Island clerk, took a series of pictures of immigrants who had been stranded at Ellis Island. Sherman took more than 250 of what he called "immigrant type photographs" between 1905 and 1920. As I will show, these images became incredibly popular at the time, circulated as postcards, framed and displayed in prominent locations, reprinted in periodicals, religious texts, and governmental reports. Most of the photographs simply capture an ethnic group or racial category on film, and label the subjects: for instance as "Russian Hebrews," "South Italians," "North African Immigrant"; or sometimes he labels a type more generally as, for example, "Eastern European Immigrant." As Ellis Island chief registry clerk from 1892 to 1925, Sherman had special access to potential subjects for his photographs. Andrea Temple writes that he told staff, "If you see an interesting face [. . .] contact Gus Sherman immediately!" (Temple and Tyler 16). He sought out the strange—"there could never be [. . .] anything too exotic to capture on plate" (16). He photographed only detained immigrants—those who could sit still for a long photo shoot because their future was uncertain. These were people who had been already processed through the snapshot diagnosis of the line inspection and viewed as somehow questionable. They then became available for further viewing and "capture" on film because they were, at least temporarily, not allowed into America.

David Bate argues that we should pay close attention to the "surfaces of emergence" of photographic practice—the set of practices, institutions, and relationships that must be considered when undertaking an archaeology of photography (4). Similarly, Walter Benjamin suggests that photographs—in the age of mechanical reproduction—must be considered in terms of their production, reproduction, and circulation. He identifies an "absolute emphasis on the exhibition value of art" ("Work of Art" 6)—and these contexts and vectors are particularly important when studying the "album" of images I will describe.

Because of the length of the photographic process, and the cumbersomeness of the technology, Sherman was compelled to capture subjects in a literal state of limbo—without a country. Those with nowhere to go could be made to be still long enough to be photographed. Sherman photographed his subjects in their full ethnic costume, capturing them in their traditional dress often for the last time—before they were rejected and sent home, or made their way to New York, leaving their traditional dress behind nearly as soon as they landed in Manhattan. If these immigrants did eventually make it to New York, they almost immediately began the process of assimilation, leaving their old identity behind, Sherman's images perhaps the fading evidence of their previous lives. It has been noted that the newly arriving immigrants' immediate removal of traditional dress left a literal "sea of clothing" at Battery Park (Temple and Tyler 16). As Andrea Temple writes, Augustus Sherman "captured these people as they would never look again, as they might want to forget they had ever looked" (17).

Under two different Ellis Island commissioners—Frank Sargent and then William Williams—Sherman worked as the unofficial photographer of immigrants. Sherman often photographed specific individuals and groups at Commissioner Williams's request. He was eventually promoted to senior clerk and personal secretary to the commissioner of immigration (under Williams) and often served on the Boards of Special Inquiry that were held there daily, to determine the fates of possibly undesirable immigrants. He became an important bureaucratic cog and Ellis Island personality, involved and instrumental in all of the immigration station's machinations.

Sherman's photographs are examples of the emerging form of "documentary photography" in this era. This "documentary photography" was also popularized by Lewis Hine and Jacob Riis. These two men also had close connections to Ellis Island and the immigrant experience, and both are most famous now for their bleak photographs documenting the impacts of industrialization and urbanization in America. Yet Peter Mesenhöller makes a key distinction between the photographs of Hine and those of Sherman. His suggestion is that while Hine represented immigrants as victims of industrialization, Sherman represented immigrants as *types*—his photographs serve as a form of "human documentation" and as "effigies of people who have no social status" (Mesenhöller 19). This propensity for human documentation overlaps with the rhetorical function of the *Manual* photos, as physiognomic and comparative texts. Indeed, having an inventory of over 250 photos, each labeled according to race and ethnicity, allows for a cataloging and sorting of bodies. Further, the idea that these images are also effigies is noteworthy. In a 1907 *National Geographic* article featuring Sherman's photographs, the unnamed author begins by noting that the immigrants photographed "are here shown just as they landed, most of them being still clad in their native costume, which will be discarded, however, within a few hours" ("Some" 317). This commentary attests to the "authenticity" of the photographs, and also to the notion that immigrants who made it through inspection would be forced to quickly assimilate. A significant power is then also lent to the photograph to capture a truly liminal moment and space. The pictures speak at once to the foreignness from which an immigrant has come, and to the demand (however impossible) to shed this history; capturing the edge between the two imperatives. While the photographs are part of a program of assimilation, they are also part of a process of abjection.

Mesenhöller suggests that the photographed subjects at Ellis Island then became "effigies" used to "classify and control deviance" across the nation (Mesenhöller n. pag.). Ellis Island held up the defective, alien body as a warning to the rest of the country—this alien, this exclusion, could be you. Interestingly, Ellis Island, before it became an immigration station, was also at one point called Gibbet's Island, so named after the gibbet, a somewhat medieval device, a kind of wire cage, used to suspend and preserve the bodies of dead pirates, after they had been hanged, and to hold these bodies up in New York Harbor for passing sailors to see, and therefore to recognize the perils of the pirate life. This statement of corporal, corporeal power, this display of force, this use of the specter of the Other body, might be viewed as a powerful symbol of what later took place on this same island once it became an immigration station. Sherman's photographs could be held up as examples and effigies of the bodies the nation had rejected, and thus as threats and warnings to all bodies in America and on their way to America.

PHOTOGRAPHIC NEGATIVES

Augustus Sherman's pictures of immigrants hung for several decades in the Manhattan headquarters of the federal immigration service. This context can be considered part of what David Bate calls the "surfaces of emergence" of photographic practice—the set of practices, institutions, and relationships that must be considered when undertaking an archaeology of photography (4). Peter Mesenhöller also writes that Ellis Island commissioners "gave copies of Sherman's haunting photographs to official [read: important] Ellis Island visitors as mementoes" (n. pag.). Sherman's pictures were first widely published in 1906 in a book entitled *Aliens or Americans?*, by Howard Grose, a Baptist minister, a text very much in the same genre as the religious books cataloging immigrant groups by Woodsworth and others, examined earlier. Grose's book devotes chapters to describing given races of the "new immigrants" and making finer distinctions within races. For instance, in the chapter on "Italians," Grose writes that

> most northern Italians are of the Alpine race and have short, broad skulls; southern Italians are of the Mediterranean race and have long, narrow skulls. Between the two lies a broad strip of country, peopled by those of mixed blood. (132)

While allowing for variation within each "race," the book advocates for a fine set of divisions within each group, and a multiplication of differentializing characteristics. The question posed by the title of the book is, finally, just a rhetorical one. These are all Aliens, until they can be fully converted to Christianity. Each chapter of the book is also followed by a set of questions, designed to reinforce Grose's didactic message about the need to religiously convert the masses. But in this schoolbook format, we also recognize that the question of the title of the book applies to each of the pictures, as in a test— look at each image, and you decide whether these people belong. Clearly, the images are meant to look foreign—the viewer is meant to understand that these people are Aliens, *not* American until they can be converted. In this way, the diagnostic glance of the immigration inspector is transferred to the reader, to all good Christian Americans. Sherman's photographs accompany each chapter and provide visual evidence of racial differentiation.

In the same way, the "Dictionary of Races or Peoples," presented as part of the 1911 *Dillingham Immigration Commission Report* to Congress, and discussed in the first section of the book, is a key parallel text for my analysis of the Sherman photographs. The Dictionary was co-authored by a group of immigration restrictionists, the Immigration Restriction League, many of whom had links to the American eugenics movement. This dictionary was used as a guide by the immigration service at Ellis Island and elsewhere from 1911 until the early 1950s. It is quite possible that immigration agents, on a daily basis, referenced both the Dictionary and Sherman's photographs—yet it is impossible to know exactly how the two artifacts were put to use. Yet the photos, their placement in Grose's book, and the similarities between Grose's book and the Dictionary all speak to a broader sociocultural trend, a movement toward new racial classifications and thus "new" forms of racism.

In the Dictionary, to distinguish between races and then *within* them, the Commission focused on skin color; on "psychic disposition"; on head measurements; and on not just language but also perceptions of literacy. The key to the Dictionary was its subcategorization: moving beyond the five primary colors of early twentieth-century ethnology to create hierarchies within ethnic groups. This Dictionary both borrows from and slightly evolves from the key preceding ethnological text, William Z. Ripley's 1899 *The Races of Europe,* which divided Europe into Alpines, Nordics, and Mediterraneans, basing these divisions on physiognomy, somatotype, and skin color, as well as social and cultural distinctions, and rooting all divergence in heredity.[2] As Robert Ziedel has written, the Dictionary had a "complex understanding of race, showing it to involve an imprecise mixture of physical, cultural, and social characteristics" (107). Nevertheless, the Dictionary was based on the idea of "ineradicable race distinctions," granting great power to this imprecise mixture of factors (107). There were now many more ways to be racially abnormal. As with the *Manual* photographs, immigrant type photographs and discursive descriptions were now useful for creating physiognomic distinctions and classifications that could further multiply hierarchical assertions of human worth.

Yehudi Webster shows that "the *sighting* of races is a function of usage of specific criteria of classification" (45; italics mine). Siobhan Somerville argues that "the significations of the body are not predetermined loci of difference, but a deeply problematical and asymmetrical production" (4). The Dictionary was a key text in setting these specific criteria of classification, each a deeply problematical and asymmetrical production. In these ways, the "Dictionary" became a discursive analogue and counterpart to Sherman's images, both in the ways the text and image actually overlapped and in the ways they conceptually inter-animate. Together, these texts stack the snapshots of race distinction that eugenicists would opportunistically shuffle.

As discussed previously, Matthew Frye Jacobson has written that in this era, the concept of "variegated whiteness" became prominent, and it was important to be able to mark ethnic others, even if they may have been previously understood as "white," as now somehow not authentically or fully white. He explains that "the salient feature of whiteness [before this era] had been its powerful political and cultural contrast to nonwhiteness," yet artifacts like the "Dictionary" and Sherman's photographs reveal how "its internal divisions, too, took on a new and pressing significance" (41). In his estimation, the "Dictionary" was "fundamentally a hierarchical scale of human develop-

---

2. The Dillingham Commission also submitted a report titled "Changes in the Bodily Forms of Descendants of Immigrants," authored by anthropologist Franz Boas, a text that was actually read as an argument against the idea of a set constellation of races, and for the idea of biological plasticity. It did not have the same rhetorical impact as the Dictionary.

ment and worth" based on this idea of both marking out non-whiteness, and on selective distinctions in a field of variegated whiteness (79). The Dictionary manufactured brand-new populations of non-whites, or not-fully-whites. Sherman's pictures further helped people to "see" these new populations and to define the American through the creation of the alien.

Looking at the somewhat simple "immigrant type photographs" of Sherman, we may think a rather harmless cataloging is all that is at work. Yet these photographs provide evidence of a much larger project of racial division. It is not that Sherman himself intended for his photographs to enable a "new racism," yet the divisions he catalogs, and the use of this catalog, specifically between 1900 and 1924, allowed for this "new racism" to be experimented with and perfected at Ellis Island. For instance, Jewish peoples from varying backgrounds and geographies became Jews; then they became "Russian Jews"; then they also became, as Ellis Island doctor J. G. Wilson wrote in 1911 "a highly inbred and psychopathically inclined race," whose defects are "almost entirely due to heredity" (493). And Sherman's photographs became ways to identify these specific bodies, and to superimpose these eugenic value judgments through the rhetoric of the glance. The Dictionary could then write these distinctions into an enforceable hierarchy, and books like Grose's could imprint these divisions on the popular consciousness. "Russian" was no longer simply a nationality; "Jewish" did not simply connote religion; both became racial labels, rhetorically expedient in the creation of classifications and divisions that could be further solidified with quack genetic science.

As Jeffrey Melnick argues, "The practice of racial naming (and unnaming) has acted as a gatekeeping force in American life" and always entails "the unnaming of whiteness itself as a racial identity" (265). Roland Barthes, John Fiske, and Patricia Williams have all written about this process of "exnomination"—and this is how the Dictionary functioned rhetorically, to produce an abundance of "scientific" information about those who were not white, and in the process to avoid examining or naming whiteness. Siobhan Somerville argues that "U.S. culture [still] anchors whiteness in the visible epistemology of black skin" (21). Likewise and often concurrently, the idea of who is American is established through differentiating practices such as those fostered by Grose's book, containing Sherman's images: by training the individual to recognize who is defective, marked, tainted, and thus alien.

Thus, when Sherman's images are linked to texts like Grose's, or like the Dictionary, then the explosion of the flashbulb not only renders a vision of the Other, but this vision can be persuasively linked to an increasingly variegated and very hierarchical genetic order, to a scientific "truth." To figure out who was American, one had to scientifically create, locate, mark, and showcase the expulsion of he and she who were not. The "exnomination" of the American was realized through the photographic negative.

NATIONAL GEOGRAPHIC AND THE FREAK SHOW

The process of exnomination creates an identity by arranging deviance and difference around the blank space of the "norm." This process, as it unfolded at Ellis Island for instance, relied on the creation of new medicalized categories of "defect." As Matthew Frye Jacobson shows, for anyone who arrived at Ellis Island before 1924, "race was the prevailing idiom for discussing citizenship and the relative merits of a given people" (9). Within this idiom, disability was the accent applied to differentiate and hierarchize. Race and disability rhetorically reinforced one another and worked together to stigmatize. Howard Markel and Alexandra Minna Stern summarize this propensity: "In an era in which differences of skin color and physical characteristics were becoming increasingly medicalized, it is not surprising that exclusionary labels of disease and disability became an essential aspect of" immigration restriction (1328). Jacobson adds that the categories of the physically and mentally defective were created and used in service of racism, as a means of darkening a group of ethnic others with the stigma of disability (access *Whiteness*). Ellis Island as a rhetorical space helped to construct disability as we know it today. This construction continues to inflect our understandings of race, "normalcy," and difference and continues to shade and shadow how we look at others and ourselves. Sherman's photographs neatly reinforce the links that I have suggested exist, and they also locate the technology of photography, and its attendant, rhetorically persuasive, surfaces of emergence in this co-construction of race and disability.

We shouldn't understate the fact that Ellis Island officials truly felt that this "scientific" categorization was part of their mission. The chief surgeon at Ellis Island, Howard Knox, himself wrote of discovering a "Stone Age" man—a Finnish man who was "deported because he approached too nearly the missing link that has been sought by scientific men for the last century" ("Eugenists" n. pag.). In an article published in the *New York Times,* Knox describes the man in great detail and concludes that "people from certain countries who are coming here at the present time are almost all physical inferiors, and with the present laws, we are absolutely powerless to stop them" (n. pag.).[3] This was the level of sophistication of the scientific inquiry of the immigration

---

3. The apocryphal story about this article is that Knox's future wife read it and was thereafter determined to meet him.

station's chief medical officer, describing an immigrant Sherman likely would have wanted to have photographed—and this story places the photos within a specific frame. At Ellis Island there was an active search for a kind of biological difference that could justify restrictions and that reinforced the evolutionary advancedness of whites with Western European ancestry.

The original Sherman photographs contain short captions, written on the photographs themselves in pen or typed. These include simple classifications like "Russian Giant" or "Burmese"; histories of arrival and origin; or a combination of histories of origin, classifications, and specific diagnoses ("Perumall Sammy, Hindoo, ex SS Adriatica April 14, 1911, certified for congenital deformity of the abdomen, two arms and legs being joined at the abdomen"). Walter Benjamin suggests that the captions that accompany a photograph carry an "altogether different character than the title of a painting" ("Work of Art" 6). These captions are often "directives," and can be "explicit" and "imperative" (6).

In contrast to the directive nature of the caption, what about the affective, reflective power of these images? It is important to ask what happened to people like Sammy Perumall. The fact that he was being photographed does not bode well: he was at least in detention, and likely waiting to be deported, though this is impossible to know with certainty. But if we don't at least ask what happened to these people, then they simply become symbols or effigies. If Sammy Perumall was deported, did he have family in India to return to? Was he separated from family who traveled with him? Did he have sponsors in the United States who could come to his defense and prove that he should be allowed to stay?

Sherman's own, handwritten captions catalog difference but also direct our view explicitly, training us to classify each individual according to race and ethnicity at a glance. The captions also urge the viewer not to view Sammy, or the Ruthenian girl, for instance, as fully human. Further, in the images that Sherman captures of bodily "abnormality," the scribbled caption asks us to view the human as the sum of his or her dysfunctional parts and to fuse race and supposed bodily "abnormality" or disability: not just a giant, a "Russian Giant." In this way, the photographs of Augustus Sherman extend the rhetorical work of the "Dictionary of Races and Peoples." Specifically, the photographs work to fuse pseudo-scientific "evidence" of racial difference with "evidence" of bodily "abnormality."

In their fusion of the image with a sort of diagnosis, these photos develop much of their rhetorical power from their allusion to the frames of the anatomy textbook, as mentioned earlier, and to the police archive. As Martin Elks has suggested, at this time the "camera became a "diagnostic tool" providing empirical proof of psychiatric sympotomology and physiognomy" (372). Barthes also wrote that "the photomat always turns you into a criminal type" (12). Susan Sontag agreed that "in one version of its utility, the camera record incriminates" (5).[4] Allan Sekula writes that "every work of photographic art has its lurking, objectifying inverse in the archives of the police" (16). Photography has drawn "an unmistakable line between the professional reader of the body's signs—the psychiatrist, the physiologist, criminologist, or industrial psychologist—and the 'diseased,' 'deviant,' or 'biologically inferior' object of cure, reform, or discipline" (18). The key to Sherman's rendering of the "deviant" other was the fact that this reading of the body's signs was connected to a clear nationalist project at Ellis Island. As mentioned before, while the photographs are part of a program of assimilation, they are also part of a process of abjection. The photographs construct a binary relationship between the American reader and the Alien subject, a ghostly national type as the inverse of an array of criminal and "defective" types.

In addition to their original public emergence, reproduction, and circulation in Grose's book, Sherman's pictures were also published in *National Geographic,* in 1907, in a segment entitled "Some of Our Immigrants." These photographs are accompanied by simple captions such as "Arabs" or "Typical Southern Italian Girl," or, as described above, "Ruthenian Girl."

The key accompanying content in this 1907 article is statistics about the numbers of each racial group admitted to the United States. The main concern seems to be the sheer number of immigrants flowing into the country: "No migration in history is comparable to the great hordes that have crossed the Atlantic during the past 20 years to enter our territory" (317). This is analogous with widespread panic about the immigration explosion at this time, and the images put faces to this threat. When Sherman's photographs appear in *National Geographic* magazine again in 1917, however, many of the same pictures are given slightly different captions, and now, notably, several of the pictures follow Sherman's own mantra that "there could never be . . . anything too exotic to capture on plate" (Temple and Tyler 16). The shift in the rhetoric on these pages from 1907 to 1917 reflects the historical shift from panic *about* immigration to eugenic action *against* immigration. Importantly, eugenic action against immigration more clearly connects the immigrant body with notions of "deviance" and "abnormality." While the 1917 issue of *National Geographic* does not include Sherman's images of Sammy Perumall, Subramaino Pillay, or Thumbu Sammy (nor

---

4. For instance, access Lombroso's criminal anthropological photographs or August Sander's "tremendous physiognomic gallery" of German citizens (Benjamin, "Small History" 252).

does the 1907 version), it does end with pictures of a "Russian Giant" and a Burmese "dwarf."

As Foucault has noted, medicine constructs bodies by "limiting and filtering" what we see through classification systems, and then transcribing difference into language (*Birth* 135). This might proceed according to what Foucault called "the nomination of the visible," wherein the definition and coherence of difference is located in the skin and skull (132). In Sherman's photographs, we can understand how the exnomination of whiteness and the intense nomination of the visibility of nonwhiteness worked in concert. In the photo of a Russian "giant" and a Burmese "dwarf," this relationship is shown quite notably: the white men flanking these two non white "specimens" serve as the normate backdrop to their Otherness—the white men do not even need to be named or labeled in the photo.

These photos mark and manufacture the genetic differences between aliens and Americans. For instance, the following captions accompany these final two pictures in the series:

A Russian Giant, seven feet nine inches tall, with two men of normal size. The Russians who come to American are a sturdy, hardy, seasoned race. But not all of them are as tall as this giant. (130)

A dwarf from Burma. He is not too small to enjoy his cigarette nor to be proud of his bracelet. (129)

These *National Geographic* photos are also staged in a particular way, so as to accentuate difference. While I have suggested that Sherman's photographs fit somewhat into the genre of "documentary photography," and overlap with the genres of the scientific and criminological catalog, these photographs are also quite at home on the pages of *National Geographic,* where, as Catherine Lutz and Jane Collins have shown, photographs have traditionally reflected clear patterns of racial power (access *Reading National Geographic*). These are images of the exotic Other, analogous with *National Geographic* pictures that manufacture a colonial gaze. As George Stocking and others have shown, *National Geographic,* since its very first issue in 1896, can be characterized by imperialist racial and sexual politics (access *Race, Culture, and Evolution*). These politics have also been consistently reinforced by the "scientific mission" of the magazine. As Philip Pauly (and, again, many others) have argued, the magazine has always had a specifically scientific purpose, eventually somewhat diluted to create more popular appeal, yet always attendant to the editorial mission of the magazine (access "The World and All That Is in It").

In these ways, Sherman's photographs fit also into the genre of the anthropological photograph, a form of exoticizing "evidence" that reinforces the primacy of white Americans. As Christopher Vaughan writes, this was a dominant photographic trope in the era: "Human beings and their cultural trappings were collected, like baskets and buttons, or bugs in a jar, for the study and more often the amusement of curious Westerners intoxicated by images of freaks" (232). This use of the word "freak" is interesting, particularly when considering a time in which the other dominant images of embodied "deviance" came from actual freak-show photographs.

STAGING

Image Nine: "Gen. Tom Thumb, Miss Lavinia Warren, Commodore Nutt and The Giant"
Brady-Handy Photograph Collection (Library of Congress) Portrait photographs 1850–70

In this photo, "General Tom Thumb" is on the far left, wearing a military outfit and holding a military hat in their hand. The military outfit has been specially tailored for Tom in a small size. Beside Tom is Lavinia Warren, slightly taller, wearing an elaborate white gown. "The Giant" wears a three-piece suit and stands beside Warren, fully twice Lavinia's height. On the far right is Commodore Nutt, also wearing a three-piece suit. Nutt is about the same height as Tom and Lavinia, and all three are much shorter than "The Giant"—this is the contrast that the image is seeking, and which Sherman's photos seem to mimic. The photo is available in the above-mentioned archive of accompanying images.

Borrowing Robert Bogdan's categories for the "staging" of freak-show photographs, we can recognize that Augustus Sherman also used common freak-show "modes of presentation" for his subjects at Ellis Island (104). That is, there are very common "techniques, strategies, and styles" for representing supposedly disabled subjects photographically so as to exaggerate physical difference (104).[5] Several of the Sherman photographs evidence what Bogdan calls the "exotic mode"—in which the "emphasis was on how different and, in most cases, inferior the person in the exhibit was" (108). The exotic dress

5. The techniques were first used in the criminal anthropological photos of Lombroso in the 1880s (access *L'Homme Criminel*) and later used by Tredgold in his 1908 text on mental deficiency and in Henry Goddard's landmark 1914 text on feeblemindedness.

of the immigrant is often accentuated—an "Eastern European Immigrant," for instance, is pictured playing his pipe, as though this is his natural pose. And this elaborate dress often combines unfortunately with the fact that each subject has recently survived a harrowing sea journey (not to mention the Ellis Island inspection process). The subjects are exotic in part because of their dress, and conveniently dirtied and "darkened" by the duress of their circumstances.

The *Manual* photos discussed at the beginning of this section also exhibit one of Bogdan's key "modes." These photographs provide evidence of what Bogdan described as the strategy of including "helping hands" in the frame of photographs depicting "low-grade" subjects (106). You can view these hands holding the chins of several immigrants in the *Manual*. Further, in Sherman's pictures of "giants" and "dwarfs," for instance, he uses a simple visual contrast to accentuate difference: the smaller or larger (and also "darker," ethnically "marked") immigrant is buffeted on either side by medium-stature, well-dressed white men who act as the ground against which difference comes into relief. The same two white men accompany both the "Giant" and the "dwarf," suggesting that either these photos were staged simultaneously or this staging was commonplace. The men's presence in the frame, like the presence of the steadying hand in the frame of the photos in the *Manual,* reveal something of the visual rhetoric of these modes of presentation. The men seem to literally support the "Giant." And these hands, or the bodies of these "normal" white men, metaphorically transport the viewer into the frame as well, asking the white American, "normal" viewer to hold this specimen for themselves, to compare their physiognomy against this "enfreaked" example. The white hands and white figures accentuate the exotic mode, and they act as "helping hands" to facilitate the othering of the racially and corporeally exotic alien.

The "Russian Giant" and the "Burmese" photograph of a diminutive man also evidence what Bogdan calls the mode of "aggrandizement" (108). Compare these photographs to a hugely popular "aggrandized" freak-show photo picturing General Tom Thumb, Miss Lavinia Warren, Commodore Nutt, and "The Giant," described above. Clearly, the same contrasts between the diminutive "freak" and the subject of "normal" height can be recognized in both this photograph and the Sherman "giant" and "dwarf" photos, as they appear across the genre of freak-show photographs. The presence of the single "normal" subject functions again as an invitation to the viewer to compare themselves against the "freak." In the "aggrandized" mode, the subject is also often fancily dressed, almost to the point of irony. For instance, in one Sherman picture, the "Russian Giant" wears a top hat and tails; the "Burmese" subject wears a three-piece suit, his hat in his hand. This mode "emphasized how, with the exception of the particular mental, physical, or behavioral condition, the freak was an upstanding high status person" (Bogdan 108). The entailments can be both positive and negative—can lead to respect or ridicule. Certainly, we should respect men who look so dapper after crossing the ocean. But the freak show's simple visual syntax incites more simple reactions based on the supposed incongruity of "abnormal" bodies in civilized dress.

Extending this simple grammar of incongruity, Sherman also pairs or groups "abnormalities" that most sharply contrast with one another as when he gathers hydrocephalics and microcephalics, arraying them in a line. For instance, view the above image of "Perumall Sammy, Subramaino Pillay, and Thumbu Sammy." Clearly, these photographs have both the physiognomic and comparative function that Benjamin and others allude to. We are to recognize the racial others in Sherman's photographs as also deviantly embodied, and as "feeble," as we are invited to abject these images from our developing notion of a eugenically progressive North America. Rosemarie Garland-Thomson extends this line of argument in her scholarship on the freak show, arguing that there are cultural processes which make physical abnormality or particularity "a hypervisible text against which the ['normal'] viewer's indistinguishable body fades into a seemingly neutral, tractable and invulnerable instrument of the autonomous will" ("From Wonder to Error" 10). The excessiveness and Otherness of the disabled body *allow* for the construction of a mythical norm. It is only against an Othered body that the normal body is allowed to perpetuate its deceit (of transparency, of being standard, of being whole).

DEVELOPING DISABILITY AND RACE

As Walter Benjamin suggests, photographs—in the age of mechanical reproduction—must be considered in terms of their production, reproduction, and circulation. He identifies an "absolute emphasis on the exhibition value of art" ("Work of Art" 6). At this time, many people collected photographs, and freak-show photographs were a very popular part of most collections. As mentioned, these immigrant photos would have fit, in many ways, into the genre of the freak-show postcard photograph, investigated at length by Robert Bogdan and Rosemarie Garland-Thomson, among others. Sherman's photographs also overlapped with the genre of the anthropological photograph of the exotic, primitive, colonized other, as well as medical and criminological archive photos. While the Ellis Island photographs borrow from these visual vocabularies, they also sent another message, particularly as they hung in the foyer of the immigration service offices, as they were circulated as mementos given to privileged visitors to Ellis Island, and most markedly as they were used by line inspectors to aid in identification of racial and ethnic "types." The photographs became a key part of the immigration restriction machine of Ellis Island. The photographs develop, in the functionaries *and* the products of this machine, the power of the snapshot diagnosis to make distinctions and discriminations, (conditionally) assuring the viewer of their own normalcy. Moreover, while they catalog strangeness and difference, they also attest to and facilitate the arrest of this difference at Ellis Island.

In the years of peak immigration, from the late 1800s until the clamp-down on immigration in the mid-1920s, an era that coincides exactly with Sherman's tenure at Ellis Island, thousands of immigrants were processed through Ellis Island every day. Sherman's photographs are a key documentation of this process, as they also facilitated this process through their use as referents. Further, as part of an emerging eugenic scientific catalog, the photos shape and are shaped by the space of Ellis Island, itself shaped by American eugenic anti-immigration rhetoric. As Vicki Goldberg and Robert Silberman show, Sherman "made images of foreign peoples as 'documents'" (31). He used the photograph as a "cataloguing and institutional record-making device" (32). This usage, they suggest, "can underscore race and ethnicity and nationality and fortify an accepted sense of order in the world based on visual characteristics—in this case, costume, physiognomic features, and skin color" (32). Most importantly, while this cataloging may have had scientific purposes—may have created new "racial knowledge"—the key function of Ellis Island was to sort out and to exclude undesirable aliens, and thus this became a key rhetorical function of the photos.

Douglas Baynton has shown that "the *concept* of disability has been used to justify discrimination against other groups by attributing disability to them" ("Disability" 33). The use of disability as a darkening mark applied to the body of an arriving immigrant later allowed for the accent of disability to be applied to entire "racial" groups. This momentum can be recognized in Sherman's own, handwritten notes on his photographs, particularly the photos that most clearly evidence the grammar of the "freak show" photograph. When he writes "Perumall Sammy, Hindoo, ex SS Adriatica April 14, 1911, certified for congenital deformity of the abdomen, two arms and legs being joined at the abdomen," the viewer effectively relates congenital deformity to the "Hindoo" race. Gathering and photographing Perumall Sammy, Subramaino Pillay, and Thumbu Sammy together is a means of highlighting their Otherness—hydrocephalic beside microcephalic, "dwarf" standing beside another sitting subject, and so on. But most importantly, these three are all also non-white. They are effectively "darkened" by both disability and race. When *National Geographic* publishes photos of a Russian "giant" and a Burmese "dwarf," there is a clear eugenic message: these foreign others, clearly and starkly unlike the white men who surround them, come from different and possibly dangerous genetic stock. The images and their framing reveal that, as Natalia Molina has shown, it is "not only that race, immigration, and disability studies are intimately connected but also that often it is difficult to discern where one ends and the other begins" (33).

As Vicki Goldberg and Robert Silberman have argued, "racial stereotyping did not of course originate with photography, but photography has proven to be an unusually powerful instrument for reinforcing and propagating racial (and racist) imagery" (32). My argument is that photography at Ellis Island industrialized a visual rhetoric that manufactured new classifications of race and disability. The visual rhetorics established at Ellis Island certainly didn't originate there, and their development are the product of a variety of overlapping attitudes that spread forwards and backwards from the moment I am looking at, and radiate outwards from the space I am looking at. But I want to make the tenuous claim that Ellis Island was instrumental in incorporating and interpellating a certain way of looking.

Between 1900 and 1925, it was at Ellis Island that new forms of racism and nationalism could be best implemented: thousands of immigrants poured through every day. The ways that these immigrants were processed and viewed, then, became a eugenic product. A vision of the foreign other could be fixed, developed, and reproduced on a grand scale. The power of the snapshot diagnosis employed by Ellis Island inspectors was then transferred to the viewer of these photographs. Finally, to view one of Augustus Sherman's photos was to become an inspector oneself, and also to hold up a mirror—to practice a glance that you would train on yourself as well, anxiously policing your own normality. As my epigraph by W. J. T. Mitchell suggests: "Whatever a picture is . . . we ourselves are in it." In the end, perhaps this is the most important surface of emergence to study when examining any photograph: the existence of the image and its rhetorics in our own thoughts and actions. Thus, the final visual rhetoric of Ellis Island was this: training the glance upon yourself.

ROGUE'S GALLERY

Henry Laughlin, a key eugenic spokesperson and the chairman of the American Immigration Restriction League, was invited to testify in front of the U.S. Congress several times in the early 1920s, on the issue of immigration restriction. Whenever he testified, he brought charts, graphs, pedigree charts, and the results of hundreds of IQ tests as evidence of "the immigrant menace." In his 1922 testimony, Laughlin plastered the Congress committee room with charts and graphs showing ethnic differences in rates of institutionalization for various degenerative conditions, and he presented data about the mental and physical inferiority of recent immigrant groups. These data included a "rogue's gallery" of photographs of "defectives" taken at Ellis Island, which purported to show, menacingly, "Carriers of the Germ Plasm of the Future American Population" (Gelb et al.). These photographs were those taken by Augustus Sherman. Clearly, across Sherman's photographs we can recognize the clear and effective uses of a visual grammar to conflate alienness and defect. This conflation led to the rejection of thousands of immigrants, but it also shaped attitudes that may linger in American culture, and that may in fact shape persistent visual rhetorics, technologies, and ways of "seeing."

In fall 2016, the New York Public Library, owners of the copyright for many of Sherman's images, released "colorized" versions of many of his "immigrant type" photos. The images circulated rapidly via social media, as part of the campaign by the brand Retronaut to create a book based around the images (among others). Interestingly, earlier books by Retronaut had been published in part by *National Geographic*. As these newly colored images circulated, attention was drawn to the "incredible outfits" worn by the immigrants, with no attention paid to Sherman, nor to the process by which they had likely been detained and photographed. In the midst of a contentious election, immigration was at the forefront of the North American cultural conversation in fall 2016. Yet, despite this, the images seemed to make Americans nostalgic for another time, back when immigration seemed simpler. Of course, as I discussed in the first section, as Aristide Zolberg shows, American immigration policy has always had a double logic: "boldly inclusive" *and* "brutally exclusive" (432). He argues that the United States has never been laissez-faire about immigration (2). That is, immigration has always been a matter of keen public and political concern—as the public has shaped immigration, so has it shaped the public. We need look no further than current American political rhetoric about building a wall between the U.S. and Mexico to understand this power. When Sherman's photographs are colored and recirculated in the present, they may not be used to guard the borders any longer, but they must be read against the construction of new immigrant threats, from south of the border, Syria, and a range of other locations, all framed as alien.

Sherman's archive became an extension and a reinforcement of Ellis Island as a rhetorical space, and transferred the incriminating gaze of the snapshot diagnosis to film and into an embodied practice. Sherman's photographs and those of the "feeble-minded" become training manuals for other inspectors, and for the new citizens of America as they carried Ellis Island with them into their new lives. The Ellis Island photographs of Augustus Sherman worked in concert with eugenic rhetoric, protocols for the inspection of aliens, narrowing immigration legislation, and texts such as the "Dictionary of Races and Peoples" to create new hierarchies of race and disability. The texts, along with the technology of photography, reached into and rearranged bodies. This coding and technologization were perfected at Ellis Island, and we recognize this intersection frozen in these images. The photographs were then instrumental in the project of immigration restriction. As Elizabeth Yew has shown, thanks to the work of the American eugenics movement, by the early 1920s, "with the inferiority of certain races proven by science, America could, at last, close her doors" (508). The doors did close, and tightly, beginning with the racial quota laws of 1921. But the rhetorical effect is much more far-reaching, as well. As Eithne Luibheid asserts, the examination process at Ellis Island "individuated" each person examined, and "tied [her or him] in to [a] wider network of surveillance" placing "immigrants within lifelong networks of surveillance and disciplinary relations" (*Entry Denied* xii; xvii). Every immigrant became an agent. Every person who picked up *Aliens or Americans?* or *National Geographic* became an agent.

So, finally, I want to suggest that we all carry Ellis Island and this history with us today. We are subject to the same gaze, governed by the same rhetorical vision. I think that studying these photographs, together with the rhetorical space of Ellis Island, and the discursive explosion of eugenics, allows us to recognize unique and complicated connections between spaces, words, images, and bodies. As bleak and pessimistic as the message may be, I also think that studying these texts allows us to recognize the historical—and the current—predominance of specific visual rhetorics. This study should hopefully allow us to "see" the other ways that, through technologies like photography, or through other "explosions" of media, we continue to frame and develop race and disability, as we freeze and arrest difference.

Affective spaces of eugenics

The archive becomes a site of lost origins and memory is dispossessed
[but] it is also within the archive that acts of remembering and regeneration occur, where a suture between the past and present is performed,
in the indeterminate zone between event and image, document and
monument.

—Okwui Enwezor, *Archive Fever* 47

EXAMINING the photographers and photographs that captured images of
"undesired" immigrants in Canada and the United States at the turn of the
twentieth century, we can begin to understand the development of photography as a eugenic technology, crucial to our evolving understanding of disability and race in North America. We can also refigure the engagement with
visual culture that we are developing in fields such as rhetoric and disability
studies. This engagement focuses not just on photographs themselves but on
the archaeology of photography as a technology, on its surfaces of emergence,
its modes of reproduction and circulation, and on the ways that disability is
revealed or ignored in archives. This approach then offers tools for interpretation and investigation that might be taken up by others and applied across
eras and images, as well as across disciplines. Less neatly, this affective work
also, as Okwui Enwezor suggests in the epigraph, sutures, and does so incom-
pletely, imperfectly. It sutures because the archive is torn, broken, disabled.
This final section is about gaps and absences; what has been cut out, ignored,
set aside, excluded. But also how an understanding of these exclusions creates
the possibility for change.

    We have been exploring a continent and a series of borders that pose as
solid, immovable, permanent, natural. But as Rachel Adams argues, a continent can only "describe the coexistence and interpretation of diverse cultures
and languages within a loosely configured territory that encompasses multiple

regions and nation-states" (7). Moreover, continents are "fluid and malleable assemblages whose boundaries have shifted over time" (7). Retaining a focus on change and transformation is essential—this allows us to see how borders can be picked up and laid down across groups and bodies, how, as Adams writes, paraphrasing Thomas King, people cross borders but borders also cross people (32). These borders, importantly, are subject to revision, as are the stories and the images we have been visiting, of the people who have crossed them, and who have been crossed by them. In this final section I propose an archive—a shadow archive—that allows us to better focus on the ways that the border has been, for many, an indeterminate zone. This is not to say that the hard edges of the border haven't been felt, haven't been used. But to create space for critique, it is useful to remember that borders shift and can be changed.

FRANK WOODHULL

Image Ten: "Lived 15 years as a man: woman wore disguise until halted at Ellis Island"
New York Daily Tribune, 5 October 1908, p. 14.

Much earlier in the book, I quoted historian Erica Rand, who has argued that there are "limited resources about sex, normative or otherwise, regarding Ellis Island" and thus "studying sex at Ellis Island requires strategies of embodiment, with attention to the particular bodies inhabited and to the complexity, messiness, and contradictions of sexed bodies in their historical specificity" (15). I examined how sex was constructed through the line inspection process but then, largely, sex, gender, and sexualization have been submerged in my analysis—except for in the powerful, unstated sense that eugenics itself is always about sex. In what follows, I hope to more carefully locate the "fixing" of sex within the processes of immigration restriction.

In a lengthy section of *The Ellis Island Snow Globe*, Rand explores the origins of one specific photo that she finds displayed on a banner at the Ellis Island museum, a black-and-white photograph of a subject with a mustache, wearing a top hat and spectacles. The image turns out to be a picture of one of the most "famous" detainees in the history of Ellis Island: Frank Woodhull.[1]

---

1. The story of Frank Woodhull was famous at the time of the photo's capture, covered in newspapers in New York and across the United States. But the story then quickly faded from memory, to the point that Frank's picture can now appear at Ellis Island with no explanation provided.

And the image was taken by Augustus Sherman, an Ellis Island agent who had unique access to potential subjects for his photographs—as we know from the previous section. He photographed only immigrants who were being detained and could sit still for one long photo shoot because their future was uncertain. This detention happened for this subject because, while in line for inspection, Frank Woodhull was suspected of having tuberculosis based on a visual assessment, and he was removed for a full medical inspection, at which point Frank admitted his previous identity. As Sherman reveals in his handwritten note on this photograph, Frank Woodhull had previously been Mary Johnson of Canada—and Frank had "dressed 15 yrs. as a man."

Frank's case is a particularly interesting one. Frank was not actually detained at any great length, he was not deported, yet his picture served important rhetorical purposes—it argued that the camera eye and the eye of the immigration inspector (in this case a compound) could not be fooled. As shown, the Ellis Island photographs of Augustus Sherman worked in concert with eugenic rhetoric, protocols for the inspection of aliens, narrowing immigration legislation, and the rhetorical space and choreography of Ellis Island itself to create new hierarchies of race and disability. In this way, the technology of photography reached into and rearranged bodies. Similarly, Frank's case shows us how Ellis Island worked to "fix" sex and sexuality. Inspection, we are to believe, could *discover* one's real sex and one's real sexual preference and *demand* heterosexuality. As Eithne Luibhéid has shown, at Ellis Island "photography enabled new forms of subjugation through the body" (*Entry Denied* 47). "Bodies were photographed, divided into zones, and classified into taxonomic schemes"; and "sanctioned sexualities became consolidated by delineating and penalizing categories of 'others'" as a function of eugenic practice (48; ix). When you were sorted through the immigration process, we are to believe that something like sex could be policed and enforced. The process could take the concepts or ideas that North Americans may have been most anxious about—race, ability, sex, sexuality, political affiliation—and set them straight.

A *New York Times* headline at the time said, "Mary Johnson, Who Has a Mustache, Will Earn Living Attired in Trousers" ("Woman in Male Garb" n. pag.). Frank Woodhull was detained only long enough for this picture to be taken, and then moved along with their life. Yet when Sherman labels the photo "Mary Johnson," and the image is circulated, Frank Woodhull becomes a spectacle. In the photo, Frank wears a black suit and tie, with a white collar. Frank is light-skinned and has a dimpled chin and a white mustache, and wears circular spectacles with a small chain leading from the right lens back toward the ear. The black top hat on Frank's head is made of a heavy material with a wide brim and sits low on Frank's forehead so that the forehead is fully obscured and Frank's eyes are shadowed. Sherman's caption, handwritten on the photo above Frank's head, says "Mary Johnson, 50, Canada came as 'Frank Woodhull' SS New York Oct. 4 '08 Lived 30 yrs. in U.S. Dressed 15 yrs. In men's clothes." This image, like all the others mentioned in the book, can be accessed on the accompanying website.

In addition to the flexible and interchangeable use of racial and ability criteria, inspectors at Ellis Island also looked keenly for signs of sexual deviance. For instance, questions about sexual preferences and histories were part of almost every medical inspection. The 1917 Immigration Act listed "abnormal sex instincts" as a "constitutional psychopathic inferiority" (29). The alignment of these terms is a great example of the ways that pseudo-scientific language could make brains, instincts, genes, and bodies defective by nesting negatives within negatives. As Jennifer Terry has written, "eugenic doctrine of the first half of the 20th century placed both racial and sexual purity at the top of its agenda . . . white phobia about miscegenation and racial passing paralleled a growing sex panic that inverts and perverts were everywhere, but difficult to detect visually hence, an apparatus for identifying and isolating them could be justified as a matter of social hygiene" (138). Martha Gardner also suggests that the "Dictionary of Races and Peoples" "argued for a link between sexual deviance and visible racial-ethnic otherness" (66). Through this "Dictionary," "immigration officials [. . .] defined moral deviance as a *visible procedure* long before federal courts would confirm the visual common sense of racialized and sexualized identities" (51; italics mine). Research by historians Heather Lee Miller, Michael Rembis, and David Serlin also reinforces this relationship between insinuations of genetic inferiority and insinuations of sexual and gendered deviance, fused through eugenic policies and procedures in the era.

Indeed, a key feature of Ellis Island's inspection procedures were discursive and visual interrogations of sexuality. Clearly, the tensions about both sexual and genetic normalcy that were ubiquitous in the rest of the country could surface and achieve a sort of exorcism at Ellis Island. As Jennifer Terry writes, "The sex deviant, like the passing negro, became a confusing border creature, who existed between man and woman, who traversed class and racial boundaries, and whose masquerade was treacherous" (139). Ellis Island was one place where this creature could be caught. For instance, Kim Nielson writes about the case of Donabet Mousekian, an Armenian Turk who was rejected at Ellis Island because he "lacked male sexual organs" and, despite the fact that he himself had made a living as a photographer, was deemed a public charge and "really repulsive in appearance" (107).

Rand's book, *The Ellis Island Snow Globe,* uses the example of Frank Woodhull to make a larger argument about how the Ellis Island museum has rewritten history and hidden truths to suit commercial interests—like the selling of souvenir snow globes. But I would suggest that Woodhull's story also reminds us that in combination with the flexible and interchangeable use of racial and ability criteria, inspectors at Ellis Island also always looked keenly for signs of sexual deviance. The most "exotic" differences were then photographed. In Frank's case, a quick visual scan that revealed an "abnormality" suggesting tuberculosis then led to a much more invasive inspection.

As Erica Rand did, I will also be examining specific images. But in searching for some answers and some loose ends, I will make a series of further arguments about photography as a eugenic technology, crucial to our evolving understanding of disability and race in North America.

INDEXES

As mentioned earlier, for many years now, I have been doing archival research, looking at the ways that disability was constructed through immigration processes, practices, discourses, artifacts, and images in the peak period of North American immigration, 1900–25, which was also the peak period of North American eugenics. In this work, and of course throughout the earlier parts of this book, I have tried to build on the work of disability historians such as Natalia Molina, Catherine Kudlick, Douglas Baynton, James Trent, and Kim Nielson in situating disability at the very center of North American immigration history. We know that such work requires extreme effort and diligence. Because, as I have written elsewhere, disability has been ignored, submerged, and overwritten throughout history and throughout the historical record (*Disability Rhetoric* 72).

As part of this research, I began visiting the archives at Ellis Island in New York City and at the location of the former Pier 2 and Pier 21 immigration stations, now the Canadian Museum of Immigration in Halifax, on the east coast of Canada (as well as at other national archives holding materials relating to these spaces). Most Canadians think of Pier 21 as the "Canadian Ellis Island"—though this is far from a good comparison for a variety of reasons. A different space called Pier 2 was the actual immigration station for most of the first quarter of the twentieth century, not Pier 21. Still, Pier 21 is the immigration location in the forefront of the Canadian cultural imagination. As I have already shown, my research on immigration in the Canadian context, frankly, has been much more difficult than research in the American context. While at Ellis Island it was relatively easy to discover the ways that anti-immigration activists and nascent eugenicists influenced the immigration process, to sense how and where new forms of "racial knowledge" fused disability and race, using Ellis Island as a space for experimentation, Pier 2 and Pier 21 offered at once a much more messy and a much more spare history.

Ellis Island in the early 1900s became the key laboratory and operating theater for American eugenics, the scientific racism that can be understood as defining a unique era of Western history, the effects of which can still be felt today. Ellis Island offered an extremely attractive set of possibilities for eugenicists. In addition to the "negative" eugenic programs of sterilization, lynching, and so on, carried out over decades across the country, immigration was ideal for "positive" eugenics, literally offering opportunities to control and edit the gene pool, using Ellis Island as an elaborate sieve.

My hypothesis is that Pier 2 and Pier 21 also functioned eugenically. I have certainly found discursive evidence to this effect. But the major impediment that I have found, and it is an impediment that many disability scholars have also encountered, is that disability is difficult to locate in canonized histories but also in archives. As I have shown, archives in Canada and elsewhere are being destroyed by austerity measures—further, archives are tremendously inaccessible spaces.[2] Moreover, in an era of "alternative facts," these archives become even more endangered. When a president needs to manipulate images to alter the reality of his own inauguration, on his very first day in office, it becomes clear that protecting images of the past will be difficult, crucially important work.

But then, poring over boxes of archival materials, I discovered an image of a young man, sitting on a gurney, likely in the Pier 2 infirmary. The photo is labeled "deformed idiot to be deported." The photograph was most likely taken by John Woodruff, the government photographer for the department responsible for immigration at this time. He had been commissioned to document the immigration process for purposes of promotion. (More on this promotion soon.)

Image Eleven: "Deformed Idiot to be Deported"
Library and Archives Canada

The image, which you can access yourself on the accompanying website, depicts a young light-skinned person sitting upright on a medical gurney with

---

2. A recent Canadian initiative to provide greater access to Canadian archival materials, the Initiative for Equitable Library Access project, was simply abandoned, and the Conservative government in place at the time of its discontinuation refused to either answer questions about why it was scrapped, or to answer questions about how the $3 million budget was spent. It seemingly wasn't spent to make even one archival file more accessible (Jodhan).

legs stretched out in front, wearing a suit with a vest, a white shirt, and no tie. The pant legs are pulled up and the subject's feet are bare, and the feet are in the foreground of the photograph, resting on a pillow, slightly blurred. The toes seem to point toward one another and the feet are misshapen. The subject has black bands around both calves, perhaps garters, suggesting that the socks and shoes have been removed. The subject has short-cropped hair and looks directly into the camera. A tag is pinned onto the lapel of the subject's jacket with the letter X written on it. If the subject used mobility aids, they are not in the frame.

When I found this image in an album of photographs, I could easily classify and recognize it according to the visual rhetorics and grammars of disability studies: placing it within criminological archives, within the pathological frame of the medical textbook, within the history of the freak show. I also could easily classify and recognize this image according to the images of disability from Augustus Sherman's archive. Like these images, this one utilizes what I have called faciality: the move to locate mental deficiency in the face and body of the immigrant. The appearance of the feet in the front of the image directly connotes the "deformity" of the caption; we are invited to attach the label "idiot" to the subject's face. Indeed, even the X written on the piece of paper on the lapel of the jacket seems to connote the same thing that such markings did at Ellis Island, where "defective" individuals were marked and indexed with codes, letters written on the lapels of their jackets in chalk. Though, of course, I could find no further evidence that Canadian inspectors ever used such codes.[3] Yet the idea that a photographer visiting—or working—at an immigration station might take the opportunity to frame images of difference certainly made sense. Furthermore, the idea that disability was the condition that rendered this subject available for photographic capture, and also left them at least temporarily without a state, is also unfortunately unsurprising. Tanya Titchkosky and Rod Michalko have argued that people with disabilities are often viewed as "draw[ing] out the intentions of an environment" via the "limits it inscribes [on] their lives and bodies" (217). The "deformed idiot" photograph can be understood not just as reproducing and perhaps sensationalizing the image of disability; we can also trace the exclusive intentions of Canadian immigration policy and practice, and the exclusive space of Pier 21, across this body. The immigration station has always been a "cultural location of disability," a loca-

---

3. As the Ellis Island mental inspection guide stated, "Should the immigrant appear stupid and inattentive to such an extent that mental defect is suspected, an X is made on his coat at the anterior aspect of his right shoulder" (Mullan 740). Some of the other code letters were *L* for lameness, *Pg* for pregnancy, and *H* for heart.

tion in which, as Snyder and Mitchell suggest, "disabled people find themselves deposited, often against their will" (3). These locations are revealed to be "sites of violence, restriction, confinement, and absence of liberty" (x). The photograph not only documents what happened in this cultural location; photography was a key technology doing its eugenic work. In this case, we can imagine that disability deposited this young person in the infirmary even though there is no evidence that they needed treatment of any sort. I will repeat: there is no evidence that the young person needed treatment. The stay in the infirmary was much more likely to have been for the "education" of young doctors, many of whom trained at immigration stations early in their careers so that they could broaden their medical experience (as shown by Birn). This photograph also extended this medical training, in addition to the cultural work it may have been intended to do.

When I did find this photograph at Library and Archives Canada, though I could guess about its uses and contexts, I was surprised that I couldn't actually discover, with any authority, how such an image was used or circulated at the time of its "capture" in 1908.[4] Then I found another image that I hoped would provide some context. It wasn't found in the same album at the Library and Archives Canada, though it was taken by either William James Topley or the aforementioned John Woodruff at an immigration station in Quebec in 1910, and filed in an album of "immigration views." Like Woodruff, Topley had been commissioned to document immigration in this period, also for purposes of promotion.[5]

This image was simply labeled "immigrants to be deported." It pictures a large group of immigrants, and seemingly the photographer wanted to present a true variety of human difference, all of it having been recently rejected. Eight subjects in male attire, two in female attire, and one child can be viewed in the image. The young child in the photograph, front and center, standing on crutches, presents a particularly powerful and memorable image. The child wears a small wool cap, a sweater, and a jacket. The child has short blond hair,

4. I have since sought further information about these images at several other archives, and in correspondence with many other historians across Canada, with no success.

5. Carlevaris writes that "though [the group of immigration images from which this one comes] are usually attributed to William Topley there is a suggestion that they may have been produced by John Woodruff who was the official government photographer for the department of the interior (the dept. responsible for immigration)" (34). Woodruff is given credit for the "deformed idiot" photo, and it is likewise possible that this was a Topley photo. Regardless, these were likely the two most prominent Canadian photographers of the first half of the twentieth century. Both were thus hired, at different times, to photograph immigration for the purposes of documenting—and forming—national culture.

cut straight across the forehead. Wooden crutches appear to prop the child up—the crutches seem just slightly too large. The subject wears tall boots, and their left foot appears to be raised just a bit higher than the right. The image can be viewed on the accompanying website.

Image Twelve: "Immigrants to be Deported"
Library and Archives Canada

Like the "deformed idiot to be deported," viewing this young subject, just over half the height of the adults around them, should spur the audience to imagine what comes next for this child. Because the child is also set apart from the adults around them, we have to imagine that they have been separated from their family *through* this deportation. This image has been somewhat widely reproduced, for instance on the cover of Barbara Roberts's very important *Whence They Came,* the key Canadian text on the history of immigration restriction. Yet Roberts doesn't actually discuss the image in the book. Anna-Maria Carlevaris does discuss the photo at some length in her dissertation, and provides an interpretation of the symbolism of the image:

> The crippled [*sic*] boy is centered in the composition and stands apart from the group behind him; he probably has been positioned there by the photographer. Neither the group, nor the boy, are close enough to the camera to evoke feelings of intimacy from the viewer but neither are they far enough away not to be recognized [. . .] by lessening the personalizing or honorific aspect of the photograph a distance between the viewer and the subject is constructed [. . .] the boy with crutches, so "obviously" defective, dispassionately gazes back across an infinite gulf of silence. The boy wears the sign of his difference; his body displays the reason for his deportation. The other figures, because they are members of this group, are also defective in some way [their proximity to the boy is incriminating]. Their failure does not announce itself physically, but it is implied by association. (38)

Carlevaris's interpretation does important work to reveal the symbology of disability in the photography (and in any photograph) as well as the symbology of disability in the historical immigration narrative: even by association, disability is incriminating. To frame nationhood, and acceptance, you need to project and reject and index difference through disability. These two mysterious photographs, unfortunately, are part of a larger catalog: they reveal how mental and physical differences twisted together in the frame; how whenever such apparent "differences" presented themselves on the border, the camera quickly transformed the subjects into spectacles of exclusion; such bodies were disposable after they had been frozen on film. Unlike Frank Woodhull, the life stories of these unnamed subjects seem impossible to uncover, even as their images have become "historical." It is important to point out this indignity, to carefully recognize my own role in this problematic dynamic.

CATHEXIS

The images of young men "to be deported" that I found on my archival journeys provide perfect examples of Kérchy and Zittlau's thesis that when we witness images of people with disabilities who have been "enfreaked," we should recognize that these bodies "are made to circumscribe and enforce the boundaries of normality in spatio-temporally specific modes that result from traumatic historical circumstances, decisive geographical contextualizations, as well as related socio-political concerns and communal anxieties" (10). More simply, there is a traumatic history likely to be attached to each of these images, and this trauma is likely geopolitical; it is likely a trauma that the viewer themselves may be implicated in or may even be in some way responsible for. Indeed, the image of the "deformed idiot to be deported" clearly reveals—even just in its name—both a normative and a geographical boundary, and this young person's exodus to Canada may very well have been initiated by trauma, and/or very likely resulted in it; the image also makes much larger communal and political statements about who can and who cannot be Canadian. Anyone claiming the identity or the citizenship of a "Canadian" viewing the image should understand that the image itself is part of the creation of this identity and this status. The same process was in place in the capture and circulation of Sherman's images in the United States. That is, these photographs functioned as "indexes" that provided pseudo-scientific evidence upon which eugenics was built and immigration restriction was based (Stange xiii). But they were also a form of *cathexis*—investments of emotional and mental energy in an individual; *emotionally charged*.

The term cathexis refers to the concentration of mental energy on one particular person, idea, or object, and, post-Freud, generally means that this focus is happening to an unhealthy degree. Freud did also use the term to refer to less pathologized focus, something more like longing. Here I mean to use that latter definition, as well as a slightly more etymological interpretation, one that calls up German associations such as physical occupation or dwelling, as well as electrical charge. The Greek word *kathexis* generally means "holding fast" or "retaining," and these are useful meanings as well, as we are referring to images that have been somewhat erased or ignored. The images are charged with and hold the trauma of these individuals, but also a eugenic legacy and a colonial legacy.

Adria L. Imada, in an excellent essay on a large archive of photos of Hawaiian leprosy patients, each of whom is soon to be excluded from society, albeit excluded *together,* suggests that "perhaps this leprosy archive is not so different from other colonial archives in betraying its anxieties and indexing its own failures" (28). That is, though the archive was certainly part of the colonial effort to exoticize but also medicalize racial difference, "the affective and sensory excess of the photographs disrupts the criminality of these visual profiles. [. . .] Their portraits, then, documented each individual patient's imminent emergence as a criminal suspect, as well as the growing bonds with one another—a new collectivity born out of violent dislocation. These gestures within and just outside the frame were acts of love, connection, and farewell prior to exile. The photographs anticipate the affective possibilities of touch and physical proximity that patients would experience and recreate in communities at the leprosy settlement" (28). Imada's work is remarkable for the capaciousness, the care, of its interpretation. Instead of reading these images as abject, Imada searches for a more generous, more human interpretation. But nowhere in my own archival search did I find any evidence of disabled, refused immigrants forming bonds with one another. The images are remarkable, instead, for the markings of the bonds that have been broken: a child standing alone on crutches, in a stack of dozens of other photographs of families, together. Like Imada, I am studying these archives as in-process, subject to a variety of reuses and recirculations, and making the effort to recognize when there might be what Imada calls "affective excess" in- and outside of the frame. Amada's excess leads in the direction of touch and proximity. Unfortunately, mine does not.

I want to suggest that, while I quickly began to recognize and place these images within the eugenic history of picturing disability, my first—and indeed my enduring—response has been sadness and anger. It is crucial to recognize the young people in these images, without sentimentalizing them, as much more than pictures. Both likely traveled to Canada with family and/or friends, with big plans, using all their family resources to make the trip. The future back "home" after deportation would have to be uncertain, as it is unlikely that family or friends could afford to travel back with them. While the capture and circulation of images like these can be read now for what consequences they may have had in the formation of something as large as a "nation" or even a "technology," there were real consequences that these events set into motion at the level of the individual, the family, the community. As Susie

Linfield argues, while photography, very importantly, exposes violence and injustice, we also know "how limited and inadequate such exposure is" (33). Her argument is that we can and should embrace this failure: "by offering us a glimpse of a reality we can neither turn away from nor grasp, photographs teach us that we will never master the past. They teach us about human limits and human failures" (98). I choose to remain in this uncertain space: unsure whether even reproducing these images in my archive is anything but a further harm—to these individuals, maybe even to you. As Rebecca Schneider shows, the archive is ironic in the way that it anticipates the presence or encounter of the body of the researcher while emphasizing the disappearance of the body (or bodies) that it preserves. How does this anticipation of the body of the researcher fail to anticipate the affective weight of this disappearance of historical bodies?

On the other hand, Leigh Raiford argues that for black political cultures, lynching photographs have "been a constitutive element of black visuality" as they also "intervene in the classification and subjugation of black life" (112). And Jane Lydon suggests that "as a form of Indigenous memory the photographic archive may address the exclusions and dislocations of the recent past, recovering missing relatives and stories, and revealing a history of photographic engagement between colonial photographers and Indigenous subjects" (173). In these examples, photographic archives that were at first full of intentions that varied from abject violence to exoticization have been mobilized in new ways. It is quite possible that images of "deported," rhetorically disabled immigrants could be used in similar ways. But my difficulty first in finding the images, and then in finding answers about their rhetorical uses, has activated another ethical concern: that the exclusionary, eugenic history of North American immigration is simply not being told, and is in fact further vanishing from the available record as time goes on. And this vanishing, in turn, relates to the broader manner in which the colonial past is hidden from the public record. As Stoler argues, this is the result of "affective practices that both elicit and elude recognition of how colonial histories matter and how colonial pasts become muffled and manifest" (122).

Here, in the case of the images I am discussing, I will suggest that not wanting to reproduce difficult, disturbing moments and images is part of the way that we might allow the dominant narratives of colonialism to endure. What does it mean that disability is being erased from history, being made in-visible? And what tools do we have as disability historians and as cultural critics for carefully relocating disability at the center of not just the "visible" record but also history and culture?

Beyond the analysis of Carlevaris, there is no knowledge about how exactly the second image of the child on crutches was reproduced or circulated, no idea how it was *used*; and the same goes, of course, for the first image of the young person on the gurney, which I have only hypotheses about. So I will argue that we can not only analyze the photos themselves, as many theorists have done with other images of disability, but also search for their connected practices, institutions, and relationships, leading us not to an analysis of photos but to an archaeology of photography—examining how the technology was used historically as well as how these uses have since been remembered and misremembered (Bate 4). We can investigate the production, reproduction, and circulation of images in the age of mechanical reproduction, as Walter Benjamin argued we must do (1). We can also analyze the "surfaces of emergence" of images, to borrow a phrase from David Bate (4).

I gesture to "archaeology" here (and elsewhere in the book) as a way to suggest that this work is not just historical. That is, as Jussi Parikka writes of media archaeology more broadly, the goal is to understand technological and media cultures as "sedimented and layered" but also to question the "regimes of memory and creative practices" that allow us to interpret and use media and technologies, currently (3; 2). So, as a historian I might find and reproduce a series of images. As a media archaeologist I will continue to analyze these photographs in terms of their possible reproduction and emergence, and I will attempt to formulate a working thesis about what these images tell us about photography as a eugenic technology, in the past and in the present. Finally, as a researcher invested in the affective power of these images, I encourage the reader to think carefully about motivations to view the archive. It is available to all, and it has been made very accessible. But it is not simply reproduced here. I leave the choice to the reader. Likewise, I am not arguing that other researchers should follow my lead and address visual archives of disability in the same way that I have.

CONTEMPORARY IMMIGRATION IMAGES

In stark contrast to these past images of immigrants "to be deported," the primary images of immigration restriction in our current era come in the form of images of people killed by immigrants. Donald Trump used these images as props throughout his presidential campaign, and used them again during a press conference about the signing of executive orders to build a border wall between the United States and Mexico and to establish an "Office for Victims of Crimes Committed by Removable Aliens" while calling for the publication of a weekly list of these crimes.

These images harness pathetic rhetorical power, but they also powerfully obscure other realities. It is terrible that these people lost their lives. But immigrants are much less likely to commit any sort of crime, let alone violent crime, than American or Canadian "citizens." A series of studies, and studies of studies, establishes this fact (access Press). Regardless, when confronted with this reality, Trump has called reporters naïve or called these "wrong statistics" (access Press). What Trump knows, however, is that the rhetorical construction of immigrants, and in particular Muslims and Mexicans, as criminals will be the lasting impact of any of these orders or acts. Recall that the final "chief success" of eugenicists in the early twentieth century was not necessarily a drastic increase in restriction and deportation focused on specific groups of immigrants, though eugenic rhetoric allowed this to happen. Instead, the chief success was "in popularizing biological arguments" (McLaren 61). And, as Francis Galton wrote in his 1909 *Essays in Eugenics,* the first goal of eugenics is simply to get people to understand its rhetoric: "Then let its principles work into the heart of the nation, who will gradually give practical effect to them in ways that we may not wholly foresee" (43). The idea of the criminal *nature* of Mexicans and of Muslims will be conveyed powerfully through visual rhetoric, like the images Trump uses. The images then work to empower not just the immigration agents and agencies who might have their forces legally expanded, but also the people whose latent xenophobic and racist attitudes have been given justification. The "remote control" over immigration restriction can then almost certainly extend to empower citizens to report immigrants or otherwise to discriminate, stigmatize, and Other.

MAGICAL (REJECTION AND PROTECTION) PROJECTIONS

For Augustus Sherman's images, production began with detention or deportation: Sherman took pictures of immigrants who had been stranded at Ellis Island. He took more than 250 of what he called "immigrant type photographs" between 1905 and 1920. Likewise, Woodruff and the Topley studio also captured "immigrant types," and photographed and cataloged "arabs," "galicians," "pure russians," "jews," and other groups as they landed in Canada.

Many of the images of both Sherman and the Topley studio used what Carlevaris calls "personalization" to humanize groups of successful immigrants, utilizing a close-up view of the immigrants' faces (36). Yet other images, such as those of the "Deformed Idiot" or the "immigrants to be deported," were framed and posed quite differently, and they clearly served other rhetorical purposes.

There would certainly be ways to simply file the Canadian photograph of a "deformed idiot to be deported" within the rhetorical frameworks of Augustus Sherman's images. But as mentioned above, Canadian immigration—specifically immigration *restriction*—was very differently organized and undertaken than American immigration. One key commonality between the nations was the explosion of eugenic rhetoric in the early part of the twentieth century.[6] Poring over the correspondence of Canadian immigration officials stationed at Halifax and Pier 21 in the 1910s and 1920s, it is clear that much of the motivation behind deportation was eugenic. It follows, then, that the examples of "immigrant type" photographs in Canada and the United States, as well as these less well understood spectacles of rejection, must be understood as evidence and as instruments of eugenics. Furthermore, the technology of photography itself can be understood as developing in these eugenic spaces and practices, though this history of technology has been neglected or left out of the frame.

Canadian eugenic approaches to immigration neither ended at, nor were ever centrally located at, Pier 2 or Pier 21. In the early twentieth century, the Canadian government, with the help of the major rail and steamship line Canadian National, was also promoting immigration *into* the country, but doing so by traveling outside the country. As mentioned, Canada was promoting the immigration of desired people from desired countries and constructing a tailored identity for Canada in the process. Canada did so by taking its show on the road and overseas. As one agent wrote in the 1922 Canadian Dept. of Immigration Annual Report, "our agents would be equipped as missionaries of Canada, carrying propaganda to the smallest town and remotest Hamlet" (25).

As mentioned earlier, Canada's two most highly regarded photographers, Topley and Woodruff, were paid to take photographs of Canada that could be used in "magic lantern slide shows" and lectures that would promote the country to potential immigrants from the United States and Western Europe.[7] Many of the photos were of summer landscapes, crops, gigantic apples and tomatoes, men at work in farm fields. The images said: We have great land and lots of work! We have genetically superior crops (and people)! Lectur-

---

6. I want to use the term "explosion" with some sensitivity here. The Pier 2 immigration station was badly damaged in the Halifax explosion of 1917, when two boats carrying explosives collided in Halifax Harbour, creating the worst man-made pre-Hiroshima explosion.

7. As mentioned, all the images that I discuss in this section are credited to the "Topley Studio" or to Woodruff, but we know that at times Woodruff worked in Topley's studio, so at times the credit is difficult to discern.

ers, when they delivered the magic lantern shows, addressed negative myths about Canada. For instance, the cold winter was reframed as having "done an enormous good in keeping out the Negro races and those less athletic races of southern Europe" (Cook).

In this way, the lantern slides document the beginning of this ongoing, oppressive, violent relationship between settlers and the natives they must be seen to include but control. So we should find it unsurprising that the Topley Studio "immigrant type" photos mentioned above were also part of this promotional push. Preferred ethnic groups were showcased in photos taken in the moments after they had passed successfully through Pier 2 or another immigration station. Carlevaris argues that many of these images "personalized" the preferred ethnic groups landing in Canada and were used as "a defense against a potentially hostile Canadian audience" about exactly who was arriving in Canada, as they were "an incentive to prospective immigrants" who could be shown to others from their country or ethnic group who had emigrated (36). These "personalized" images were a key part, then, of magic lantern shows. But what of the two images of deportees? How might their images have been reproduced and circulated?

My contention is that the inverse of the preference for and success of "personalized" ethnic groups was showcased when the ill and undesirable were pictured in the immigration detention and hospital quarters, and this is where I place the mysterious images of a "deformed idiot, to be deported" and "immigrants to be deported." I feel relatively safe making this inference simply because the photos were found in albums of images attributed to Woodruff and the Topley studios, all of which were taken during the time in which they had been commissioned to capture their immigration archive—the other images in the albums showcase landscapes, residential schools, "immigrant types," and the other scenes mentioned above. While it is not possible to prove that the "deformed idiot" or "immigrants to be deported" images were ever used as warnings or spectacles of exclusion in magic lantern shows, at the very least they were placed within the available repertoire of images.[8] I would suggest that it is highly unlikely that the images were *never* reproduced and circulated—they were printed and included in the albums found in the archive, so it is unlikely that this was their only surface of emergence. Perhaps they were simply circulated among Topley or Woodruff's associates, or among immigration agents or politicians; perhaps they were made into postcards or cabinet

---

8. Many of these lantern slide images and scripts have since been lost. Carlevaris writes that "like the actual confusion that existed in the immigration sheds and quarantine hospitals [across Canada], the management of the images themselves was an administrative problem that tended towards breakdown" (55).

cards and circulated informally. Yet they were included in an album of other images that certainly were all used in magic lantern shows. This availability meant that the specter and spectacle of the disabled body and mind may very well have been *projected* in these magic lantern shows, just as a normate vision of Canada was *protected* through these magic projections. Disabled bodies would have been held up as both a warning to those who might immigrate and as a retroactive and transubstantiated corrective to the Canadian body. They would have been emblems and examples.

The magic lantern tours promoting the immigration of desired stock to Canada provide evidence of what Snyder and Mitchell call "the eugenic Atlantic" (103). Snyder and Mitchell show that even during the Nazi regime, eugenics was a transatlantic phenomenon, a result of ongoing "collaboration," and an "unprecedented level of scientific and governmental exchange" between the United States and Europe (103). Indeed, the extensive correspondence between key industrial and national stakeholders on both sides of the Atlantic set up eugenic restrictions on the "wrong" kinds of immigration to Canada; this correspondence also facilitated the promotion of immigration among the "right" races, providing key evidence of this transatlantic exchange.

From a disability studies perspective, we can certainly understand the image of the "deformed idiot" as connoting the archives of criminology, the anatomy textbook, or the freak show. But I want to connect these images to more than just a specific set of disability studies analytic techniques. Instead, I want to place the images squarely within the archaeology of photography, examining how the technology was used and also how these uses have since been remembered and misremembered. These images reveal the eugenic nature of photography itself.

The rhetorical power of the magic lantern shows needs to be examined as well.[9] We know that the lantern shows were the chosen media form for traveling immigration agents because they were thought to be classier than cinema shows, which would "draw from the streets a class of person that we are not desirous of" (Smith). Magic lantern shows were thought to create a deeply felt embodied affect for their audiences, scrambling one's sense of time and place by jumping across eras and geographies quickly (Heard 24). Beth Haller and Robin Larsen reveal that magic lantern shows were used in the Pennsylvania Hospital for the Insane and were thought to positively "alter the patients' moods and moral behavior" (271). In their uses for immigration promotion,

---

9. As Jean-Louis Comolli argues, our obsessive focus on the camera as the "delegated representative of the whole of cinematic equipment" to the exclusion of other technologies like the magic lantern is an "operation of reduction," a repression that is not just historical and technological but ideological (125).

the shows made "overt and implicit appeals to prospective immigrants" that were "ephemeral and somewhat mysterious," with "information conveyed literally on beams of light" (Scheinberg and Rombout n. pag.).

Carol Williams has also shown how religious missionaries used magic lantern slide shows to "lure and win over [First Nations] converts in relatively isolated villages" in the Pacific Northwest. They employed the lantern shows "alternatively as magic and as science" in a conscious manipulation (29). In Germany in the late nineteenth century, such shows were used to show the "'newest results of the colonial endeavours in Central Africa' based on 'authentic reports' by the explorers Emin Pasha and Dr Carl Peters, as well as the Imperial Commissioner Major von Wissmann" (Short, as cited in Williams, 148). As John Phillip Short has shown, magic lantern shows have a deep colonial history, and the ways that the shows blended and faded from one image to the other, creating a pre-cinematic sequence of imagery, can also be understood to "structure the colonial public sphere" (Short, as cited in Williams 148). The same can be said for the ways such shows were used in Canada, showing prospective settlers a kind of magical shorthand for their potential colonialism: holding up all that they might consume and claim while also holding up all that might be abjected from this colonial ideal.

The shows provide early evidence of the ways that "histories make geographies," to borrow from Arjun Appadurai, who suggests that global "flows and networks" have traditionally been based on "models of acculturation, culture contact, and mixture" but have increasingly "brought new materials for the construction of subjectivity" (6). More simply, the slides were circulated through well-established channels based on governmental and industry collaboration, channels that created pipelines for certain types of immigration while shutting down others. But bodies weren't just moved and rearranged via these immigration "markets," they were also shaped through "new" technologies like photography and the lantern show.

Magic lantern shows, in short, had an *aesthetic*: they were designed to create specific forms of embodied and affective response within a certain group of bodies.[10] It makes sense that they would do so by putting "desired" bodies in visual contact with "undesired" bodies, and this is what Topley's and Woodruff's deportation photos do as well. It is not just the content of the photos that matters; it is how they were framed and delivered. They targeted a specific audience that was itself a specific immigrant population. In this way, once you got the right group to view the photo or the lantern show, the image of disability could then act as a safeguard, a warning, a spectacle.

---

10. I nod here to Tobin Siebers's definition of aesthetics: "aesthetics tracks the emotions that some bodies feel in the presence of other bodies" (63).

We wouldn't have "disability" as we understand it currently without photography, nor would we have the technology of photography as we know and use and see through it, without disability and its rhetorical work alongside racialization. Magic lanterns contributed to the power and circulation of this rhetorical work, involved in what Arjun Appadurai recognizes as "the relationship between the forms of circulation and the circulation of forms" (7). Some forms "meet well-established circulatory paths and circuits" while others, like Sherman's photographs and the magic lantern shows, "create circuits of circulation, which did not exist before" (7). In these cases, the technologies or forms have created transatlantic eugenic circuits that endure. These, then, were technologies of eugenics creating new eugenic geographies.

Magic lantern shows, which were already a form of pedagogy and performance, may also have used these images of deportees to "train" foreign and domestic audiences about undesired difference. Everyone who viewed this slide show—or the deportation images in whatever other ways they were reproduced and emerged—could be interpellated with the ability and the imperative to glance at themselves and at others in the manner in which the images and the show had framed difference. Perhaps this, then, is where an investigation of photography as eugenic technology will turn: toward a more inclusive archive of bodies and a full accounting of eugenic practices and techniques; also back on the viewer and the photographer her or himself. If the "chief success" of eugenics, as McLaren suggests, was not measured by the actual number of deportations but by popularizing its arguments, then a key part of this success has been in training the public to use its technologies on itself and others. This archaeology urges us to recognize as technologies of eugenics not just the camera and photograph, not just the magic lantern, but also the archive itself.

"ALTOGETHER UNSATISFACTORY"

In 1996 the Historic Sites and Monuments Board of Canada stated that Pier 21 was a "highly specialized building type associated with the theme of immigration and as such it embodies the policies, procedures and attitudes of early 20th-century Canadian immigration processes" (qtd. in McDonald et al. 28). Much like Ellis Island to the south, the idea was that Pier 21 might at once symbolize immigration history, simulate immigration processes, and contain immigration narratives and artifacts. Many have called Pier 21 Canada's Ellis Island, and this comparison is hard to shake, regardless of its inaccuracy. The idea that Pier 21 could be not just a museum space but a museum *experience* that accurately "embodied" Canadian immigration history, as the Historic Sites and Monuments Board optimistically implied in 1996, is an idea echoed in popular books, published manuscripts, documentaries, interpretation at the site and in popular media, as well as across the literature from a broad range of academic disciplines. The argument is that Pier 21, as a structure, evokes and enacts Canadian immigration as an idea. As Steven Schwinghamer, historian at Pier 21, suggested to me, "This is a pervasive assumption about a landmark historic site—but it has some serious problems" (personal communication, 2013).

To begin with, for much of the history of the site, the immigration sheds at Pier 21 were not deemed suitable at all. Through the 1910s and 1920s, thousands of immigrants from Western Europe were being processed through Pier 21. In 1925, as immigration through the site was beginning to really accelerate and to diversify beyond Western Europe, local officials argued that

> the accommodation suggested by the Canadian National Railway Company in shed 21 for Immigration purposes is altogether unsatisfactory [. . .] accommodation could never be provided in such sheds suitable for the examination of passengers and immigrants and for civil detention. (Williams to Fraser 1925)

The archival record of correspondence between immigration agents and the public evinces this sense of the unsatisfactory conditions in Halifax, as mentioned earlier when discussing the efforts of restrictionist allies within the country and their effort to tighten the border and to deport new immigrants deemed unsatisfactory.

Throughout the 1910s and 1920s, other complaints specifically about Pier 21 are more structural: that there is no place for passengers to stow baggage, that immigrants often skip the inspection process altogether or get lost en route, that there are no official inspection protocols or guides, that boards of inquiry fail to keep records of their hearings, even that the immigration agents lack a typewriter (Unattributed correspondence). Yet, at the same time as the Halifax immigration station is being referenced in newspaper articles critiquing the laxity of inspection processes, new buildings at Pier 21 are also being promoted through official visits from dignitaries, and the image of the space is carefully managed through such events. As Schwinghamer suggested, the positive presentation in historical sources and media of Pier 21 was actually a calculated campaign on the part of immigration authorities to counter negative stories of the conditions endured by arriving immigrants. The Immigration Department of the 1920s played a deliberate role in shaping the public discussion of the facilities. In 1928 the Department created and solicited good press about a newly built facility at Pier 21, an effort that altered public sentiment and rewrote much of the public record:

> If publicity could be given to this building through the press it would possibly do a great deal to off-set the stories which from time to time creep out as to the conditions under which immigrants are admitted to Canada. (Fraser to Little, 1928)

That media campaign may now be many, many decades old, yet it continues to shape impressions of Pier 21 as an intentional, organized, and smoothly run immigration station. It was not.

SHADOW ARCHIVE

As mentioned earlier, the space and processing of Ellis Island was like the choreographic and architectural brainchild of Jeremy Bentham and Henry Ford—a panopticon and an assembly line. The various structures used at Pier 21 for immigrant processing, on the other hand, were settled upon through compromises and confusion from the very beginning, and were inefficient and inconsistent in their processing of arriving immigrants. Yet the historical campaign to suppress this messy history was finally extended to its logical end, and cemented within the public register, with the designation of Pier 21 as the site of the Canadian National Museum of Immigration, ostensibly because it fully "embodied" Canadian immigration history.

Here, my goal is not to correct the historical record. Instead, I have been discussing the conflicting and contested histories of Halifax's Pier 21, arguing against a confident, certain, or "satisfactory" representation of this space. In the place of a monolithic history, I gather the doubt and uncertainty that accompanied the creation of the site, its ongoing administration and functions, and its accrued meaning at the center of an accepted Canadian immigration narrative.

Whitewashing the Canadian immigration narrative, we know, also takes on more insidious forms. As Paulette Regan and others have pointed out, public sentiment in Canada is that "Indigenous peoples have been the fortunate beneficiaries of altruism" (84). The truth is much more unsavory, and much more messy. Canadians first self-described the country as a "white settler colony," and this later became a useful way to understand its political and economic character (access Abele and Stasiulis). But this has come to describe a process in which *making* Canada white, and *keeping* Canada white, worked in very much connected ways. The elimination or assimilation of Indigenous peoples happened at the same time as, and was justified with the same types of eugenic arguments as, the restriction or deportation of particular groups of immigrants. As explored earlier, the distinctive chapter in Woodsworth's *Strangers within Our Gates* is "The Negro and the Indian," whom he feels he must point out "are so entirely different from the ordinary white population" that they "both stand out entirely by themselves" (190). This eugenic rhetoric provides clear evidence of the rhetorical co-construction of Indigenous peoples and "new" immigrants in Canada. The proud self-definition of Canada as a "white settler colony" and the later understanding of white settler colonialism as a violent and eugenic process both require that we place documents like Woodsworth's chapter at the center of our analysis, that we place artifacts like the magic lantern slides at the center of our analysis. Artifacts and narratives like these thus become a powerful "shadow archive" to haunt and to critique the official museum (Sekula). In this framing, the United States and/or Canada cannot truly lay claim to be "immigrant nations" so much as settler nations, founded on forcible colonization, slavery, and then a very selective immigration sieve.

I draw the term *shadow archive* from Alan Sekula's influential essay "The Body and the Archive." What Sekula argues is that for any photographic image to be intelligible, it must efface or ignore or submerge an entire historical reservoir of other images. When we look at an image, what we do not see is the shadow archive surrounding it. This shadow archive contains subordinate, hidden archives: archives whose interdependence with the canonical images that we do see is normally obscured (Sekula 10). Importantly, what we most often find in the shadow archives are minoritized, vulnerable bodies and social groups. So when we see images of desired and successful Canadian immigrants in the Pier 21 museum or the Ellis Island museum, what we must not see, but what makes these images possible, are the shadow archives of the undesirable, the deported. Recall that although Frank Woodhull's picture is prominently placed at Ellis Island, his story is not told. As I will show, it is only in contrast with the shadow archives of illness, disability, and abject or disciplined racial or sexual otherness that something like an immigration museum can be built.

While Canadian immigration history has always been about "grounds for exclusion"—ways to deport or reject certain bodies, minds, races, ethnicities—the ways that the current Pier 21 museum elides these messier and more sinister histories, at the same time that government cuts threaten other Canadian cultural institutions and social supports, positions the Pier 21 museum itself as a grounds for exclusion.

RHETORICAL FOUNDATIONS

To understand the diversity both suppressed and expressed at Pier 21, we should examine the new museum built there—again, as we did with Ellis Island—as what Roxanne Mountford calls a "rhetorical space." Mountford urges us to consider "the effect of physical spaces on communicative event[s]"; the ways that "rhetorical spaces carry the residue of history upon them, but also, perhaps, something else: a physical representation of relationships and ideas" (42). Richard Marback builds on this analysis, claiming that a location can be seen as a "nexus of cultural, historical, and material conditions" of oppression, and can become a "physical representation of [   ] injustice" (1). In particular, Marback has written that any island is a "special rhetorical space" (1). Piers, I'd suggest, are a subcategory of this idea. Ellis Island and Pier 21 were both infilled space—they were created and expanded and reinforced with actual soil and rocks brought from elsewhere. They are also filled with rhetorical power, built to traffic the heavy cargo of eugenic ideas. Thus a rhetorical analysis of Pier 21 will allow us to pay attention not just to how it once functioned (and failed to function) as an immigration station, how it currently signifies as *the* Canadian museum of immigration, but also how the space itself was generated out of—and continues to generate—forms of injustice.

As the location of a national museum and a national historic site, Canada's Pier 21 in Halifax is a complex heritage site. Museums as physical spaces are intersections between practice and display; the buildings embody in their architecture and visual presentation a synthesis of conflicts, provide a space of particular, located knowledge and are—as buildings—agents that influence the readings of visitors (Forgan 572). The museum's physical space is important to its character as one of Canada's key national historic sites. The subject of why and how a space shapes interpretation has received a great deal of consideration as recent museums have developed spaces that function as part of their interpretive argument. For instance, in creating the United States Holocaust Memorial Museum, museum designer Ralph Appelbaum worked from the principle that "a museum functions from the inside out" to offer a "whole environment that supported the interpretive story" (qtd. in Linenthal 407). As C. Greig Crysler writes in an analysis of this museum and the Apartheid Museum in South Africa, the spaces "constitute subject-forming mechanisms: each is comprised of narrative structures, a set of aesthetic practices, an architecture [which] attempt to contain politically charged histories in a museological past, where they can be curated, commemorated and instrumentally separated from [. . .] the global present" (30; 19).

Clearly, many museums are designed from the beginning as rhetorical spaces—as "physical representations of relationships and ideas" (Mountford 42). As Gareth Hoskins has written, "Museums and heritage operations are increasingly employing experiential forms of interpretation, including role adoption and first-person interpretation, in order to cultivate emotional bonds between visitors and the characters that populate historic sites" (101). At Pier 21, as with the Ellis Island museum that Hoskins critiques, *the very architecture is the key artifact.* This aligns Pier 21 with other "new museums" which Marouf Hasian suggests seek to physically "*become* sensory experiences that involve the co-production of meaning, as both rhetors and their audiences are involved in the process of remembrance" and where historical experience is "synthesized" ("Remembering" 70; italics mine). Like Ellis Island, the structure of the current Pier 21 museum is made to look and feel as though it hasn't been designed as a museum at all (though of course both have been retrofitted, less so or more so). In the case of Pier 21, this is a fairly substantial embellishment. While those visiting Ellis Island confront a building and a performed immigration process much like the "original," the Pier 21 museum doesn't at all resemble the sheds that were used for processing immigrants for much of the Pier's history.

Yet the Pier 21 museum exhibits are designed to take the visitor through the process of immigration. On the whole, this enacted immigration process is untroubled and smooth, though there is one small plaque, in a back corner of the main exhibit room, that offers some deportation numbers, and some students are given "deportation orders" if they have paid for the "basic" "Landed Immigrant Program." This unique space, wherein the architecture of the "new" museum seeks to mirror and reproduce the rhythms and routines of the original purposes of the immigration sheds, marks Pier 21 as much more than just a neutral warehouse for artifacts, as much more than a gallery or a performance space. Both Ellis Island and Pier 21 go much further than other purpose-built museum spaces. The museums, to a great degree, have sought to remain "authentic" to the building's actual *uses* during the period of peak immigration. The irony at Ellis Island, explored by theorists such as Erica Rand, is that many of the bodies currently moving through this space as tourists, playing a large-scale game of immigration, would have been detained or rejected one hundred years ago. Yet this process or game, utilizing the museum space itself, remains relatively "faithful" to history because of the architecture of the building at Ellis Island. And we know that "museum learning is 'sticky': it becomes attached through particular affects and has the capacity to leave a lasting impression" (Mulcahy 208). As Hoskins writes, "Visitors are encouraged to adopt the position of an immigrant. Even when not part of the formal interpretive apparatus, so resonant is the national narrative of immigration that visitors independently make associations between their own experience of arrival and that of immigrants some one hundred years previous" (102). The Pier 21 museum, on the other hand, makes Canadian immigration processing at Pier 21 seem so much more consistent, organized, and monolithic than it actually was. That one's pathway through this museum becomes part of the vicarious historical experience speaks to the ways this particular museum actually limits diverse spaces or spatial diversity: the museum building is a kind of lie.

While the museum narrows spatial interpretations and overwrites the messy history of immigration by creating order and authority architecturally, the museum at Pier 21 *also* denies the diverse times and locales of Canadian immigration. As Joachim Baur shows in his study of Pier 21, "Migrants are presented in static, often cultural categories and in heroic images, instead of showing the complexities of their social roles, including class and gender. In turn, the nation appears often as overtly focused on European immigration. Also, the host society is presented as the lucky conclusion rather than one point in complex journeys, experiences and decisions on the migrant's part, and of selection, discrimination and expectations on the part of the receiving country" (Kleist 119).[11] Thus, locating the official and only Canadian Museum of Immigration at Pier 21 elides many of the other times and places and costs of immigration, most notably but not limited to the complicated geographies of the present—but also, basically, all legacies and trajectories of non–Western European immigration. First, though Pier 21 was a major ocean port through which immigrants passed, it was certainly not the only port—many, many immigrants passed through Victoria, Vancouver, Quebec City, Montreal, or Saint John, New Brunswick, among other places. But the move to designate Pier 21 as *the* museum of immigration retroactively erases huge numbers of immigrants—those arriving after the period of peak immigration in the early to mid-twentieth century, and those not traveling by ocean liner to the east coast of Canada, for instance. This move then effectively subordinates many whole *groups* of immigrants as well.

"A SEVERER SELECTION"

In memorializing an ideal, smooth immigration process at Pier 21, the move to historicize immigration back to only the early part of the twentieth cen-

---

11. I cite here from J. Olaf Kleist's English language review of Baur's *Die Musealisierung der Migration. Einwanderungsmuseen und die Inszenierung der multikulturellen Nation* rather than trusting my own translation from the German.

tury denies the growing diversity of a country like Canada—effectively freezing history in a time when only white Europeans arrived at Pier 21. As Tamara Vukov writes, the Pier 21 museum has always been a "xenophilic spectacle" (10). In her rhetorical analysis of the space, she also focuses on the ways that inspection and processing are performed and choreographed in the space:

> If there is one critical function that Pier 21 serves as a particular construction of place then, it is in the image of the national gateway as both a marker of physical geography and national identity. The gateway and border as a place of passage is constantly linked to the iconic moment of assimilation and national becoming. Pier 21 becomes a gateway to a federalist construction of national identity and citizenship [. . .] effected through the continual focus on the physical passage through Pier 21 as a romanticized moment of passage from an old life to a new life, from old world to new, mythologizing [and enacting] the moment of arrival into nationhood. [. . .] Rooted in this official state nationalism, Pier 21 offers an institutional articulation of immigrant citizenship as a xenophilic and celebratory myth of national inclusion. (8)

In these ways—and others—the immigration museum at Pier 21 severely limits the bodies and repertoires of the Canadian immigration archive. Perhaps most notably, refusal, denial, and deportation have not been examined as part of Pier 21's history. It is in this area that I will begin populating a shadow archive of Canadian immigration.

My analysis of Pier 21 as a rhetorical space reveals that it is indeed a "nexus of cultural, historical, and material conditions" of oppression (Marback 1). And the best way to intervene in the rhetorical production of this space is to reveal the "shadow archives" around Pier 21 and the broader domain of North American immigration history. These shadow archives might then maintain our contestation and remind us of the unsettled nature not just of this site but also of the policies, procedures, and attitudes it supported. I will highlight just a few findings as a way to open up a gateway to a range of other understandings and questions, more disturbance.

I have mentioned that the positive presentation of historical Pier 21, in sources and media from its period, is linked to a calculated campaign on the part of immigration authorities to counter stories "creeping out" about the negative conditions endured by arriving immigrants. My suggestion is that we are still fighting against this campaign. We must trouble the straight story of Canadian immigration. We must do this troubling not just to find some other "real" stories of Canadian immigration but also to shift the reality and question the foundations of our Canadian *mythos* around immigration history, build as it is on such altogether unsatisfactory foundations.

Just as I have suggested that the history of the Pier 21 edifice has been messy, so too was the history of immigrant processing at the site. While the imagined inspection process enacted at the current museum can seem orderly, choreographed, and architecturally integrated, immigrant inspection during the peak years at the site rarely embodied this surety and clarity.

As Thomas Guglielmo, David Theo Goldberg, Anna Stubblefield, Matthew Frye Jacobson, Jennifer Guglielmo, and others have shown, in this period, through the process of immigration restriction in North America, a new racial "knowledge" manufactured shades of non-whiteness, using darkness to symbolize genetic inferiority and using the implication of genetic inferiority to rescind whiteness. A result was that "black color" and "dark races" came to be loaded rhetorical terms and tools, facilitated in their usage by eugenic constructions of disability. Further examples of these constructions abound in the Canadian archival record—for instance, as already mentioned, when a young woman named Louise Abbott is rejected and deported from Canada for being "feeble-minded" and the nationality on her medical certificate is simply marked down as "negro" (Louise Abbott Medical Certificate). Also mentioned earlier, but worth repeating here: Rebecca Barnett, who faced deportation in 1907 and was labeled "Undesirable (insane) (black)" (Raska n. pag.). In short, while other medical cards listed nationality by country, if one was "black" or a "negro," this superseded country of origin or made nationality immaterial at the same time that it was linked to mental and physical inferiority. As Robert Menzies reveals, between the 1920s and the outbreak of World War II, more than five thousand people were deported from Canada based on a "feeble-minded" diagnosis which was "bolstered by theories of eugenics and race betterment, and drawing on public fears about the unregulated influx of immigrants [. . .] nourished by the flood of nativist, rac(ial)ist, exclusionist, eugenicist, and mental hygenist [*sic*] thinking in Canada during this period" (135–36).

Roger Daniels shows that the protocols for racial differentiation at Ellis Island "popularized, if [they] did not invent, the category of 'old' and 'new' immigrants," with new immigrants being "both different from and inferior to" old immigrants (62). Daniels is specifically referring to the difference between pre-1880 American immigrants and those who arrived afterwards. At Pier 21 this same division may have happened later, but it is clear that officials were working to turn back the clock. This objectionable process must be recognized, however, as something compounded by the creation of a national museum at Pier 21—this also turns back the clock and separates the old from the new.

Although the mock-inspection process at the current museum acknowledges exclusionary formal policies (for instance, when some students are given deportation orders if they have paid for the "Landed Immigrant Program"), these exclusions are not explicitly linked to race or disability. Informal policies and practices such as the aforementioned inspection of the skin are just as integral to the history of the space as are the mainstream exhibits. Linking such practices to larger eugenic thinking is also important.

From the Baumgartner narrative, one thing we can infer about Pier 21 is that when disorganized processes broke down, the impulse was toward exclusion: "a severer selection is possible" (Baumgartner to England, 1927). Newspapers and public officials like those from the Toronto School Board may have complained that "The Immigration Barrier Is Not Tight Enough" (*Globe*, 1925). Yet eugenic arguments were repeatedly used to tighten the barrier. The shadow archive should be further populated with these stories: for instance when there is concern that officials might be allowing in the wrong sort of biological stock, an official reminds his inspectors that "we would rather discourage five good members of a family than take in one who was subnormal" (Unattributed correspondence). In another example mentioned earlier, but worth repeating here, immigration official Peter Bryce justifies the deportation of a young girl named Daisy Fetch by writing that though her deportation will cause "a great deal of inconvenience for her relatives [. . .] you will understand that our action is taken solely in the interest of this country and for the protection of future generations" (Bryce to unnamed official, 1926).[12] When a woman deemed insane ends up at a mental hospital in Saskatchewan as a "public charge," a letter circulates to immigration officials chastising them, and reminding them that it is not the cost of caring for the woman that is the foremost concern. Instead, the emphasis is on the "menace in the future to this country from the progeny of such persons" (Jolliffe to Clark, 1926).

While these may seem like minor episodes in Canadian immigration history, they speak to and begin to animate an important shadow archive. Beneath the mainstream narrative and its situated reiteration through the

---

12. Ironically, this is the same Peter Bryce who later lost his career when he exposed systemic abuse and maltreatment at native residential schools, an act for which he has been deified, most recently during Canada's celebration of an anniversary of 150 years in the summer of 2017. Yet this retroactive honoring of Bryce does not erase the harm he caused as an immigration official. Bryce began reporting on the sorry state of these residential schools in 1911 and continued until 1914 but was ignored and eventually relieved of his duties (Sproule-Jones 219). Right after he retired, following being passed up for the job of Minister of Health, he wrote *The Story of a National Crime*, a pamphlet revealing both the horrible conditions at residential schools and government efforts to cover this up. Bryce's role as the white savior in the story of residential school abuse needs to be troubled by his record as an immigration official.

museum space and in the historical record, Canadian immigration history is perhaps much better explained through the less-traveled corridors. From these perspectives, I recognize a peninsula surrounded by tensions, I view Pier 21 as a site of significant dispute and as the product of competing interests, I sense confusion and collusion about policies and processes. Importantly, I recognize thousands of bodies denied the ability to move through Pier 21 on to a new life, and we understand how the immigration process was leveraged to further eugenic aims.

"POSITION AS DESIRED"

In 1986, Canada received the Nansen Refugee Award from the United Nations High Commissioner for Refugees, for outstanding hospitality and service to refugees, the first time an entire nation was given the honor. Canadians and—indeed—much of the world view the country and its borders as open. The current prime minister, Justin Trudeau, has publicly and personally welcomed Syrian refugees, for instance, at the very least conveying a welcoming enthusiasm, even if the number of refugees accepted has not yet matched his campaign promises. And yet in the 1920s, Canada refused the recognize the Nansen passport, named—as was the medal—after the Norwegian statesman who used the passport to resettle almost two million displaced people (Kaprielian-Churchill 281). In fact, Canada was coldly indifferent to or actively deterred the emigration of survivors of war, revolution, and/or genocide who weren't also "of the right class" or from the right part of the world—Western Europe (Kaprielian-Churchill 293). This irony is one very few current Canadians would recognize, and this is a history very few know or understand. The Nansen Award will be remembered and commemorated. The refusal to recognize the Nansen passport, a passport developed specifically to protect the world's most vulnerable people, has been successfully relegated to the darkest shadows of Canadian history.

As Allan Sekula writes, the "shadow archive" plays a crucial role in structuring or organizing how we consume images or produce histories, yet the entirety of the shadow archive itself is barely perceived, as in the case of the Nansen passport/award. For instance, the current Canadian Museum of Immigration at Pier 21 is built upon an elaborate, man-made peninsula, one that also supported the original immigration sheds and a range of other historic buildings. As I have shown, that heritage is now largely forgotten or ignored, overwritten on paper and with bricks and mortar by newer construction. Likewise, the stories featured in this museum are just isolated parts of a much larger historical past. This larger, unseen corpus, much like the unseen underpinnings of Halifax's piers, offers the foundations of my proposed shadow archive.

With this said, it is important to understand that shadow archives are not easily fixed and static—many images or artifacts central at one point in history are now relegated to the shadows. On the other hand, current researchers at Pier 21 are constantly generating a shadow archive of stories of deportation at Pier 21, of other stories of immigration from across other times and spaces, albeit not as part of the main and permanent museum exhibit. The current Interpretive Master Plan includes the expansion of the Pier 21 website, locating other less comfortable stories and materials here (see DeVoretz n. pag.). This planning could be read as simply reinforcing the importance and authority of the physical museum space—given that the space itself makes up so much of the message. Yet it is important to remember that museums, as rhetorical spaces, are always in process. So are "nations."

At the current Pier 21, an art gallery on the main floor of the building, apart from the main museum space, has been running a series of temporary exhibits that seem to comment on and celebrate Canadian multiculturalism. Recent exhibits include "Revolutionizing Cultural Identity: Photography and the Changing Face of Immigration," and "Position as Desired / Exploring African Canadian Identity." The first collection showcased portraits of North Americans of mixed ancestry, highlighting particularly unusual combinations. The second collection focused on the question of black identity in Canada. These celebrations of diversity would certainly benefit from being put in conversation with Baumgartner's disturbing lessons about race and skin color; and the featured photo of a young African Canadian man in a parka that serves as the anchoring image for the "Position as Desired" series seems to directly repudiate Mackenzie-King's promise of a "white man's country." And yet when the main exhibit doesn't include these other racist histories, the conversation can't happen. The perhaps-intended double meaning of "Position as Desired" comes into relief. Position as *desired,* as wanted. But also, *position* as desired: place these bodies somewhere slightly outside of the dominant narrative.

We thus witness a dangerous co-optation of diversity: something to be celebrated artistically at the margins, but not something to reconcile with history or with the dominant institution. As Sekula suggests, the shadow archive "contains subordinate, territorialized archives: archives whose semantic interdependence is normally obscured by the "coherence" and "mutual exclusivity" of the social groups registered within each" (10). In this manner, an immigration history that elides the messy, racist processes of exclusion and deportation is also a history that further reinforces the mutual exclusivity of desired and undesired groups of Canadians. If you don't tell the full history of exclusion, you make it easier to hide current exclusions as well. Such a history is altogether unsatisfactory.

As mentioned, there was almost no reference to rejection or deportation as part of the official exhibit at the Pier 21 historic site—just one small plaque, hidden around the back of the main exhibit, off the beaten path through this very intentionally plotted space. A massive renovation of the space will, hopefully, remedy these exclusions. The museum's website and blog have been "publishing" many more nuanced stories of immigration restriction and deportation, like the article by Raska cited above, or the work of Schwing-hamer mentioned previously—these are important parts of the shadow archive, as are the photographic exhibitions. Yet the argument and ideology of the physical space of the museum make it difficult for these stories to gain much traction. And we have reason to be worried that the designation of the site as the National Immigration Museum will not address this problem.

In 2010, in support of the bill to name Pier 21 the Canadian National Museum of Immigration, New Democratic Party representative Megan Leslie of Halifax suggested:

> The history of Pier 21 is remarkable and has touched virtually every family in every region in Canada. We can learn so much from the different stories that are told through the history of Pier 21. Each story tells about a different era of Canadian immigration, a different school of thought, and illustrates changes to the role that Canada played in the international community. One thing is clear from any visit to Pier 21: the history of immigration in Canada is two-sided. It is both a history to be proud of but at times a history where pride is overshadowed by racist or classist policies. But it is a history that we can be honest about and a history that we can learn from. (Canada)

At the time of her comments, the museum at Pier 21 did not clearly focus on the two-sided nature of immigration in the main exhibit, and while Leslie is correct to point out (later in her statement) that there were key exhibits showcasing the rejection of Jewish refugees, the museum narrated this rejection through a single event—the 1939 refusal of all passengers on the *SS St. Louis*. The museum does not recognize how this exclusion of Jewish immigrants was systematically enforced over time, or through the refusal to recognize the Nansen passport, or any of the many other avenues for exclusion. Further, Leslie suggests that events like the refusal of the *Komagatu Maru* on the west coast of Canada are memorialized at the Pier 21 museum—at the time of her comments, it was not. Leslie also suggests that Pier 21 speaks to different eras and regions, when in fact what it does is limit *both* to the celebrated period of the early twentieth-century arrival of white Western Europeans. There are many historical, museological, and of course political reasons for the location of this museum at Pier 21, but none of these could include a sincere belief that this is the best space from which to recognize all eras of immigration, or to recognize Canada's evolving and sometimes conflicted role in the international community. The same can then be said of Ellis Island. The location of this museum on the East Coast, and the fact that it ceased being extensively used after the clampdown in the 1920s, effectively freezes its historical frame, making a convenient argument about which era and which type of immigration can be celebrated.

AUSTERE ARCHIVES

Today, the "grounds for exclusion" at Pier 21 lie not only in the historical (and current) immigration policies that the museum refuses to foreground but also in national policies of public history. In both cases, the shadow archive tells a different story than what is formally represented. In Canada, changes to the National Museums Act and the Department of Canadian Heritage have had a series of effects, including ending some programs, gutting agencies such as Parks Canada, reducing archives, and closing smaller museums. The rebranding of the Canadian Museum of Civilization in Gatineau as the Canadian Museum of History, with its implied changes to content and space, caused public outrage (access "Civilization Museum's $25M Re-Branding" n. pag.). At the same time, programs to accentuate military history and the monarchy have been given funding, sometimes directly in the face of more contested histories (See Campbell n. pag.). One example of the shift in emphasis was the replacement of the image of the Haida, one of the Indigenous First Nations, on the Canadian twenty-dollar bill, by a First World War memorial. Of course, this replacement should be read against the fact that the hundred-dollar bill has, since 2011, featured former Prime Minister Robert Borden, whose campaign slogan "A White Canada" has already been explored.

David Harvey has also suggested that the neoliberal state attempts to "reconstruct social solidarities, albeit along different lines [. . .] in new forms of associationism (around questions of rights and citizenship, for example)" (*Brief History* 81). In *The House of Difference,* Eva Mackey famously studied Canadian memorial discourses that invoke liberal multicultural practices but does so in order to protect existing economic and cultural power structures.

In contemporary Canada, we see these forces working together in ways that directly threaten public history. The government might utilize arguments for accessibility, celebrate certain forms of diversity, and emphasize certain forms of shared citizenship. Yet these liberal values, under examination, repudiate themselves: making *one* history of citizenship accessible to all is not true accessibility or diversity. The move to create one monolithic museum to celebrate certain types of immigration camouflages moves to cut other regional museums and heritage sites. As Fiona Candlin has written, "Discounting or marginalising independent museums effectively attributes expertise and knowledge to the established public institutions" (37). This, in turn, also obscures the fact that many of the other public institutions being cut are those that offer support to *current* Canadian immigrants. As Penni Stewart writes, "other victims of [the current spate of] defunding include small neighborhood organizations that work with immigrants [and] refugees" (n. pag.). As Julie Avril Minich has shown, neoliberalism, in exactly such forms of selective celebration coupled with systematic defunding, "exacerbates the racializing and disabling effects of dominant constructions of citizenship" (*Accessible* 15). Simply, memorializing Pier 21 and Ellis Island doesn't just take up the space and funding that might be used to repudiate other colonial stories and expand other archives; memorializing just these sites reinforces the racism and ableism upon which they were built and run.

Library and Archives Canada, where I searched for and found some of my "shadow archive" material, recently cut or severely limited the roles of 235 workers, over 20 percent of its workforce (Curry n. pag.). All reference services are now by appointment only. As Susan Crean has shown, as of 2012 the current budget for acquisitions was basically zero (n. pag.). The Canadian National Archival Development Program was eliminated completely by the conservative Stephen Harper government, no longer in power. Rare materials are being sold off or farmed out to storage facilities, where they are endangered. (Such a storage facility is where the "deformed idiot to be deported" image is kept. To view it at the main Library and Archives Canada site, you need to put in an advance request for it to be shipped from Gatineau Quebec.) Further, the push to digitize some existing materials instead of acquiring new material is essentially normative—only the most appealing and popular materials will survive. As Crean has argued, the digitization of materials, under the neoliberal banner of democratization and access, actually erects significant barriers and allows for very interested processes of selectivity (n. pag.). A code of conduct introduced in 2013 and stressing a "duty of loyalty" to the government for archivists and librarians also left many feeling they were being "muzzled" (Munro n. pag.).

Disturbingly, Citizenship and Immigration Canada's own library is closing. Representative Remi Lariviere said in 2012 that this print/media collection, which is geared to support policy development relevant to citizenship, immigration, refugees, settlement, integration, and multiculturalism, has "very low demand" (qtd. in Teresa Smith, n. pag.). And he said that, while "a great deal of reference material is available online," important documents will be housed offsite with a private-sector provider (n. pag.). As Jeffrey Simpson argues, Canadian governments have been "systematically reducing the role of the informed and the neutral in explaining the country to Canadians, while enhancing the capacity of the government to cherry-pick what it chooses to highlight" (n. pag.).

The space to find and tell other stories, and to locate other bodies in Canadian history, is being streamlined and right-sized, privatized, made liquid. The renaming of the existing Pier 21 as *the* Canadian National Museum of Immigration in 2011 did not simply centralize immigration history in one place—it made room for such ideological amendments and decisions. Its mission as the Canadian National Museum of Immigration was drastically different. The location and focus of the Pier 21 museum of Canadian immigration has subordinated histories and cultures from its inception, particularly since the land on which Pier 21 is built has its own much longer aboriginal history that has been overbuilt by colonization and not recognized at the site.

Such propaganda has always been central in Canadian immigration history. The positive rhetoric in historical sources and media of Pier 21 was actually a calculated campaign on the part of immigration authorities to counter stories "creeping out" of the poor conditions endured by arriving immigrants in the early part of the twentieth century. The danger now is that propaganda will compose the only available public history on Canadian immigration. Even more importantly, modern eugenic rhetoric, while not as overt as the sentiment in the 1920s and 1930s, continues to inflect citizenship debates and to shape both disability and race today. As Menzies argues, "while the mentally and cognitively afflicted are no longer singled out for prohibition in Canadian law, the codewords of dependency and risk have become convenient discursive substitutes for lunacy and feeble-mindedness" (172). It is estimated that two million Canadian immigrants currently undergo mental and physical examination each year; approximately four thousand are deported, and this number is "almost certain to include an abundance of people deemed psychiatrically ill" or physically unfit (172). A Canadian Council for Refugees report to the UN, written in 2000, "highlights a number of ways in which Canadian immigration policies are discriminatory and racist," including "policies that directly target certain racialized groups, based on profiling, stereotyping, and public annoyance," leading to "continuing signs of xenophobia" (18). The impact of such attribution and typing must be interrogated, and a strong public historical recognition of these conditions would seem essential. Better understanding our restrictive past surely wouldn't hinder us in interrogating our restrictive present.

The grounds for these exclusions, as we have seen, were historically based on a messy and disorganized process at locations like Pier 21, albeit a process which, when in doubt, focused and enforced eugenic fears: "we would rather discourage five good members of a family than take in one who was subnormal"; "a severer selection is possible." These grounds for exclusion are not recognized in the national museum. The parallel that the museum unwittingly gets right is that Pier 21 *itself* has always been a grounds for exclusion—as a selective filter of Canadianness then, and as a limited and limiting testament to the Canadian immigrant experience now. Yet it is through shadow archives like the one I have presented here that we can and must trouble the clean and organized story of North American immigration—and emigration throughout the world—as we create new spaces for critique.

Stephanie Wheeler argues that "if we continue to overlook how eugenicist logic has the capacity to thrive at the foundations of social justice legislation, bodies will continue to become effaced and forgotten" (387). Her point is a powerful one: eugenic logic doesn't just reside within and around laws and policies that are clearly discriminatory; it can also hide within and around laws and policies and social practices intended on the surface to right these wrongs. Wheeler's work shows how human rights legislation like the Americans with Disabilities Act needs to be read alongside racist immigration laws (like those from the early twentieth century that I discuss in this book), because much of the eugenic logic that empowered the harm of vulnerable groups will remain active in the reparative actions we take. This may be particularly true when exploring the ways that something like eugenics does (and does not) get publicly memorialized. This memorialization can, in Wheeler's words, efface and forget bodies very effectively.

THE DISABLED IMMIGRANT EFFECT

January 12, 2017: Canadian Prime Minister Justin Trudeau is holding a town hall meeting in Kingston, Ontario, taking questions from the audience. A young woman, Ella Sheldon, is given the microphone and tells Trudeau that, though she would have voted for the Green Party in the recent election, she is happy with the job he is doing as prime minister. Then she tells him a story:

her sister Maggie is disabled. She has lived in Canada for eleven years, since age two, but she was born in the United States. And the law dictates that an immigrant with disabilities cannot stay. "What are you doing to prevent this?" she asks (LiveWorkPlay). Trudeau, sitting down, spends two minutes avoiding the question. Instead, he starts talking, in a self-congratulatory tone, about how welcoming Canada has been to Syrian refugees, an issue he has personally invested in, and one he has made a conscious attempt to create positive press around, and to take credit for. His efforts with Syrian refugees have certainly created a sort of spectacle of acceptance, one in which his face is always in the picture. When he does get around to addressing Ella's question, he simply promises "we will look into it," suggesting that Maggie's is a singular case. But then he also qualifies that he would "deal with it in a way that is fair for all Canadians and for everyone who wants to come to Canada" (LiveWorkPlay). Canadian Ministers of Parliament have indeed begun to "look into it," though it is unclear what actions might be taken. The subtle message underlying this answer is the idea that allowing immigrants with disabilities to come or to stay in Canada is somehow not fair to all Canadians. Much like the dangerous myth that immigrants are criminal, which has been very clearly refuted, the myth is that immigrants are a drain on health care.

Yet research in the United States shows that "health care expenditures are substantially lower for immigrants than for U.S.-born persons" on a strictly per-person basis, and the difference is significant: 55 percent lower for adults and 74 percent lower for children (Mohanty et al. 1431). Despite this, in the United States, the Personal Responsibility and Work Opportunity Reconciliation Act (1996) and other connected acts make it incredibly difficult for immigrants to even access health care (Costich 1043). On the whole, "immigrants have lower rates of health insurance, use less health care, and receive lower quality of care than U.S.-born populations" (Derose, Escarce, and Lurie 1258). In Canada, there are thousands of pages of research on the "healthy immigrant effect," naming a phenomenon in which new immigrants are at first more healthy than the "average" Canadian, but their health declines over time. Scientists and medical practitioners and economists then want to find out why this happens, seemingly because the only good immigrant is a totally healthy one. But the entire framework of this "effect" is built around the fact that over time, what immigrants "regress" to in terms of health is simply "towards that of the native-born population," not worse (Newbold 77). Let me repeat that point: immigrants start out healthier than the average North American, and *never get less healthy*, on average.

So while you might argue that health care expenditures for immigrants are lower because the border has been selective in keeping out those who might become a "burden," these numbers factor in only a small number of immigrants, those who fully access health care. Most do not. You might argue that because of the "healthy immigrant effect," immigrants are not suited to the "environment," be it social or ecological, of their destination countries. But on your way down this slippery slope, you'd encounter "native-born" North Americans, whose health is already below that of immigrants. Of course, you also might question what exactly is meant by health, and this would be a very reasonable thing to ask. Yet if these arguments are being used against immigrants, at the very least we should refute them on their own terms, and then move on to questioning the terms (like "health") themselves.

This matters because the picture painted by current immigration restrictionists, and even by seemingly progressive leaders like Trudeau, creates uncertainty about the worth and viability of immigrants with disabilities, doubt which flies in the face of the facts. So we confront a series of absurdities. Speaking generally, those North Americans who are least likely to use the health care system, and who are the least costly to the system, are immigrants, who are also simultaneously constructed as the greatest threat to this system.

Finally, for a leader like Trudeau as much as for a leader like Trump, there must be other reasons—political and rhetorical—for ignoring these facts and for constructing immigrants as such latent or overt threats, as inherently disabled or disabling. Those reasons, I would suggest, are eugenic. Or, at the very least, the arguments and embedded sentiments used against immigration have never come fully detached from their eugenic roots.

Responsibility for tomorrow

DANIEL ENWEZOR suggests that we understand the archive itself as rhetorically, generatively, broken: in the "indeterminate zone between event and image, document and monument" (47). Because what can really be said about images that have effectively been disappeared from history? Most likely, we can't know with any authority how the Canadian archival images of immigrants "to be deported" were used. Very likely, we will never know what happened to the young people in the photos, in the infirmary, on the docks, or those like Louise Abbott and Rebecca Barnett, deported from within the country. At the very most, we can have what Brophy and Hladki call a "tenuous beholding" of these images and stories, one that wraps the real trauma of rejection for these subjects in our own empathic rejections (264). Perhaps this is a rejection of responsibility for this injustice; perhaps this is a rejection of the ongoing politics that perpetuate such deportations.

We do know that it is unlikely that the unnamed subjects discussed in this book continued on with their life in the way that Frank Woodhull did after he passed through Ellis Island. What happens, however, when we refuse to leave these gaps, these unknowns, these displacements, in the past? What happens when we move from indexes to cathexis, from the scientific or political purpose of such photos to their emotional impact? What happens when we recognize that even our recirculation of the images, now, offers only a "limited and inadequate" response to their past violence, and reveals just as much about our own "limits and failures" as those of the time? (Linfield 33). As Derrida reminds us, "The question of the archive is not, we repeat, a question of the past" but rather "a question of the future, the question of the future itself, the question of a response, of a promise and of a responsibility for tomorrow" (36). In what ways can the history of disability discrimination through immigration practices and processes elicit an embodied response or responsibility?

Further, as Edwards and Mead show, "the photographic invisibility of the colonial past" in museums, in history books, in classrooms, in cultural artifacts "is not a question of ignorance"; instead it is intentional and systematic (36). So what does it mean that so little of the history of North American immigration comes to consider immigration along a violent continuum of disablement with colonialism? And what can we learn from the fact that even some historians looking at immigration history are not making efforts to understand racism and ableism intimately and violently together, for instance, but instead trying to argue, as Baynton does, that immigration restriction was mostly about disability *rather than* race.

In writing about the history of slave auctions, Katherine McKittrick suggests that "bodily inscriptions can be scrutinized not for their measurable oppressive corporeal signifiers, but rather for thinking about how practices of subjugation are socially produced and evidence of a larger, unfinished, geographic story" (*Demonic* 90). I would suggest that the ways that borders have been inscribed upon bodies also tell a larger, unfinished, geographic story. One that extends much further than the "peak immigration era" or the early twentieth-century "eugenics movement," and certainly beyond Pier 21 and Ellis Island. Indeed, these inscriptions tell a story that continues today in very real, very violent ways. Margaret Jacobs writes of the "intimacy of borders" to describe how they are "fluid sites of affective and emotional cross-cultural encounters where colonial relations played out on an often daily basis" (165). They still do.

In North America, the last few decades have seen attitudes towards immigration that one might not exactly classify as boldly inclusive *and* brutally exclusive, as Zolberg suggests of American immigration history. Instead, we might call these attitudes cautiously inclusive and then interchangeably, brutally exclusive again. Importantly, the descriptors here outline affective, rhetorical powers: "bold," "brutal," "cautious."

As an example of bold exclusion: the 1996 Personal Responsibility and Work Opportunity Reconciliation Act in the United States made it impossible for immigrants to get Social Security, including the disability supports that so many disabled Americans rely on and, as Kurt C. Organista points out, this included "*legal permanent residents*" (302; italics his). And then cautious inclusion: as Susan Schweik has shown, President Barack Obama's proposed DREAM act sought to protect alien minors, but only those who could go to college or into the military, leaving many with disabilities without any protections ("Disability" 433). As Schweik writes, "democratic citizenry binds itself together through an internal logic that, even as it attempts to manage the incorporation of disabled subjects, drives disability down or assumes it away" (419). One can only assume that these same sorts of small steps towards inclusion, steps that have still traditionally driven disability down, will be hard to come by in "Donald Trump's America." Already, graffiti on college campuses has been discovered urging the deportation of "DREAMers" (access Brennan et al.).

Trump has also made concrete steps towards the creation of a border wall, a rhetorical spectacle of exclusion perhaps even more monumental than Ellis Island. Kurt C. Organista reveals how a previous Mexican border fence created drastic death and disablement. A militarized border, and a fourteen-mile-long steel wall erected as part of "Operation Gatekeeper" in 1994, drove many to cross at much more dangerous locations (303). We know that immigration restriction has always needed to create, construct, and invent disability, disabled bodies, and to denigrate racialized others through the use of disability. As restriction increases, so will these forces. While a border wall likely won't dissuade much movement, the wall does reveal that borders are mainly ideas. If there is a ten-foot wall, there will be eleven-foot ladders. But Trump and many others know that the wall as an *idea* is much, much more powerful than it is as a boundary. This border wall, when it is picked up and laid down across real bodies, all across North America, will have a profound impact.

As Allan Levine wrote in his sweeping history *The Devil in Babylon,* "during the thirties, Canadian and American physicians and scientists watched almost with envy as Hitler and the Nazis imposed their own eugenics program. In their view, it was something to behold" (138). Later, in 1946, at the trial of Nazi doctors held at Nuremberg, "one physician after another stated that they had modelled their system after the one in the United States," and the key origin for this modeling was immigration restriction (138). This reality has been submerged.

But perhaps even more arrestingly, this submersion, this evasion of responsibility, makes it easier for new forms of eugenics to thrive in North America. Turda and Gillette have shown that since Latin eugenics has been able to dodge an association with Nazism, "eugenicists in Latin countries found it easier to adapt to post-WW2 realities" (241). The same might be said of North American eugenics—massaging the historical record to turn Nazi doctors from friendly colleagues into enemies has been rhetorically effective.

But Nancy Stepan shows that "the history of eugenics should alert us to the politics of scientific interpretation. As we enter a new stage in genetics, biotechnology, and reproductive physiology, we have to be constantly aware that our sciences, and the social messages we derive from them, are never 'simply scientific' but are complex constructions that always involve struggles over meaning and values" (201). It is not just in the arena of negotiations over immigration that we can find eugenics operating—we need to remember that none of the current research in genetics, pharmacology, aging, wellness, even agriculture is "simply scientific," and that all of these fields of research may simply be camouflaging their eugenic roots.

As Kuhl has shown, "race-based eugenics" was an international movement, crystallizing around written correspondence that has now been made broadly available, but also around academic journals and conferences all with a "positively-defined end value—the genetic improvement of the race" (4). Regardless of where the eugenics came from, discourse revealed "striking interdisciplinary connections between various cultural and political discourses" (Turda, *Hungary* 239). It is this diversity and interdisciplinary that Turda and others note, again and again, about eugenics all over the world—it is at once social and medical and legal and political, literary and visual, strident and gentle. Eugenics could leverage and utilize nearly every avenue of persuasion. Thus, eugenics also gathered all sorts of actors and spokespeople, from every station of life. And yet beyond these similarities, there were many climates for eugenics. As Kuhl argues, "The original orthodox race-oriented eugenics [. . .] has come to be considered as only one among several variants of eugenics" (2).

Importantly, turn-of-the-twentieth-century eugenics was very malleable, perhaps because its science was much more rhetorical than factual. This malleability meant that if the argument was that certain bodies were genetically suited to certain lands, this argument could be used to suit settler colonial interests or to protect ethnic minorities. In East-Central Europe, for example, Turda shows that there were eugenic ideas about the protection of minority groups' racial makeup based on ideas of the "natural" links between the land and the bodies that claimed ownership over it. Eugenics was, in many ways, about making arguments that support the natural suitability of certain bodies to certain lands, but there was no need to actually be "from" this land for the claim to be made. Turda has also argued that, in East-Central Europe, "minority eugenics offered more than just a scientific remedy for the decline of the ethnic community's health; it also provided a defensive biological strategy" based on "protecting the hereditary qualities of the ethnic community, while simultaneously protecting it from miscegenation and assimilation" (East-Central xx). In North America, on the other hand, eugenics could be an offensive biological strategy that supported colonization, and then a defensive strategy against "new" forms of immigration. The science of eugenics has always been opportunistic and suspect. Unfortunately, we do not seem to be moving towards popular science that is any more nuanced or agnostic.

David Harvey calls this linking of land and biology the "longstanding trick" of environmental determinism. In his scheme, we attribute "global inequalities to the effects of geography, construed as physical environmental and locational conditions rather than, say, market forces, policy choices, and imperialist practices changes radically how we think of political possibilities" because policy choices are "trumped by [environmental] determinism" (*Cosmopolitanism* 209). Currently, then, we find political actors and cultural commentators "attributing our ills to natural environmental causes and fixed spatial orderings, about which we can supposedly do little or nothing, rather than to societal malfunctioning, about which we can take strong action," and this "makes a huge difference in how we might understand, feel responsible for, and attempt to confront global inequalities and political repressions" (209).

What makes this environmental determinism so tricky currently is that, on the other hand, we have powerful discourse blaming environmental risk and degradation on immigration. Jessica LeAnn Urban outlines the function of this discourse, suggesting that currently, through a "greening of hate," immigration can be constructed as a scapegoat for environmental harm (205). Of course, she argues that it is not immigration but rather inequitable social and economic systems, systems made even more inequitable by immigration restriction, that cause environmental harm. But even the discourse of many environmentalists seems prone to blaming immigration (205). The Catch-22 then, is that Othered bodies and peoples can be described as inferior based on where in the world they were born, based on their environments. And yet if these bodies attempt to move, or are moved by forces well outside their control, they are described as causing environmental harm. We have evolved not very far at all from the concept of "climatic suitability" that was used to keep Canada a "white man's country." If anything, the derogatory power of linking particular bodies with particular environments has gained momentum.

Whether the consideration is "natural" or economic, disability is a key rhetorical vector. In Canada the "excessive demands" provision of the current immigration system makes individuals with disabilities inadmissible if they are "expected to be medically or socially expensive and thereby prevents family unification where the overseas relative has a disability" (Mosoff 149). This is what is happening to Maggie and Ella's family. Currently, this policy is explained away as an economic consideration, but "the history and underlying inconsistencies of immigration policy suggest that financial arguments mask a more fundamental stereotype that immigrants with disabilities will not be worthwhile members of Canadian society" (149). One can quite easily recognize the lie of true inclusion for people with disabilities within Canada or the United States by recognizing how easy it is to argue that these people should not be allowed to emigrate. When, within the country, the feeling is that the social safety net is in danger, it is clear that the groups of people who are held up as costly and dangerous to this system are likely to be the least valued—and these people, over and over again, are people with disabilities; both citizens *and* potential immigrants.

In situations where this movement is forced, the treatment of disabled people can be clearly recognized. Currently, over 350,000 immigrants are detained by U.S. Immigration and Customs Enforcement (ICE) each year. An unknown fraction of these detainees have serious mental illnesses and are taken into ICE custody even though a criminal court has ordered them to enter inpatient mental health care (Venters and Keller 377). As the total number of persons held within the U.S. immigration detention system has grown, the number of detained persons with severe mental illnesses has grown as well. A growing detention system also has exponentially growing "legal and mental health care disparities" (Ochoa et al. 392). There are very few "legal protections for immigration detainees with severe mental illnesses, such as no right to appointed legal counsel and no requirement for mental competence before undergoing deportation proceedings" (392). No wonder Jennifer Aronson calls immigration detention of people with mental disabilities "inexplicable shoals"—we might also call these islands or piers or heterotopias of deviation (145). These detentions are also subject to the sorts of temporal extensions that made Ellis Island and Pier 21 capable of suspending personhood. After September 11, 2011, "aliens" could be detained for an undefined "reasonable period of time" (Dow 23). The "flow of information" about these detentions was also arrested, with immigration hearings often closed (27; 22). Trump's previously mentioned executive orders in late January 2017 promised to triple the number of ICE agents, surely also extending these powers exponentially.

Similarly, as Serena Parekh shows, the average time that international refugees spend displaced in camps is seventeen years, thus "the treatment of people during their displacement because it is regular and enduring, not exceptional and temporary, ought to be subject to rigorous ethical consideration" (3). As Mansha Mirza has argued, the transformation of refugee camps from "temporary safe havens to landscapes of humanitarian confinement" has had a huge disabling impact, as it has had a disproportionate impact on disabled people (219). Both groups—refugees and people with disabilities— are already constructed as those in need of confinement until they can be "returned" or "rehabilitated" into a normal state, and thus disabled refugees are the least likely to escape the "shoals" of camp confinement; they are threats to security and they are threats to the social support system of countries they might emigrate to. Trump's executive order banning refugees from Syria and from a series of other Muslim-majority countries will surely exacerbate these conditions.

Moreover, just as enforcement moved outwards from Ellis Island and Pier 21 after the clampdowns in the 1920s, there is a new type of "remote control" in North America currently, with "more intimate contact of local police with residents to assist in the detection and removal of unauthorized immigrants" (Provine et al. 42). And historical constructions of immigrants as contagious, as threats, and as burdens have given way to the contemporary construction of "nearly every immigrant as a potential source of danger" despite the fact that immigrants commit less crime than "native-born" North Americans (Kubrin, Zatz, and Martinez 235). This construction then works to justify even greater strategies of control like, for instance, Donald Trump's campaign promises to deport all "illegal" aliens, or to identify and card all Muslims, or his creation of the category of "removable alien."

As Lisa Marie Cacho shows, the 1882 Chinese Exclusion Act "produced Chinese 'illegal aliens,'" the first legal usage of this term (5). When this act was repealed in 1943 (61 years later!) more Chinese people may have been able to enter, "but it didn't change the vulnerable legal status of the 'illegal alien,'" a status which forms the basis of immigration and naturalization law (5). The law is thus "dependent upon the permanence of certain groups' criminaliza- tion" (6). Immigration law needs "illegals." Likewise, it needs some form of "darkness," it needs "poor physique," it needs the "climatically unsuitable," and it needs "feeble minds" even after these categories are erased from the law.

In these tangled, stacked, and complicated current realities, we find our- selves located frustratingly close to, feeling uncanny resonance with, the his- torical stories of immigration, racialization, and ableism that have been told throughout this book. How is it possible that we are still, one hundred years later, living in a culture that might best be characterized by anthropologists, hundreds more years in the future, as obsessed with borders and driven to exclude? How are we still a culture that vilifies disability and disables racial otherness? I've asked you to visit a few spaces of immigration, and to expe- rience and interrogate eugenic technologies. But these spaces visit us, too, and we still utilize similar technologies for racialization and disablement.

We might recognize the ways that Ellis Island and Pier 21, or other border spaces, travel with each of us wherever we go. But we can make an effort to challenge the spectacles and interpellations of these borders and these border technologies, and we can imagine the resistance and subversion they might have engendered and might still. Finally, in viewing these piers and islands as rhetorically constructed spaces in which the key grammars were derogation and exclusion, we might also recognize the possible power of any rhetorical or cartographic construction, or of any technology, for reimagining the individual, social, and political body more carefully and critically.

In the beginning of the book, I suggested that the individual snapshots I offer throughout could, generally, be read in any order, accessed in a variety of ways. In general, you could open this book in almost any place and be offered a version of North American immigration history, or a snapshot of North American eugenics, that dominant historical narratives have generally suppressed, and that conventional archives and memorializations will not make available. Moreover, once you experienced enough of these snapshots or postcards, the goal was to make it less and less easy to impose a spatial or historical distance between yourself and the stories that are told here.

And you were warned: this book asks an important favor. The responsibility of the reader is to work to recirculate these snapshots or postcards through their own research, teaching, and advocacy, and to do so in a careful, respectful, and responsible way. *Disabled Upon Arrival* was written because these artifacts and images are on the edge of our collective memory, on the precipice of forgetting, and because the power of eugenics is growing even and exactly because it is becoming harder to recognize.

But there is much more that can be done. We need to look for other shadow archives, and work to recirculate them. But we also need to search for new iterations of the coded language of eugenics, the creation of wastebasket terms, the ways that biological difference gets projected upon the faces and bodies of people. We need to examine the ways that industry exerts particular forms of pressure on immigration. We need to interrogate how politicians harness the power of xenophobia, and how immigration is used to pit future North Americans against current ones, current ones against "old stock," and so on. We need to look at the ways bodies are linked to environments or blamed for environmental change, or how religion gets transformed into ethnicity.

On the policy side, we need to refuse to allow immigration to be an arena for "positive" eugenics. It's not terrifically complex. Do you have any citizens with disabilities in your country? Yes? Then how could it not be eugenically opportunistic of you to limit the movement of people with disabilities across your borders? Somewhere around 20 percent of immigrants will have disabilities, just like 20 percent of the people in your country currently do. If your immigration, refugee, or naturalization policies exclude people with disabilities, then you need to understand that this is eugenic editing. You need to understand exactly what message this editing sends to your own citizens, whether disabled or temporarily able-bodied, and what message this editing sends to the rest of the world. And then those in power need to be held to account for this eugenics.

Making America Great Again, Trump's tagline, or keeping Canada a White Man's Country, or Returning to Normalcy, these powerful rhetorical phrasings have all relied on scapegoating, denigrating, and making a spectacle of bodies deemed un-American or un-Canadian. This book has traced some of the spaces, technologies, and discourses involved in this work. The immigration laws and measures that these lines justify have had a huge impact on the shape of the world. But the eugenic beliefs that they have empowered and that they have told citizens to enforce have had an even more sweeping and dangerous effect. As mentioned at the beginning of this book, just days after Trump's executive order, Canadian terrorists killed seven Muslim citizens praying at a mosque in Quebec City, Canada. In the early part of the twentieth century, mobs murdered thousands of Mexicans in the United States, with 547 cases recorded but many more occurring. The lynchings occurred not only in border states but also far from the border in places like Nebraska and Wyoming (access Jaret; Carrigan and Webb). Anti-immigration rhetoric and its connection to violence has been pervasive—one of the most dangerous forces in North America. This violence, fueled by eugenic ideas about immigration, continues, seemingly daily.

When Donald Trump signed executive orders to ban refugees and immigrants from majority-Muslim countries, or to report on crimes committed by immigrants, these actions fell outside of American and international law. Hopefully, the orders will be successfully challenged or resisted. But it is also clear that the legal frameworks put in place to correct and atone for eugenic immigration laws in the past need to be revisited and reinforced. The attitudes that made bans based on national origins popular in 1924 began in the late 1800s and never went away. Those countries that can counteract the impact of these current orders must do so. In Canada, this should mean overturning the "Safe Third Country Agreement" that prevents refugees fleeing persecution or violence from seeking refuge in Canada if they land in the United States first. Not doing so would simply extend the ongoing complicity with which Canada and the United States have shaped immigration restriction over more than a century. Individuals—scholars, citizens, industry leaders—putting pressure on the government, at all levels, is what allowed eugenicists to shape the first of these laws. Individuals have avenues—practical and rhetorical—to challenge these restrictions now. After the clampdown on immigration in Canada and the United States in the 1920s, there was a huge growth in Immigrant Aid Societies (access Moya). Current international organizations such as the American Civil Liberties Union, the Arab American Civil Rights League, the International Refugee Assistance Project, No One Is Illegal, Solidarity Across Borders, the Council on American-Islamic Relations, and the Human Rights First lobby raise money for legal challenges and protect individuals. Citizens and citizen groups still have work to do to effect change.

One thing is certain: we can't continue to tell sanitized and selective stories about immigration and eugenic history. We have been here before. We know that biological and other arguments about immigrants have reshaped the continent, most often with terrible consequences. As groups and individuals, over time, have been disabled upon arrival, these ideas and attitudes have never left.

BIBLIOGRAPHY

"500 Reds at Ellis Island; Prisoners Taken in Raids Hurried to This Port for Deportation." 1920. Ellis Island Archives.

Abele, Frances, and Daiva Stasiulis. "Canada as a 'White Settler Colony': What about Natives and Immigrants?" *The New Canadian Political Economy* (1989): 240–77.

Adams, Rachel. *Continental Divides: Remapping the Cultures of North America*. Chicago: University of Chicago Press, 2010.

Appadurai, Arjun. "How Histories Make Geographies." *Transcultural Studies* 1 (2010): 4–13.

Aristotle. *Rhetoric*. Ed. George A. Kennedy. New York: Oxford University Press, 1992.

Aronson, Jennifer L. "The Kafkaesque Experience of Immigrants with Mental Disabilities: Navigating the Inexplicable Shoals of Immigration Law." *Interdisciplinary Journal of Human Rights Law* 6 (2011): 145–66.

Asch, Adrienne. "Critical Race Theory, Feminism, and Disability." *Gendering Disability*. Ed. Bonnie G. Smith and Beth Huchinson. New Brunswick: Rutgers University Press, 2004. 9–44.

Backhouse, Constance. *Colour-coded: A Legal History of Racism in Canada, 1900–1950*. Toronto: University of Toronto Press, 1999.

Balibar, Étienne. *Race, Nation, Class: Ambiguous Identities*. With Immanuel Wallerstein. Trans. Chris Turner. London & New York: Verso, 1991.

Barthes, Roland. *Camera Lucida: Reflections on Photography*. London: Hill and Wang, 1982.

Bate, David. "The Archaeology of Photography: Rereading Michel Foucault and the Archaeology of Knowledge." *Afterimage* 35.3 (Nov.–Dec. 2007): 1–14.

Baumgartner to England. Zagreb, 22 July 1927. Immigration Fonds, Library and Archives Canada, RG 76, vol. 623, file 938332, pt. 2.

Baur, Joachim. *Die Musealisierung der Migration: Einwanderungsmuseen und die Inszenierung der multikulturellen Nation*. Bielefeld: Transcript, 2009.

Baynton, Douglas C. *Defectives in the Land: Disability and Immigration in the Age of Eugenics*. Chicago: University of Chicago Press, 2016.

———. "Disability and the Justification of Inequality in American History." *The New Disability History: American Perspectives*. Ed. Paul K. Longmore and Lauri Umansky. New York: New York University Press, 2001. 57–65.

Benjamin, Walter. "A Small History of Photography." *One-Way Street, and Other Writings.* Trans. Edmund Jephcott and Kingsley Shorter. London: NLB, 1979. 240–57.

———. "The Work of Art in the Age of Mechanical Reproduction." *Illuminations: Chapters and Reflections.* New York: Schocken Books, 1969. 217–52.

Berlin, James, Susan Jarratt, Sharon Crowley, Victor J. Vitanza et al. "Octalog: The Politics of Historiography." *Rhetoric Review* 7 (1988): 5–49.

Bier, David J. "Trump's Immigration Ban Is Illegal." *New York Times,* 27 Jan. 2017. Web. 28 Jan. 2017.

Bird, Randall D., and Garland Allen. "The J. H. B. Archive Report: The Papers of Harry Hamilton Laughlin, Eugenicist." *Journal of the History of Biology* 14.2 (1981): 339–53.

Birn, Anne-Emanuelle. "Six Seconds per Eyelid: The Medical Inspection of Immigrants at Ellis Island, 1892–1914." *Dynamis* 17 (1997): 281–316.

Black to Blair. Montreal, 6 September 1927. Immigration Fonds, Library and Archives Canada, RG 76, vol. 623, file 938332, pt. 2.

Bogdan, Robert. *Freak Show: Presenting Human Oddities for Amusement and Profit.* Chicago: University of Chicago Press, 1990.

Boyko, John. *Last Steps to Freedom: The Evolution of Canadian Racism.* Victoria, BC: J. Gordon Shillingford, 1998.

Brennan, Leah, Rosie Kean, Natalie Schwartz, Christine Condon, Scott Gelma, and Rosie Kean. "Seven UMD Student Groups Will March to Administration Building on 'May Day of Action.'" *The Diamondback,* 27 Apr. 2017. Web. 26 May 2017.

Brophy, Sarah, and Janice Hladki, eds. *Embodied Politics in Visual Autobiography.* Toronto: University of Toronto Press, 2014.

Brown, Elspeth H. *The Corporate Eye: Photography and the Rationalization of American Commercial Culture, 1884–1929.* Baltimore: Johns Hopkins University Press, 2005.

Bryce, Peter Henderson. *The Story of a National Crime: Being an Appeal for Justice to the Indians of Canada: The Wards of the Nation, Our Allies in the Revolutionary War, Our Brothers-in-arms in the Great War.* Charleston, SC: BiblioLife, 2009.

Bryce to unnamed official. 4 May 1926. Immigration Fonds, Library and Archives Canada, RG 76, vol. 269, file 228124, pt. 14.

Benjamin, Walter. "A Small History of Photography." *One-Way Street, and Other Writings.* Trans. Edmund Jephcott and Kingsley Shorter. London: NLB, 1979. 240–57.

———. "The Work of Art in the Age of Mechanical Reproduction." *Illuminations: Chapters and Reflections.* New York: Schocken Books, 1969. 217–52.

Berlin, James, Susan Jarratt, Sharon Crowley, Victor J. Vitanza et al. "Octalog: The Politics of Historiography." *Rhetoric Review* 7 (1988): 5–49.

Bier, David J. "Trump's Immigration Ban Is Illegal." *New York Times,* 27 Jan. 2017. Web. 28 Jan. 2017.

Bird, Randall D., and Garland Allen. "The J. H. B. Archive Report: The Papers of Harry Hamilton Laughlin, Eugenicist." *Journal of the History of Biology* 14.2 (1981): 339–53.

Birn, Anne-Emanuelle. "Six Seconds per Eyelid: The Medical Inspection of Immigrants at Ellis Island, 1892–1914." *Dynamis* 17 (1997): 281–316.

Black to Blair. Montreal, 6 September 1927. Immigration Fonds, Library and Archives Canada, RG 76, vol. 623, file 938332, pt. 2.

Bogdan, Robert. *Freak Show: Presenting Human Oddities for Amusement and Profit.* Chicago: University of Chicago Press, 1990.

Boyko, John. *Last Steps to Freedom: The Evolution of Canadian Racism.* Victoria, BC: J. Gordon Shillingford, 1998.

Brennan, Leah, Rosie Kean, Natalie Schwartz, Christine Condon, Scott Gelma, and Rosie Kean. "Seven UMD Student Groups Will March to Administration Building on 'May Day of Action.'" *The Diamondback*, 27 Apr. 2017. Web. 26 May 2017.

Brophy, Sarah, and Janice Hladki, eds. *Embodied Politics in Visual Autobiography*. Toronto: University of Toronto Press, 2014.

Brown, Elspeth H. *The Corporate Eye: Photography and the Rationalization of American Commercial Culture, 1884–1929*. Baltimore: Johns Hopkins University Press, 2005.

Bryce, Peter Henderson. *The Story of a National Crime: Being an Appeal for Justice to the Indians of Canada: The Wards of the Nation, Our Allies in the Revolutionary War, Our Brothers-in-arms in the Great War*. Charleston, SC: BiblioLife, 2009.

Bryce to unnamed official. 4 May 1926. Immigration Fonds, Library and Archives Canada, RG 76, vol. 269, file 228124, pt. 14.

Buller, Charles. *Lord Durham's Report on the Affairs of British North America*. Vol. 3: *Appendixes*. Oxford: Clarendon, 1912.

Butler, Judith. *Bodies That Matter: On the Discursive Limits of "Sex."* London: Routledge, 1993.

Cacho, Lisa Marie. *Social Death: Racialized Rightlessness and the Criminalization of the Unprotected*. New York: New York University Press, 2012.

Campbell, Clark. "For Tories, Diefenbaker Is on Top of Icon List." *Globe and Mail*, 8 Feb. 2011, http://www.theglobeandmail.com/news/politics/for-tories-diefenbaker-is-top-of-the-icon-list/article1899825/

Candlin, Fiona. 2012. "Independent Museums, Heritage, and the Shape of Museum Studies." *Museum and Society* 10.1 (2012): 28–41.

Canada. 14 June 2010. House of Commons Hansard #62 of the 40th Parliament, 3rd Session.

Canada, Canadian Department of Immigration and Colonization, Annual Report, 1922 at 25.

Canada v Singh [1914], 20 BCR 243.

Canadian Council for Refugees. "Report on Systemic Racism and Discrimination In Canadian Refugee and Immigration Policies." 1 Nov. 2000.

Canadian Department of Immigration and Colonization, Annual Report, 1922. Print.

Canguilhem, George. *The Normal and the Pathological*. New York: Zone Books, 1989.

Capurri, Valentina. "The Medical Admissibility Provision vis-à-vis the Charter of Rights and Freedoms." *Left History* 16.1 (2012): 91–113.

Carey, Allison C. "Beyond the Medical Model: A Reconsideration of 'Feeblemindedness,' Citizenship, and Eugenic Restrictions." *Disability & Society* 18.4 (2003): 411–30.

Carlevaris, Anna-Maria. *Photography, Immigration and Canadianism: 1896–1921*. MA thesis, Concordia University, 1992.

Carlson, Elof Axel. *The Unfit: A History of a Bad Idea*. Cold Spring Harbor, NY: Cold Spring Harbor Laboratory Press, 2001.

Carrigan, William D., and Charles Webb. "When Americans Lynched Mexicans." *New York Times*, 20 Feb. 2015. Web. 30 Jan. 2017.

Caufield, Timothy, and Gerald Robertson. "Eugenic Policies in Alberta: From the Systematic to the Systemic?" *Alberta Law Review* 35 (1996): 59–79.

Cavell, Janice. "The Imperial Race and the Immigration Sieve: The Canadian Debate on Assisted British Migration and Empire Settlement, 1900–30." *The Journal of Imperial and Commonwealth History* 34.3 (2006): 345–67.

"CBSA Rushes Deportation of Men Rounded Up in Racial Profiling Anti-Immigrant Raids." *No One Is Illegal,* n.d., http://toronto.nooneisillegal.org/node/871

Chadha, Ena. "'Mentally Defectives' Not Welcome: Mental Disability in Canadian Immigration Law, 1859–1927." *Disability Studies Quarterly* 28.1 (2008). Web.

Chang, Robert. *Disoriented: Asian-Americans, Law, and the Nation-State.* New York: New York University Press, 1999.

Chinese Immigration Act 1885, SC 1885, c 71, s 4.

Chinese Immigration Act 1923, SC 1923, c 33, s 5.

Chocano, Carina. "Dreams Just beyond Reach through the Golden Door." *New York Times,* 1 June 2007. Web. 15 Sept. 2010.

"Civilization Museum's $25M Re-Branding." *CBC News,* 16 Oct. 2012, http://www.cbc.ca/news/canada/ottawa/story/2012/10/16/ottawa-canadian-museum-civilization-becomes-canadian-museum-history.html

Clark, Jane Perry. *Deportation of Aliens from the United States to Europe.* New York: Columbia University Press, 1931.

Coal Mines Regulation Act 1877, c 84, as am. SBC 1903, c 17, s 2.

Coal Mines Regulation Act 1877, SBC 1877, c 84, as am. SBC 1890, c 33, s 1.

Cogdell, Christina. 2004. *Eugenic Design: Streamlining America in the 1930s.* Philadelphia: University of Pennsylvania Press.

Cohen, Adam. "Harvard's Eugenics Era." *Harvard Magazine* (2016). Web.

———. *Imbeciles: The Supreme Court, American Eugenics, and the Sterilization of Carrie Buck.* New York: Penguin, 2016.

Cole, Teju. "A Too-Perfect Picture." *New York Times,* 2 Apr. 2016. Web. 14 Jan. 2017.

Coleman, Matthew. "A Geopolitics of Engagement: Neoliberalism, the War on Terrorism, and the Reconfiguration of US Immigration Enforcement." *Geopolitics* 12 (2007): 607–34.

Comolli, Jean-Louis. "Machines of the Visible." *The Cinematic Apparatus.* Ed. Teresa De Lauretis and Stephen Heath. New York: St. Martin's, 1980. 121–42.

The Constitution Act, 1867, 30&31 Vict, c 3, s 91(25), 95.

Conway, Lorie. *Forgotten Ellis Island: The Extraordinary Story of America's Immigrant Hospital.* New York: HarperCollins, 2007.

Cook, W. Hennessy. Lantern Slide Lecture, "If England Only Knew." Immigration Fonds, Library and Archives Canada. RG 76, vol. 560, file 808468, pt. 1, p. 2.

Coolidge, Calvin. "Whose Country Is This?" *Good Housekeeping,* Feb. 1921, 13–14.

Costich, Julia Field. "Legislating a Public Health Nightmare: The Anti-Immigrant Provisions of the Contract with America Congress." *Kentucky Law Journal* 90 (2001): 1043–70.

Crean, Susan. "National Archives Blues." *Literary Review of Canada,* Jan.–Feb. 2011, http://reviewcanada.ca/essays/2011/01/01/national-archives-blues/

Crysler, C. Greig. "Violence and Empathy: National Museums and the Spectacle of Society." *Traditional Dwellings and Settlements Review* 17.2 (2006): 19–38.

Curran, Henry H. "The New Immigrant." *Saturday Evening Post,* 15 Aug. 1925.

Curry, Bill. "Parks Canada Hit Hard as Ottawa Doles out Nearly 4,000 Job Notices." *Globe and Mail,* 30 Apr. 2012, http://www.theglobeandmail.com/news/politics/ottawa-notebook/parks-canada-hit-hard-as-ottawa-doles-out-nearly-4000-job-notices/article4106781/

Daniels, Roger. *Guarding the Golden Door: American Immigration Policy and Immigrants since 1882.* New York: Hill and Wang, 2004.

———. *Not Like Us: Immigrants and Minorities in America, 1890–1924.* Chicago: Ivan R. Dee, 1997.

Daniels, Roger, and Otis Graham. *Debating American Immigration, 1882–Present.* Lanham, MD: Rowman and Littlefield, 2001.

Daschuk, James. *Clearing the Plains: Disease, Politics of Starvation, and the Loss of Aboriginal Life.* Regina, SK: University of Regina Press, 2012.

Davenport, Charles B. *Heredity in Relation to Eugenics.* New York: Henry Holt, 1911.

———. "Memorandum re: Eugen Fischer, 1927." American Philosophical Society Archives, Philadelphia, PA.

Davis, Lennard J. *Enforcing Normalcy: Disability, Deafness, and the Body.* New York: Verso, 1995.

De Courcy Ward, Robert. "Immigration and the War." *The Scientific Monthly* 2.5. (May 1916): 438–52.

"Definition of Feeble-Minded." *Eugenical News* 1 (1916): n. pag.

"Definitions of Various Terms Used in Medical Certificates." BMS Am 2245 (1059) Compositions, 1906. Houghton Library, Harvard College Library, Harvard University.

"Deported, Disabled U.K. Citizen Arrives in Britain." *CBC News,* 20 Jan. 2009, http://www.cbc.ca/news/canada/manitoba/deported-disabled-u-k-citizen-arrives-in-britain-1.845793

Derose, Kathryn Pitkin, José J. Escarce, and Nicole Lurie. "Immigrants and Health Care: Sources of Vulnerability." *Health Affairs* 26.5 (2007): 1258–68.

Derrida, Jacques. *Archive Fever: A Freudian Impression.* Trans. Eric Prenowitz. Chicago: University of Chicago Press, 1996.

DeVoretz, Sacha. "Canada's National Immigration Museum Expanding Online." *Vancouver Observer,* 15 Jan. 2013. Web. 16 Aug. 2017.

Dillingham Commission. "Dictionary of Races or Peoples" [Serial set no. 5867, Senate document 662, session 61–3, session-date: 1910, 1911]. Reports of the Immigration Commission. Washington, DC: Government Printing Office, 1911.

Dirks, Gerald E. *Canada's Refugee Policy: Indifference or Opportunism?* Montreal: McGill-Queen's University Press, 1977.

Dolmage, Jay. *Disability Rhetoric.* Syracuse: Syracuse University Press, 2013.

———. "Disabled Upon Arrival: The Rhetorical Construction of Race and Disability at Ellis Island." *Cultural Critique* 77 (Winter 2011): 24–69.

———. "Framing Disability, Fixing Race: Photography as Eugenic Technology." *Enculturation* 17 (Winter 2014). Web.

———. "Grounds for Exclusion: Canada's Pier 21 and Its Shadow Archives." *Diverse Spaces: Examining Identity, Heritage and Community within Canadian Public Culture.* Ed. Susan Ashley. Cambridge: Cambridge Scholar's Press, 2013. 100–121.

Dolmage, Jay, and Jen Rinaldi. "'Of Dark Type and Poor Physique': Law, Immigration Restriction, and Disability in Canada, 1900–1930." *Disabling Barriers: Social Movements, Disability History, and the Law.* Ed. R. Malhotra and B. Isitt. Vancouver: UBC Press, 2017. 98–122.

Dow, Mark. *American Gulag: Inside US Immigration Prisons.* Berkeley: University of California Press, 2004.

Dowbiggin, Ian Robert. *Keeping America Sane: Psychiatry and Eugenics in the United States and Canada 1880–1940.* Ithaca: Cornell University Press, 2003.

Dwyer, June. "Disease, Deformity, and Defiance: Writing the Language of Immigration Law and the Eugenics Movement on the Immigrant Body." *MELUS* 28.1 (Spring 2003): 105–21.

Edwards, Elizabeth, and Matt Mead. "Absent Histories and Absent Images: Photographs, Museums and the Colonial Past." *Museum & Society* 11.1 (2013): 19–38.

Edwards, Peter. "'Old Stock Canadians' Comment Gives Chills to Professor." *Toronto Star,* 18 Sep. 2015, http://www.thestar.com/news/canada/2015/09/18/old-stock-canadians-phrase-chills -prof-ignites-twitter.html

Efremkin, Evgeny. "Canada's Invisible Nationality Policy: Creating Ethnicity, Managing Populations, Imagining a Nation." *Journal of the Canadian Historical Association / Revue de la Société historique du Canada* 24.2 (2013): 263–310.

Eliot, Charles W. "Suppressing Moral Defectives." *The Journal of Education* 74.7 (Aug. 1911): 175–76.

Elks, Martin. "Believing Is Seeing: Visual Conventions in Barr's Classification of the 'Feeble-Minded.'" *Mental Retardation: A Journal of Practices, Policy and Perspectives* 42.5 (2004): 371–82.

Elliot, Louise. "Syrian Refugee Plan Has Officials 'Working around the Clock,' McCallum Says." *CBC News,* 7 Nov. 2015, http://www.cbc.ca/news/politics/canada-mccallum-syrian-refugee -plan-1.3307788?cmp=rss

Enwezor, Okwui. *Archive Fever: Uses of the Document in Contemporary Art.* New York: International Center on Photography, 2008.

Epps-Robertson, Candace. "The Race to Erase Brown v. Board of Education: The Virginia Way and the Rhetoric of Massive Resistance." *Rhetoric Review* 35.2 (2016): 108–20.

Erevelles, Nirmala. *Disability and Difference in Global Contexts.* London: Palgrave MacMillan, 2011.

"Eugenists Hear of Real Missing Link." *New York Times,* 20 June 1914. http://query.nytimes.com/ mem/archive-free/pdf?res=940DE3DA133EE733A25753C2A9609C946596D6CF

Fairchild, Amy. *Science at the Borders: Immigrant Medical Inspection and the Shaping of the Modern Industrial Labor Force.* Baltimore: Johns Hopkins University Press, 2004.

Ferguson, Lindsay. "Constructing and Containing the Chinese Male: Quong Wing v. The King and the Saskatchewan Act to Prevent the Employment of Female Labour." *Saskatchewan Law Review* 65 (2002): 549–65.

Finnegan, Cara A. "Doing Rhetorical History of the Visual: The Photograph and the Archive." *Defining Visual Rhetorics* (2004): 195–214.

Fitzgerald, David S., and David Cook-Martin. "The Geopolitical Origins of the US Immigration Act of 1965." *Migration Policy Institute, Migration Information Source* 18, 5 Feb. 2015, http://www.migrationpolicy.org/article/geopolitical-origins-us-immigration-act-1965

Forgan, Sophie. "Building the Museum." *Isis* 96.4 (2005): 572–85.

Foucault, Michel. *Abnormal: Lectures at the Collège de France, 1974–1975.* Ed. Valerio Marchetti and Antonella Salomoni. Trans. Graham Burchell. New York: Picador, 2004.

———. *The Birth of the Clinic: An Archaelogy of Medical Perception.* New York: Vintage Books, 1973.

———. *Discipline and Punish: The Birth of the Prison.* New York: Vintage Books, 2012.

———. *The Order of Things: An Archaeology of the Human Sciences.* New York: Vintage Books, 1973.

Foucault, Michel, and Jay Miskowiec. "Of Other Spaces." *diacritics* 16.1 (1986): 22–27.

Fraser to Little. Ottawa, 1 March 1928. Immigration Fonds, Library and Archives Canada, RG 76, vol. 666, file, 1594, pt 2.

Fresko, David. "Muybridge's Magic Lantern." *Animation: An Interdisciplinary Journal* 8.1 (March 2013): 47–64.

Galton, Francis. *Essays in Eugenics.* London: Macmillan, 1909.

Gardner, Martha. *The Qualities of a Citizen: Women, Immigration, and Citizenship, 1870–1965.* Camden: Princeton University Press, 2005.

Garland-Thomson, Rosemarie. *Extraordinary Bodies: Figuring Physical Disability in American Culture and Literature.* New York: Columbia University Press, 1997.

———. "From Wonder to Error." *Freakery: Cultural Spectacles of the Extraordinary Body.* Ed. Rosemarie Garland Thomson. New York: New York University Press, 1996. 1–19.

Gelb, Steven A. "'Not Simply Bad and Incorrigible': Science, Morality, and Intellectual Deficiency." *History of Education Quarterly* 29.3 (1989): 359–79.

Gelb, Steven A., Garland E. Allen, Andrew Futterman, and Barry A. Mehler. "Rewriting Mental Testing History: The View from the American Psychologist." *Sage Race Relations Abstracts* 11.2 (May 1986): 18–31.

Gerber, David A. "Comment: Immigration History and Disability History." *Journal of American Ethnic History* 29.3 (2012): 49–54.

Gerken, Christina. *Model Immigrants and Undesirable Aliens.* Minneapolis: University of Minnesota Press, 2013.

Gerstle, Gary. *American Crucible: Race and Nation in the Twentieth Century.* Princeton: Princeton University Press, 2001.

Goddard, Henry Herbert. *Feeble-Mindedness, Its Causes and Consequences.* New York: Macmillan, 1914.

———. *Manual of the Mental Examination of Aliens.* Treasury Department of the United States Public Health Service, Miscellaneous Publication 18. 1918.

———. "Mental Tests and the Immigrant." *Journal of Delinquency* 2 (1917): 243–77.

Goldberg, David Theo. *The Racial State.* Oxford: Basil Blackwell, 2001.

Goldberg, Vicki, and Robert Silberman. *American Photography: A Century of Images.* New York: Chronicle, 1999.

Gonzalez, Ed. "Review: Golden Door." *Slant Magazine.* 2 Mar. 2007.

Greenland, Cyril. *Charles Kirk Clarke: A Pioneer of Canadian Psychiatry.* Toronto: University of Toronto Press, 1966.

Grose, Howard B. *Aliens or Americans?* New York: Young People's Missionary Movement, 1906.

Grubbs, Samuel B. *By the Order of the Surgeon General.* Greenfield, IN: William Mitchell, 1943.

Guglielmo, Jennifer, and Salvatore Salerno, eds. *Are Italians White? How Race Is Made in America.* London: Routledge, 2003.

Guglielmo, Thomas A. *White on Arrival: Italians, Race, Color, and Power in Chicago, 1890–1945.* New York: Oxford University Press, 2003.

Hall, Prescott F. "Immigration Restriction and World Eugenics." *Journal of Heredity* 10.3 (Mar. 1919): 125–27.

———. "Immigration and the World War." *The Annals of the American Academy of Political and Social Science* 93.1 (1921): 190–93.

Haller, Beth, and Robin Larsen. "Persuading Sanity: Magic Lantern Images and the Nineteenth-Century Moral Treatment in America." *The Journal of American Culture* 28.3 (2005): 259–72.

Hanes, Roy. "None Is Still Too Many: An Historical Exploration of Canadian Immigration Legislation as It Pertains to People with Disabilities." *Council of Canadians with Disabilities,* n.d., http://www.ccdonline.ca/en/socialpolicy/access-inclusion/none-still-too-many

Harvey, David. *A Brief History of Neoliberalism.* Oxford: Oxford University Press, 2005.

———. *Cosmopolitanism and the Geographies of Freedom.* Oxford: Oxford University Press, 2005.

Hasian, Marouf. "Remembering and Forgetting the 'Final Solution': A Rhetorical Pilgrimage through the U.S. Holocaust Memorial Museum." *Critical Studies in Media Communication* 21.1 (2004): 64–92.

———. *The Rhetoric of Eugenics in Anglo-American Thought.* Athens: University of Georgia Press, 1996.

Heard, Mervyn. "The Magic Lantern's Wild Years." *Cinema: The Beginnings and the Future.* Ed. C. Williams. London: University of Westminster Press. 24–32.

Hernandez, Kelly Lytle. "Distant Origins: The Mexican Roots of Border Patrol Practice and American Racism, 1924–1954." UCLA Second Annual Interdisciplinary Conference on Race, Ethnicity, and Immigration. 18 May 2002. Ellis Island Manuscript Collection IM-158.

"Heterotopy." *Oxford English Dictionary Online,* 2nd ed., 1989, http://dictionary.oed.com/cgi/entry/50105565?

Hetherington, Kevin. K. *The Badlands of Modernity: Heterotopia and Social Ordering.* London: Routledge, 1997.

Higham, John. *Send These to Me: Jews and Other Immigrants in Urban America.* New York: Athenaeum, 1975.

Hollihan, K. Tony. "'A Brake upon the Wheel': Frank Oliver and the Creation of the Immigration Act of 1906." *Past Imperfect* 1 (1992): 93–112.

Holloway, Pippa. *Sexuality, Politics, and Social Control in Virginia, 1920–1945.* Chapel Hill: University of North Carolina Press, 2006.

Hoskins, Gareth. "Poetic Landscapes of Exclusion: Chinese Immigration at Angel Island, San Francisco." *Landscape and Race in the United States.* Ed. Richard H. Schein. New York: Routledge, 2006. 95–112.

House of Commons Debates, 9th Parl, 2nd Sess (29 April 1902) at 3740.

House of Representatives, 41st Congress, 2nd Session. U.S. Congressional Documents and Debates, 1774–1875. Library of Congress.

Hudak, John. "Four Realities about Executive Actions: Moving Beyond the Rhetoric of Immigration Reform." *Brookings,* 29 July 2016. Web. 28 Jan. 2017.

Imada, Adria L. "Promiscuous Signification." *Representations* 138.1 (2017): 1–36.

The Immigration Act 1886, RSC 1886, c 65.

The Immigration Act, RS 1906 c 6, s 30, as am. RS 1908, c 33, s 30.

Immigration Act, RS 1910, c 27, s 38(a)(c).

"Immigration Barrier Is Not Tight Enough." *Toronto Globe,* 12 Nov. 1925. Immigration Fonds, Library and Archives Canada.

Jacobs, Margaret. "Crossing Intimate Borders: Gender, Settler Colonialism, and the Home." *Gendering Border Studies.* Ed. Jane Aaron and Henrice Altink. Cardiff: University of Wales Press, 2010. 165–91.

Jacobson, Matthew Frye. *Whiteness of a Different Color: European Immigrants and the Alchemy of Race.* Cambridge, MA: Harvard University Press, 1999.

Jaret, Charles. "Troubled by Newcomers: Anti-immigrant Attitudes and Action during Two Eras of Mass Immigration to the United States." *Journal of American Ethnic History* (1999): 9–39.

Jodhan, Donna J. "Letter to the Auditor General of Canada Regarding the Initiative for Equitable Library Access (IELA) Project." *Alliance for Equality of Blind Canadians,* 1 Mar. 2014, http://www.blindcanadians.ca/news/correspondence/2013-01/2600-letter-auditor-general-canada-regarding-initiative-equitable-librar

Jolliffe to Clark. 4 May 1926. Immigration Fonds, Library and Archives Canada, RG 76, vol. 269, file 228124, pt. 14.

Jones, Chelsea Temple. *Writing Intellectual Disability: Glimpses into Precarious Processes of Re/Making a Cultural Phenomenon.* Ph.D. diss., York University, 2016.

Kallen, Evelyn. *Ethnicity and Human Rights in Canada.* Don Mills, ON: Oxford University Press, 2010.

Kaprielian-Churchill, Isabel. "Rejecting 'Misfits': Canada and the Nansen Passport." *International Migration Review* (1994): 281–306.

Karzel, Emil. Ellis Island Metaform Collection Box 39 No. 1 (New Box 99) "General Research Files: AARP Letters." 22 November 1985.

Kelley, Ninette, and Michael Trebilcock. *The Making of the Mosaic.* Toronto: Toronto University Press, 1998.

Kérchy, Anna, and Andrea Zittlau, eds. *Exploring the Cultural History of Continental European Freak Shows and Enfreakment.* Newcastle, UK: Cambridge Scholars, 2012.

King, Thomas. *The Inconvenient Indian: A Curious Account of Native People in North America.* Toronto: Doubleday Canada, 2012.

Klautke, Egbert. "'The Germans Are Beating Us at Our Own Game': American Eugenics and the German Sterilization Law of 1933." *History of the Human Sciences* 29.3 (2016): 25–43.

Kleist, J. Olaf. "Rev. of Baur, Joachim, *Die Musealisierung der Migration. Einwanderungsmuseen und die Inszenierung der multikulturellen Nation.*" *Memory Studies* 4.1 (2001): 119–22.

Kline, Wendy. *Building a Better Race.* Berkeley: University of California Press, 2001.

Knox, Howard A. "A Diagnostic Study of the Face." *New York Medical Journal,* 14 June 1913, 1227–28.

———. "Tests for Mental Defects." *Journal of Heredity* 5.3 (March 1914): 122–30.

Knowles, Valerie. "Forging Our Legacy: Canadian Citizenship and Immigration, 1900–1977," 15 Jan. 2000, http://publications.gc.ca/site/eng/91366/publication.html

Kotker, Norman, Shirley C. Burden, Charles Hagen, Robert Twombly, Susan Jonas, Klaus Schnitzer, and Brian Feeney. *Ellis Island: Echoes of a Nation's Past.* New York: Aperture, 1991.

Kraut, Alan. *Silent Travelers: Germs, Genes, and the "Immigrant Menace."* New York: Basic Books, 1994.

Kremer, Emmie. "Personal Correspondence with AARP." Ellis Island Archive Metaform Collection Box 39 No. 1 (New Box 99) "General Research Files: AARP Letters."

Kubrin, Charis Elizabeth, Marjorie Sue Zatz, and Ramiro Martinez, eds. *Punishing Immigrants: Policy, Politics, and Injustice.* New York: New York University Press, 2012.

Kudlick, Catherine. "Comment: Comparative Observations on Disability in History." *Journal of American Ethnic History* 29.3 (Spring 2005): 59–63.

Kühl, Stefan. *For the Betterment of the Race: The Rise and Fall of the International Movement for Eugenics and Racial Hygiene.* New York: Palgrave Macmillan, 2013.

La Guardia, Fiorello H. *The Making of an Insurgent: An Autobiography, 1882–1919.* Westport, CT: Greenwood, 1948.

Laughlin, Henry H. "Correspondence with Charles B. Davenport, Eugenics Record Office January 8, 1921." Charles B. Davenport Papers, American Philosophical Society.

———. "Report of H. H. Laughlin for the Year Ending August 31, 1922." Charles B. Davenport Papers, American Philosophical Society.

Lee, Victor. "The Laws of Gold Mountain: A Sampling of Early Canadian Laws and Cases that Affected People of Chinese Ancestry." *Manitoba Law Journal* 21 (1992): 301–24.

Levine, Allan. *The Devil in Babylon: Fear of Progress and the Birth of Modern Life*. Toronto: McClelland & Stewart, 2005.

Linenthal, Edward. "The Boundaries of Memory: The United States Holocaust Memorial Museum." *American Quarterly* 46.3 (1994): 406–33.

Linfield, Susie. *The Cruel Radiance*. Chicago: University of Chicago Press, 2010.

LiveWorkPlay. "Young Citizen (Ella) Questions PM Trudeau about Disability and Immigration." *YouTube*, 14 Jan. 2017. 16 Jan. 2017. https://www.youtube.com/watch?v=vOghwdEG-jM

Lombroso, Cesare. *L'Homme Criminel*. Paris: Félix Alcan, 1895.

Louise Abbott Medical Certificate. 24 March 1925. Immigration Fonds, Library and Archives Canada, RG 76, vol. 269, file 228124, pt. 13.

Lowe, Lisa. *Immigrant Acts*. Durham: Duke University Press, 1996.

Luibheid, Eithne. *Entry Denied: Controlling Sexuality at the Border*. Minneapolis and London: University of Minnesota Press, 2002.

———. "Heteronormativity and Immigration Scholarship: A Call for Change." *GLQ: A Journal of Lesbian and Gay Studies* 10.2 (2004): 227–35.

Lutz, Catherine A., and Jane L. Collins. *Reading National Geographic*. Chicago: University of Chicago Press, 1993.

Lydon, Jane. "Return: The Photographic Archive and Technologies of Indigenous Memory." *Photographies* 3.2 (2010): 173–87.

Mackenzie King, William Lyon. "Diaries of William Lyon Mackenzie King 1893–1950," https://www.bac-lac.gc.ca/eng/discover/politics-government/prime-ministers/william-lyon-mackenzie-king/Pages/search.aspx

———. Report by W. L. Mackenzie King, C. M. G., Deputy Minister of Labour, on Mission to England to confer with the British Authorities on the subject of Immigration to Canada from the Orient and Immigration from India in Particular. Ottawa: S. E. Dawson, 1908.

Mackey, Eva. *The House of Difference: Cultural Politics and National Identity in Canada*. Toronto: University of Toronto Press, 2002.

———. "Tricky Myths: Settler Pasts and Landscapes of Innocence." *Settling and Unsettling Memories: Essays in Canadian Public History*. Ed. Nicole Neatby and Peter Hodgins. Toronto: University of Toronto Press, 2012. 310–39.

Marback, Richard. "The Rhetorical Space of Robben Island." *Rhetoric Society Quarterly* 24.2 (Spring 2004): 7–28.

Markel, Howard, and Alexandra Minna Stern. "Which Face? Whose Nation?" *American Behavioral Scientist* 42.9 (1999): 1314–31.

Matje, Thelma I. "A Pursuit of Happiness through Ellis Island." Ellis Island Archive Metaform Collection Box 39 No. 1 (New Box 99) "General Research Files" "Immigration Experiences: First-Person Accounts."

McDonald, R. H., Joe O'Brien, Robert P. Moody, Krista Dempsey, Cindi MacNeill, Robert Todd, and William Naftel. *Pier 21 Commemorative Integrity Statement*. Parks Canada, 2004.

McIntosh, William R. *Canadian Problems*. Toronto: Presbyterian Church in Canada Committee on Young People's Societies, 1910.

McKittrick, Katherine. "'Their Blood Is There, and They Can't Throw It Out': Honouring Black Canadian Geographies." *Topia: Canadian Journal of Cultural Studies* 7 (2002): 28–37.

———. *Demonic Grounds: Black Women and the Cartographies of Struggle*. Minneapolis: University of Minnesota Press, 2006.

McLaren, Angus. *Our Own Master Race: Eugenics in Canada, 1885–1945*. Toronto: McClelland & Stewart, 1990.

McMahon, Thomas L. "The Final Abuse of Indian Residential School Children: Deleting Their Names, Erasing Their Voices and Destroying Their Records after They Have Died and without Their Consent." 4 May 2016. Available at SSRN: https://ssrn.com/abstract=2812298 or http://dx.doi.org/10.2139/ssrn.2812298

"Medical Examination of Immigrants to Canada." *British Medical Journal* 1.3675 (13 June 1931): 1040–41.

Melnick, Jeffrey. "Immigration and Race Relations." *A Companion to American Immigration*. Ed. Reed Ueda. Malden, MA: Blackwell, 2006. 255–73.

Menzies, Robert. "Governing Mentalities: The Deportation of 'Insane' and 'Feebleminded' Immigrants out of British Columbia from Confederation to WWII." *Crime and Deviance in Canada: Historical Perspectives*. Ed. Chris McCormick. Toronto: Canadian Scholars, 2005. 161–86.

Mesenhöller, Peter. *Augustus F. Sherman: Ellis Island Portraits 1905–1920*. New York: Aperture, 2005.

Miller, Heather Lee. "Sexologists Examine Lesbians and Prostitutes in the United States, 1840–1940." *NWSA Journal* 12.3 (2000): 67–91.

Minich, Julie Avril. *Accessible Citizenships: Disability, Nation, and the Cultural Politics of Greater Mexico*. Philadelphia: Temple University Press, 2013.

———. "Enabling Whom? Critical Disability Studies Now." *Lateral* 5.1 (Spring 2016). Web.

Minna Stern, Alexandra. *Eugenic Nation: Faults and Frontiers of Better Breeding in Modern America*. Berkeley: University of California Press, 2005.

Mirza, Mansha. "Refugee Camps, Asylum Detention, and the Geopolitics of Transnational Migration: Disability and Its Intersections with Humanitarian Confinement." *Disability Incarcerated: Imprisonment and Disability in the United States and Canada*. Ed. Liat Ben-Moshe and Allison C. Carey. New York: Palgrave Macmillan, 2014. 217–36.

Mitchell, Don. *Cultural Geography: An Introduction*. Oxford: Blackwell, 2000.

Mitchell, W. J. T. *What Do Pictures Want? The Lives and Loves of Images*. Chicago: University of Chicago Press, 2005.

Modood, Tariq. "Muslims and the Politics of Difference." *The Political Quarterly* 74.s1 (2003): 100–115.

Mohanty, Sarita A., Steffie Woolhandler, David U. Himmelstein, Susmita Pati, Olveen Carrasquillo, and David H. Bor. "Health Care Expenditures of Immigrants in the United States: A Nationally Representative Analysis." *American Journal of Public Health* 95.8 (2005): 1431–38.

Molina, Natalia. "Medicalizing the Mexican: Immigration, Race, and Disability in the Early-Twentieth-Century United States." *Radical History Review* 2006.94 (2006): 22–37.

"More Tong Wars." *Time,* 5 Oct. 1925. Ellis Island Archives.

Moreno, Barry. *The Encyclopedia of Ellis Island*. New York: Greenwood, 2004.

Mosoff, Judith. "Excessive Demand on the Canadian Conscience: Disability, Family, and Immigration." *The Manitoba Law Journal* 26 (1998): 149–79.

Mountford, Roxanne. "On Gender and Rhetorical Space." *Rhetoric Society Quarterly* 31.1 (Winter 2001): 41–71.

Moya, Jose C. "Immigrants and Associations: A Global and Historical Perspective." *Journal of Ethnic and Migration Studies* 31.5 (2005): 833–64.

Mulcahy, Dianne. "'Sticky' Learning: Assembling Bodies, Objects and Affects at the Museum and Beyond." *Learning Bodies: The Body in Youth and Childhood Studies.* Ed. Julia Coffey, Shelley Budgeon, and Helen Cahill. Singapore: Springer, 2016. 207–22.

Mullan, E. H. "Mental Examination of Immigrants: Administration and Line Inspection at Ellis Island." *Public Health Reports* 33.20 (18 May 1917): 92–103.

Munro, Margaret. "Federal Librarians Fear Being 'Muzzled' under New Code of Conduct that Stresses 'Duty of Loyalty' to the Government." *National Post,* 13 Mar. 2013, http://news.nationalpost.com/2013/03/15/library-and-archives-canada/

Murray, Robert K. *The Politics of Normalcy.* New York: Norton, 1917.

Newbold, Bruce. "Health Status and Health Care of Immigrants in Canada: A Longitudinal Analysis." *Journal of Health Services Research & Policy* 10.2 (2005): 77–83A.

Ngai, Mae M. *Impossible Subjects: Illegal Aliens and the Making of Modern America.* Princeton and Oxford: Princeton University Press, 2004.

———. "The Strange Career of the Illegal Alien." Ellis Island Manuscript Collection IM-157.

Nielson, Kim. *A Disability History of the United States.* Boston: Beacon, 2012.

Ochoa, Kristen C., Gregory L. Pleasants, Joseph V. Penn, and David C. Stone. "Disparities in Justice and Care: Persons with Severe Mental Illnesses in the US Immigration Detention System." *Journal of the American Academy of Psychiatry and the Law Online* 38.3 (2010): 392–99.

O'Gallagher, Marianna. *Grosse Île: Gateway to Canada, 1832–1937.* Ste. Foy, Québec: Carraig Books, 1984.

Oliver, Frank. Canadian House of Commons, *Debates,* 12 Apr. 1901, 2939.

Oliver, Michael. *The Politics of Disablement: A Sociological Approach.* London: St. Martin's, 1990.

Ordover, Nancy. *American Eugenics: Race, Queer Anatomy, and the Science of Nationalism.* Minneapolis: University of Minnesota Press, 2003.

Organista, Kurt C. *Solving Latino Psychosocial and Health Problems: Theory, Practice, and Populations.* Hoboken, NJ: Wiley, 2007.

"Our Foreign-Born Citizens." *National Geographic* 31.2 (Feb. 1917): 95–130.

Parekh, Serena. *Refugees and the Ethics of Forced Displacement.* New York: Routledge, 2016.

Parikka, Jussi. *What Is Media Archaeology?* London: Polity, 2012.

Pauly, Philip J. "The World and All That Is In It: The National Geographic Society, 1898–1918." *American Quarterly* 31 (1979): 517–32.

Paupst, K. "A Note on Anti-Chinese Sentiment in Toronto before the First World War." *Canadian Ethnic Studies* 9.1 (1977): 54–59.

Pearse to Egan. 27 October 1925. Immigration Fonds, Library and Archives Canada, RG 76, vol. 269, file 228124, pt. 14.

Pernick, Martin. *The Black Stork: Eugenics and the Death of "Defective" Babies in American Medicine and Motion Pictures since 1915.* New York: Oxford University Press, 1996.

Photographs of Ellis Island 1902–1913. New York Public Library. The Miriam and Ira D. Wallach Division of Art, Prints and Photographs: Photography Collection.

Pickens, Donald K. *Eugenics and the Progressives.* Nashville: Vanderbilt University Press, 1968.

Press, Eyal. "Trump and the Truth: Immigration and Crime." *The New Yorker,* 17 Oct. 2016. Web. 28 Jan. 2017.

Price, Margaret. "Disability Studies Methodology: Explaining Ourselves to Ourselves." *Practicing Research in Writing Studies: Reflexive and Ethically Responsible Research.* Ed. Katrina M. Powell and Pamela Takayoshi. New York: Hampton, 2012. 159–86.

Provine, Doris Marie, Monica Varsanyi, Paul G. Lewis, and Scott H. Decker. "Growing Tensions between Civic Membership and Enforcement in the Devolution of Immigration Control." *Punishing Immigrants: Policy, Politics, and Injustice.* Ed. Charis E. Kubrin, Marjorie S. Zatz, and Ramiro Martinez Jr. New York: New York University Press, 2012. 42–61.

Quackenbos, Mary Grace. "Why They Come." *Pearson's Magazine,* Dec. 1910, 737–47.

Quayson, Ato. *Aesthetic Nervousness: Disability and the Crisis of Representation.* New York: Columbia University Press, 2007.

Quong Wing v R, [1914] 49 SCR 440 [Quong Wing].

Raiford, Leigh. "Photography and the Practices of Critical Black Memory." *History and Theory* 48.4 (2009): 112–29.

Rand, Erica. *The Ellis Island Snow Globe.* Raleigh: Duke University Press, 2005.

Raska, Jan. "Facing Deportation: The Curious Cases of Rebecca Barnett and Rebecca Grizzle." *Canadian Museum of Immigration at Pier 21,* 2013, http://www.pier21.ca/blog/jan-raska/facing-deportation-the-curious-cases-of-rebecca-barnett-and-rebecca-grizzle

Reaume, Geoffrey. "Disability History in Canada: Present Work in the Field and Future Prospects." *Canadian Journal of Disability Studies* 1.1 (2012): 35–81.

Regan, Paulette. *Unsettling the Settler Within: Indian Residential Schools, Truth Telling, and Reconciliation in Canada.* Vancouver: UBC Press, 2010.

Rembis, Michael A. "'I Ain't Been Reading While on Parole': Experts, Mental Tests, and Eugenic Commitment Law in Illinois, 1890–1940." *History of Psychology* 7.3 (2004): 225–47.

"Report of the Joint Special Committee to Investigate Chinese Immigration, 1877." Senate Reprint No. 689, 44th Cong., 2d Sess. at p. 1172 (1877).

Richards, Penny L. "Points of Entry: Disability and the Historical Geography of Immigration." *Disability Studies Quarterly* 24.3 (2004). Web.

Richardson, Theresa R. *The Century of the Child: The Mental Hygiene Movement and Social Policy in the United States and Canada.* Albany: State University of New York Press, 1989.

Ripley, William Z. *The Races of Europe: A Sociological Study.* New York: Appleton, 1899.

Roberts, Barbara. *Whence They Came: Deportation from Canada 1900–1935.* Ottawa: University of Ottawa Press, 1988.

Robertson to Cory. Ottawa, 13 December 1918. Immigration Fonds, Library and Archives Canada, RG 76, vol. 642, file 947852, pt. 1 [Robertson to Cory].

Rossiter, Kate, and Annalise Clarkson. "Opening Ontario's 'Saddest Chapter': A Social History of Huronia Regional Centre." *Canadian Journal of Disability Studies* 2.3 (2013): 1–30.

Royal Commission on Chinese and Japanese Immigration: Sess 1902, 2 E VII, A 1902, at 224.

Safford, Victor. *Immigration Problems: Personal Experiences of an Official.* New York: Dodd, Mead, 1925.

Sander, August. *August Sander: Citizens of the Twentieth Century Portrait Photographs 1892–1952.* Cambridge: MIT Press, 1986.

Sanger, Margaret. *The Pivot of Civilization.* New York: Brentano, 1922.

Sargent, Frank P. "Dept. of Commerce and Labor, Bureau of Immigration Correspondence with Immigration Restriction League" 17 April 1905. BMS Am 2245 (916) US Immigration and Naturalization Service. Correspondence with IRL, 1896–1920. Houghton Library, Harvard College Library, Harvard University.

Scheinberg, Ellen, and Melissa K. Rombout. "Projecting Images of the Nation: The Immigration Program and Its Use of Lantern Slides." *The Archivist* 111 (1996).

Schneider, Rebecca. *Performing Remains: Art and War in Times of Theatrical Reenactment*. London and New York: Routledge, 2011.

Schweik, Susan. "Disability and the Normal Body of the (Native) Citizen." *Social Research* 78.2 (2011): 417–42.

———. *The Ugly Laws: Disability in Public*. New York: New York University Press, 2009.

Scott, William Duncan. "Immigration and Population." *Canada and Its Provinces*, vol. 7. Ed. Adam Shortt and Arthur G. Doughty. Toronto: Brook, 1914. 517–30.

Sears, Alan. "Immigration Controls as Social Policy: The Case of Canadian Medical Inspection 1900–1920." *Studies in Political Economy* 33.1 (1990): 91–112.

Sekula, Allan. "The Body and the Archive." *October* 39 (Winter 1986): 3–64.

Senate Debates, 19th Parl, 3rd Sess (19 Mar. 1903).

Serlin, David. "Touching Histories: Personality, Disability, and Sex in the 1930s." *Sex and Disability*. Ed. Robert McRuer and Anna Mollow. Durham: Duke University Press, 2012. 145–64.

Seth, Patricia, Marie Slark, Josée Boulanger, and Leah Dolmage. "Survivors and Sisters Talk About the Huronia Class Action Lawsuit, Control, and the Kind of Support We Want." *Journal on Developmental Disabilities* 21.2 (2015): 60–68.

Shepard, R. Bruce. *Deemed Unsuitable: Blacks from Oklahoma Move to the Canadian Prairies in Search of Equality in the Early 20th Century, Only to Find Racism in Their New Home*. Toronto: Umbrella, 1997.

Shilliam, Robbie. *The Black Pacific: Anti-colonial Struggles and Oceanic Connections*. London: Bloomsbury, 2015.

Short, John Phillip. *Magic Lantern Empire: Colonialism and Society in Germany*. Ithaca: Cornell University Press, 2012.

Siebers, Tobin. "Disability Aesthetics." *Journal for Cultural and Religious Theory* 7.2 (Spring–Summer 2006): 63–73.

———, ed. *Heterotopia: Postmodern Utopia and the Body Politic*. Ann Arbor: University of Michigan Press, 1994.

Sikka, Annette, Katherine Lippel, and Jill Hanley. "Access to Health Care and Workers' Compensation for Precarious Migrants in Quebec, Ontario and New Brunswick." *McGill Journal of Law and Health* 5.2 (2011): 203–69.

Simpson, Audra. *Mohawk Interruptus: Political Life across the Borders of Settler States*. Durham: Duke University Press, 2014.

Simpson, Jeffrey. "Making Canada's Past a Slave to Power." *The Globe and Mail,* 10 Sept. 2012. Web. 16 Aug. 2017.

"Six Big Liners in Thrilling Race to Land Aliens." *New York Evening World,* 1 Sep. 1921. Ellis Island Archives.

Skilling, Harold Gordon. *Canadian Representation Abroad: From Agency to Embassy*. Toronto: Ryerson, 1945.

Smith, Teresa. "Conservatives Defend Cuts to Archives Canada." *Postmedia News,* 3 May 2012. Web. 16 Aug. 2017.

Smith, William George. *A Study in Canadian Immigration*. Toronto: Ryerson, 1920.

Snyder, Sharon L., and David T. Mitchell. *Cultural Locations of Disability*. Chicago: University of Chicago Press, 2006.

"Some of Our Immigrants." *National Geographic* 42 (1907): 317–34.

Somerville, Siobhan B. *Queering the Color Line: Race and the Invention of Homosexuality in American Culture.* Durham: Duke University Press, 2000.

———. *American Anatomies: Theorizing Race and Gender.* Durham: Duke University Press, 1995.

Sontag, Susan. *On Photography.* New York: Picador, 1977.

Sproule-Jones, Megan. "Crusading for the Forgotten: Dr. Peter Bryce, Public Health, and Prairie Native Residential Schools." *Canadian Bulletin of Medical History / Bulletin canadien d'histoire de la médecine* 13.1 (1996): 199–224.

"SS New York Oct 4 08 Dressed 15 yrs in men's clothes. Lived 30 yrs. in US." Mesenhöller and Sherman 93.

Stange, Maren. *Symbols of Ideal Life.* Cambridge: Cambridge University Press, 1989.

Stepan, Nancy. *The Hour of Eugenics: Race, Gender, and Nation in Latin America.* Ithaca: Cornell University Press, 1991.

Stewart, Penni. "Harper Government Puts Library & Archives Canada at Risk." *CAUT Bulletin* 58.4 (April 2011).

Stocking, George W., Jr. *Race, Culture, and Evolution: Essays in the History of Anthropology.* New York: Free Press, 1968.

Stoler, Ann Laura. "Colonial Aphasia: Race and Disabled Histories in France." *Public History* 23.1 (2011): 121–56.

Stubblefield, Anna. "'Beyond the Pale': Tainted Whiteness, Cognitive Disability, and Eugenic Sterilization." *Hypatia* 22.2 (2007): 162–81.

"Suicide." Metaform Collection Box 31 No. 3 (New Box 78) W230 and W232 "Ellis Island: Exclusion."

Suksennik, Jean. Ellis Island Metaform Collection Box 39 No. 1 (New Box 99) "General Research Files: AARP Letters." 19 May 1985.

Temple, Andrea, and June F. Tyler. "Ellis Island: A Historical Perspective." *Americans All*, https://americansall.org/sites/default/files/882-ELLIS%20ISLAND%20C_T%20MedLoRes_0.pdf

Terry, Jennifer. "Anxious Slippages between 'Us' and 'Them': A Brief History of the Scientific Search for Homosexual Bodies." *Deviant Bodies: Critical Perspectives on Difference in Science and Culture.* Ed. Jennifer Terry and Jacqueline Urla. 129–69.

Terry, Jennifer, and Jacqueline Urla. 1995. "Introduction." *Deviant Bodies: Critical Perspectives on Difference in Science and Culture.* Ed. Jennifer Terry and Jacqueline Urla. Bloomington: Indiana University Press.

Thobani, Sunera. *Exalted Subjects: Studies in the Making of Race and Nation in Canada.* Toronto: University of Toronto Press, 2007.

Tichenor, Daniel J. *Dividing Lines: The Politics of Immigration Control in America.* Princeton: Princeton University Press, 2002.

Tifft, Wilton S. *Ellis Island.* Chicago: Contemporary Books, 1990.

Titchkosky, Tanya, and Rod Michalko. "Putting Disability in Its Place: It's Not a Joking Matter." *Embodied Rhetorics: Disability in Language and Culture.* Ed. James C. Wilson and Cynthia Lewiecki-Wilson. Carbondale: Southern Illinois University Press, 2001. 200–228.

Topley, William James. Detail from "immigrants to be deported." Library and Archives Canada, RG 1939, vol. 434 NPC. PA-020910.

Trausch, Susan. "Visiting Ellis Island." *Boston Globe,* 15 June 1986. Ellis Island Archives.

Tredgold, A. F. "Eugenics and Future Human Progress." *The Eugenics Review* 3.2 (1911): 94–117.

Tremain, Shelley. "On the Subject of Impairment." *Disability/Postmodernity: Embodying Political Theory.* Ed. Mairian Corker and Tom Shakespeare. London: Continuum, 2002. 32–47.

Trent, James W. *Inventing the Feeble Mind.* Berkeley: University of California Press, 1994. Print.

Troper, Harold Martin. "The Creek-Negroes of Oklahoma and Canadian Immigration, 1909–11." *Canadian Historical Review* 53.3 (1972): 272–88.

Turda, Marius. *Eugenics and Nation in Early 20th Century Hungary.* Houndmills, Basingstoke: Palgrave Macmillan, 2014.

———. *The History of East-Central European Eugenics, 1900–1945: Sources and Commentaries.* London: Bloomsbury Academic, 2015.

Turda, Marius, and Aaron Gillette. *Latin Eugenics in Comparative Perspective.* London: Bloomsbury Academic, 2014.

Tyner, James. *Oriental Bodies: Discourse and Discipline in US Immigration Policy, 1875–1943.* Lexington: University of Kentucky Press, 2006.

Unattributed correspondence. Immigration Fonds, Library and Archives Canada, RG 76, vol. 269, file 228124, pt. 10–12.

Urban, Jessica LeAnn. *Nation, Immigration, and Environmental Security.* New York: Palgrave Macmillan, 2008.

U.S. Congress, "Immigration Act of 1917," History Research Center, Farmington Hills, MI: Gale Group, http://galenet.galegroup.com/servlet/HistRC/ [31 Jan. 2007].

Vattimo, Gianni. "From Utopia to Heterotopia." *The Transparent Society.* Trans. David Webb. Cambridge: Polity, 1992. 62–75.

Vaughan, Christopher. "Ogling Igorots: The Politics and Commerce of Exhibiting Cultural Otherness, 1898–1913." *Freakery: Cultural Spectacles of the Extraordinary Body.* Ed. Rosemarie Garland Thomson. New York: New York University Press, 1996. 219–33.

Venters, Homer, and Allen S. Keller. "Diversion of Patients with Mental Illness from Court-ordered Care to Immigration Detention." *Psychiatric Services* 63.4 (2012): 377–79.

Vukov, Tamara. "Performing the Immigrant Nation at Pier 21: Politics and Counterpolitics in the Memorialization of Canadian Immigration." *International Journal of Canadian Studies* 26 (Fall 2002): 1–17.

Wallace, Kenyon. "Family Faces Deportation over Son's Autism." *Toronto Star,* 9 June 2011. Web. 16 Aug. 2017.

Walters, Lindsey K. "Slavery and the American University: Discourses of Retrospective Justice at Harvard and Brown." *Slavery & Abolition* (2017): 1–26.

Ward, Robert DeCourcy. "Our Immigration Law from the Viewpoint of National Eugenics." *National Geographic,* Jan. 1912, 38–41.

Weatherford, Doris. *Foreign and Female: Immigrant Women in America, 1840–1930.* New York: Facts on File Press, 1995.

Webster, Yehudi O. *The Racialization of America.* New York: St. Martin's, 1992.

Weil, Patrick. "Races at the Gate: Racial Distinctions in Immigration Policy: A Comparison Between France and the United States." *Europe to North America, Migration Control in the Nineteenth Century: The Evolution of States Practices in Europe and the United States from the French Revolution to the Inter-War Period.* Ed. Andreas Fahrmeir, Olivier Faron, and Patrick Weil. New York: Berghahn Books, 2003. 368–402.

Wells, H. G. *The Future in America: A Search After Realities.* Boston: St. Martin's, 1987.

Wheeler, Stephanie K. "The Construction of Access: The Eugenic Precedent of the Americans with Disabilities Act." *Continuum* 31.3 (2017): 377–87.

William Lyon Mackenzie King. See Mackenzie King, William Lyon.

Williams to Fraser. 20 November 1925. Immigration Fonds, Library and Archives Canada, RG 76, vol. 666, file 1594, pt. 1.

Williams, Carol. *Framing the West: Race, Gender and the Photographic Frontier in the Pacific North-west.* Oxford: Oxford University Press, 2003.

Williams, William. "Annual Reports of the Commissioner of Ellis Island, 1902–09, 1909–13." New York Public Library, Rare Book and Manuscript Collections, William Williams Papers, box 5.

Wilson, J. G. "The Crossing of the Races." *Popular Science Monthly* 2.9 (Nov. 1911): 486–95.

"Woman in Male Garb Earns Her Freedom." *New York Times,* 6 Oct. 1908. Ellis Island Archives.

Woodruff, John. "Deformed Idiot to Be Deported." Library and Archives Canada, RG 1939, vol. 434, file 2000768705. PA-20911.

Woodsworth, J. S. *Strangers within Our Gates; or, Coming Canadians.* Toronto: University of Toronto Press, 1972. Print.

Yew, Elizabeth. "Medicine, Bureaucracy, and Immigration: Medical Inspection of Immigrants at Ellis Island 1891–1924." *Bulletin of the New York Academy of Medicine* 56 (June 1980): 488–510.

Ziedel, Robert F. *Immigrants, Progressives, and Exclusion Politics: The Dillingham Commission, 1900–1927.* DeKalb: Northern Illinois University Press, 2004.

Žižek, Slavoj. *The Universal Exception.* London, New York: Continuum International, 2006.

Zolberg, Aristide R. *A Nation by Design: Immigration Policy in the Fashioning of America.* New York: Russell Sage Foundation with Harvard University Press, 2006.

INDEX

CPSIA information can be obtained
at www.ICGtesting.com
Printed in the USA
BVHW041024080719
552338BV00010B/2/P

9 780814 254677